# You Are
# Your Child's
# Best Psychologist

---

# 7  Keys to
# Excellence in
# Parenting

---

## Daniel J. van Ingen, Psy.D

ISBN-10: 1935576062
ISBN-13: 9781935576068

Published By: FEP INTERNATIONAL

# Endorsements

"You hold in your hand a very remarkable thing, something for which parents have always yearned: a how-to manual for raising children that are happy, independent and productive! In this easy-to-read book, Dr. Daniel van Ingen has provided today's parents with an invaluable aid. I have been a pediatrician in private general practice for over 30 years, and I have never read such a concise and easily navigable roadmap such as this, every parent's goal. Dr. van Ingen has a hugely successful practice in clinical psychology in Sarasota, Florida, and he and his wife Sarah, a university professor, have three lovely, and loving, children that are a testament to their parents' authority on this topic.

A wise person once said that the goal of parenting should NOT be to raise children who are happy, but to raise children who become happy adults. Dr. Van Ingen's book provides today's parents with simple, easy-to-follow instructions toward that end. Wisely, he has identified seven "keys to optimal parenting", and each is explored in its own dedicated chapter. The chapters discuss goals that include, among others, successfully reinforcing a healthy attachment to parents, teaching the child to internalize self-control, and laying out a blueprint for facing adversity in a healthy manner. My personal favorite was the chapter entitled "Drawing Out the Strength of Boldness", an insight that I consider to be a stroke of genius.

Each chapter is presented in the same format: the parenting key is identified and explained and then fleshed out with examples, both positive and negative. He then provides "reflection tips" that demonstrate to the reader how to think about incorporating the lesson of the chapter. This is followed by "words of wisdom" and more "reflection tips" that further elucidate the lessons of the chapter. Scattered throughout the chapter are quotes from other parenting experts and authors that encapsulate the insights that Dr. van Ingen is exploring. As the reader progresses through the lesson, Dr. van Ingen's recommendations become crystalized via his careful and easily understood prose. At the book's conclusion, it will be abundantly clear to the reader why Dr. van Ingen entitled his soon-to-be classic, You Are Your Child's Best Psychologist."

**Ted L Meyer MD, FAAP (Fellow of the American Academy of Pediatrics)**
**Meyer Pediatrics**
**Sarasota, Florida**

"Dr. Dan van Ingen's book "You Are Your Child's Best Psychologist" is a compelling read that lays out specific strategies that parents can utilize to help children grow up happy, healthy and well-adjusted. van Ingen weaves rich stories supported by empirical research that paints a picture of the joys and challenges of raising children in our modern world. Not everyone has an advanced degree in psychology, and each chapter provides clear and concise behaviors that parents can utilize to reinforce positive behaviors and help reduce negative ones. van Ingen's passion and understanding of the importance of raising children well is evident throughout the book. You are Your Child's Best Psychologist" is a must read for anyone who is raising or works with children!"

**John Tauer, Ph.D.**
**Author of "Why Less Is More for WOSPs (Well-Intentioned, Overinvolved Sports Parents): How to Be the Best Sports Parent You Can Be"**
**Professor & Men's Head Basketball Coach**
**University of St. Thomas**

"Dr. van Ingen has drawn upon extensive research in child development and parenting to identify seven crucial methods to become a better parent. The book is replete with illustrative examples that will aid parents and caregivers in making the most of the recommendations. Included are strategies for improved positive regard for your child, even during times of intense stress; being flexible in interactions with your child; understanding and accepting your own limitations; and making reasonable goals in order to find balance and happiness. Parents and caregivers will find this a highly readable and valuable resource while trying to navigate the often difficult, yet highly rewarding, task of raising children."

**Dean McKay, PhD, ABPP**
**Editor of "Treatments for Psychological Problems and Syndromes"**
**Professor & Fordham-Columbia Research Fellow**
**President-elect, Society for Science of Clinical Psychology**
**Past President, Association for Behavioral and Cognitive Therapies (2013-2014)**
**Fordham University**

"Dr. van Ingen has done it again! A personal touch is effectively woven throughout this book, which is a primer for professionals, validation for balanced parents, and guidance for those who have fallen off course. Realistic and practical for providers, non-judgmental of parents, this book provides insight and inspiration. Core concepts, related interventions, and resources are relevant and funny. This is a complex evidence-based resource made simple. Now, check your musts at the door, and suck a lemon when you fall off course!"

**Jame Lontz, Ph.D.**
**Executive Director, Blue Mountain**
**Neuropsychological Associates**
**Spokane, WA**

"Dr. van Ingen again demonstrates his talent for meshing personal experience with parenting research. I have had lots of conversations with parents, and this is the 'parenting handbook' all parents are searching for. This instruction book that our kids didn't come with is a great reminder of what we DO know when it comes to parenting 'right.' In my opinion, as both a parent and a psychologist, this book also presents a welcome reminder of how simple changes in day-to-day parenting can have profound impacts on the future."

**Patricia H. Price, PsyD, Licensed Psychologist**
**Author of "No More Screen Time"**
**Rochester, Minnesota**

"You Are Your Child's Best Psychologist is a delightful integration of both clinical and practical knowledge for parenting. As it states, ' all parents make mistakes.' In this realistic guide, Dr. van Ingen points out that what we do now to prepare our children through relationships has a direct impact on how our children will weather the storms of life. The impact we make on our children today will have a direct impact on their lives and the community that surrounds them. This is an excellent resource for both parents and people preparing for child rearing."

**Reverend Dr. Justin C. Kidd**
**D.Min., M.DIV. Bethel Seminary**
**Certificate, Management Studies, Gala Schools**
**Pastor Antioch Baptist Church**
**Adjunct Professor, Crossroads College**

"Too many experts can leave a reader feeling dependent and less than fully capable. Dr. Dan van Ingen achieves exactly the opposite with the most solid thinking of modern psychology. He sets out to instill confidence in parents, helping them align their best instincts with solid psychological research. The result is a book that will raise up effective parents – not groupies! Readers of You Are Your Child's Best Psychologist may wonder whether this book has three authors: a committed father, a psychological researcher, and a practicing counselor. Dr. van Ingen combines all three perspectives in a useful and readable handbook for parents. In fact, you might even hear a fourth voice, because Dan obviously listens attentively to his wife Sarah, herself a Doctor of Education. Four perspectives; one very practical book!"

**Reverend Kevin McDonough**
**Pastor, Incarnation of Minneapolis**
**President, Sagrado Corazon de Jesus**

"You Are Your Child's Best Psychologist: 7 Keys to Excellence in Parenting is a useful resource for navigating the everyday challenges of being a parent or caregiver to children and adolescents. Dr. van Ingen's clear passion for families is evident throughout the book. As a parent, I especially appreciate the practical examples and suggested tips in each chapter."

**Stacy Freiheit, PhD, LP, Mom and**
**Associate Professor of Psychology.**
**Augsburg College**

# Table of Contents

## Quick Tip Reference for Practical Parenting Skills

# FOREWORD
### by Sarah A. van Ingen, Ph.D.

The book that you hold in your hands is more than a bound stack of pages, so much more than the ink and the paper on which it is written. This book is an invitation to take a deep breath. It is an invitation to drink from a glass of cool water. At its heart, it is a reminder that you are not alone in this walk in life that we call parenting.

If this parenting thing is going well for you, if you have picked up this book because you are looking to improve what is already working, you will certainly find what you are looking for. Because of the wealth of experience that Dan has had over the years of working with thousands of families, I guarantee that he has placed in this book wisdom that even the most successful parents can learn from. At times, I think you will find that Dan has put words to something that you may have already known intuitively, and your confidence in that approach will grow. Other times, you may have always done something a certain way, and Dan will uncover some of the unintended consequences, and he will lay out a path for a more effective approach. In short, if you yourself are a bit of a parenting expert, you are in for a treat. I think you will deeply enjoy having a "conversation" with Dan about this passion of yours. These pages will affirm you and provide some of the nutrients you need to continue to grow as a parent.

But, my friend, if parenting is not going so well for you right now, I want you to know that you are not alone and that this book can be like a shelter from the storm. Let Dan come along side of you and hold you up for a bit. Page after page, you will start to be strengthened and encouraged. You will probably start to see ways in which the parenting that you received wasn't what it needed to be, and in seeing that truth, you will be able to choose something different for your own children.

There is no one perfect way to parent. We joke about it, but we all know that children don't come with a manual. And each child is so different! What works for one is almost guaranteed not to work the same way for another. So, this book is not about setting up some sort of standard of perfection, and you will not find a word of condemnation for the times when you feel you have fallen short of what you had hoped you could do for your children. No, what you will find is a book about principles and strategies. This book reveals the WHY behind the HOW. Dan has a gift for cutting through the complexity and the confusion of family relationships, and he provides simple strategies that are able to shift the direction and tone of our family relationships.

Dan has distilled the clarity that has come from his professional work as a psychologist, and he has made that available to the rest of us. As he is quick to point out, yes, there are times in the life of a family when a professional psychologist may be needed. But for all of the ordinary times, Dan's mission is to see you, the child's parent, empowered to raise up that son or daughter to be free and full of joy.

As we all know so well, parenting is not a sprint, it is a marathon. If you have ever had the opportunity to watch an Olympic marathon, you will see that there is a lot of strategy involved—it's not about who starts out the fastest. This is a book of strategy. It is a book that will help you achieve your long-term parenting goals by giving you strategy that you can use immediately. So take that deep breath. Allow hope to rise up within you. I know how important parenting is to you, and you have just found an advocate, an encourager, and a mentor in Dan. Allow Dan to take you on this journey toward greater joy and peace in parenting.

# **Dedication**

I want to dedicate this book to my three sisters—
Katherine, Jane, and Alessandra – three wonderful moms.
I am grateful for their love and laughter over the years.
When we started on these parenting adventures,
I had no idea how much kids would impact my life.

# **Acknowledgements**

There are many people I would like to acknowledge. First and foremost, I want to thank my wife Sarah for her encouragement and unconditional support. I have learned so much from her. As Kevin McDonough points out, I listen attentively to her voice of reason, wisdom, and passion for our children and her gifted understanding of youth. I am deeply grateful she is the mother of our three wonderful children. May we continue to facilitate their gifts of joy, boldness, and encouragement.

I want to thank Stacy Freiheit for her encouragement and feedback on my manuscript. Her many years of collegiality and intellectual generosity are deeply appreciated. I am grateful to Marietta Whittlesey for her editing of my earlier drafts and practical advice for writing that can be helpful to parents. Her professional insight is appreciated. I want to thank my good friend John Gislason who took time to review one of my early drafts, and for his long-time support of the vision of Parenting Doctors. Your friendship is deeply appreciated. I want to express thanks to Christopher Vye, my graduate advisor from the University of St. Thomas in Minneapolis, Minnesota. He gave me important feedback on the importance of encouraging parents to seek professional help. Consequently, I wrote out Chapter 8 as a way to clarify the many reasons why parents may need to see a professional clinician.

I want to thank Andrew Doan and his staff at FEP International for their professional expertise. I want to thank my editor Michele Berner for her helpful input and the many others who have worked on You Are Your Child's Best Psychologist.

Finally, I want to express my deep gratitude to the Father, the Son, and the Holy Spirit—the fount of love.

# Introduction

The delight of my life is raising three children – lovely, beautiful, funny, and amazing young people. The joy of my life was marrying my wife, Sarah A. van Ingen, Ph.D. and this joy is sustained raising our three children. Sarah and I balance two careers – as a university professor and as a clinical psychologist, respectively. We work hard to serve our students, clients, schools, colleagues, and the cities of Tampa, St. Petersburg, and Sarasota. Much of our professional lives consists of service for kids, tweens, and adolescents. While fully engaged in our careers, we help our kids balance school, athletics, church, and relationships. As a dad, I am a youth sports coach in soccer, baseball, and basketball, and cheer on my kids in gymnastics and swimming. As a family, we host friends for dinner on a regular basis and visit others' homes, building up our family support and engaging in a community life. And like many, attempting to balance all of this leads us to experience feelings of overwhelm as we make lunches, enforce chores, clean toilets, and engage in your usual tasks of laundry, cooking, and shopping.

On this journey of balancing our professional lives with our coaching, friendships, and the day-to-day joy-filled grind, my secondary delight has been our work with parents and families. It has been Sarah's and my joy to build up the communities of Sarasota County with our focus on equipping parents with the best information that psychology and education has to offer. Two years ago, Sarah and I started a non-profit business called the Parenting Doctors with a mission to support families as they weather the storms of life. One of our services has been our regular seminars that we voluntarily provide at schools and churches throughout Sarasota, Florida. We approach these seminars representing our areas of expertise – I teach on the major tenets of successful parents and Sarah teaches on the key strategies to accelerate learning. For several years, I have provided a weekly parenting podcast on a different parenting theme, available on my website www.danvaningen.com or via the Parenting Doctors podcasts at iTunes.

In our respective fields, as Parenting Doctors www.parentingdoctors.com, we have worked with thousands of children, tweens, and adolescents in a variety of capacities – teaching, mentoring, advising, coaching, psychological and intelligence testing, counseling, and psychological therapy. Likewise, we have worked with parents in an array of professional functions – family interventions for teenage addiction, domestic violence, couples and family counseling, individual therapy, school interdisciplinary team meetings, educational consultations, and direct parenting training. All of this experience, including the joy of raising our three children, has led us to identify the objectives of child-raising. As a result of our parenting: Our children will become solid, productive, contributing members of society. Second, as a result of their lives, our culture will be healthier. Third, our world will be a much better place in which to live because our children have been alive.

These are the three objectives of child-raising. How do we accomplish this? How do we raise children to be contributing members of society, make the culture healthier, and improve our world? Sounds idealistic. I call it the quiet revolution—bringing necessary change to the world one family at a time. How we do bridge the gap between our ideals for our children making a difference in the world and real life ordinary development? Both Sarah and I completed our respective dissertations on effectiveness research, bridging the gap between the research and academic world and the "real world." Our studies have emphasized taking evidence-based practices in controlled studies on math education and the treatment of emotional disorders (e.g. mood, anxiety) on teaching and psychological practice and applying these to real life teaching and clinical settings. As a result, we have 15 years of experience discussing the research on bridging this ideal – real gap. This knowledge base, combined with our reflections from our plentiful parenting mistakes and thousands of those made by our fellow parenting partners, has given us keen insight to develop the seven keys to optimal parenting in raising solid members of society, helping our children to be cultural difference makers, and leaving a legacy. We have identified seven keys that make a difference based on our thousands of hours of combined experience as well as our combined review of the psychology and education literature.

Several studies were also completed to lay a foundation for this book. A published study of 45 comprehensive and standardized interviews with licensed professionals such as psychologists and social workers who work full time with parents and families provided key insights into healthy and over-involved parenting. Another published study that involved interviews of 20 experienced parents who raised children with significant disabilities provided nuggets of wisdom on dealing with real life problems. The interviews provided emerging themes on healthy parenting. Additional research that was instrumental was our groundbreaking published study on the topic of helicopter parenting that became a household concept via popular media.

Additionally, I have traveled to over 100 cities in 30 states teaching all-day seminars on 3-city speaking tours and have talked with and informally interviewed thousands of counselors, social workers, psychologists, and teachers. Based on these speaking tours, I have gleaned insight into the key issues of youth and some geographical differences throughout the country. With our 15 years and thousands of hours of combined clinical and educational experience, 65 comprehensive standardized interviews, thousands of interactions with parents and professionals, and a thorough review of the psychology literature on parenting over the last 100 years, we identified the seven keys to optimal parenting: (1) Reinforcing a Secure Attachment, (2) Minimizing Reinforcement Errors, (3) Drawing out the Strength of Boldness, (4) Promoting the Reflective and Optimistic Life, (5) Establishing Purpose with an Internal Locus of Control, (6) Sustaining Cognitive Flexibility in the Face of adversity, (7) and Establishing Family Happiness Rituals. These seven Keys help parents achieve the three objectives of parenting: facilitating solid, productive, contributing members of society, making our culture healthier, and making this world a better place.

Each chapter is a key to "optimal parenting" that moves us in the direction of raising our children to be contributing members of society, to make our culture healthier, and to improve our world. Each of the chapters consist of "Words of Wisdom & Steps for Taking Action" that provide both parents and youth professionals with a knowledge base and specific skills to strengthen each of the seven keys. We have also included in each chapter "Reflection Tips" and "Reflection Exercises", developed as opportunities for reflection, and practice activities for parents and those who work with parents. These tips and exercises are provided to help parents put the keys into action and incorporate them into your daily life.

In our life together, Sarah and I have found that many of these words of wisdom, action steps, and reflections are helpful in our approach to shaping, instructing, and inspiring our kids toward excellence. I have found that some of the reflection tips and exercises are helpful in particular contexts. But, life changes and children evolve which force us all to be flexible and use wisdom as needed. In my own situations, I have figured out that great parents choose the right times to use these strategies to raise heroic kids. Most importantly, I have realized everything else is second. Doctorates, professional success, and prestige all fall short. The biggest difference we will make in this world is with our own families.

Finally, but most importantly, I want to briefly share a personal experience of faith. This is by no means a religious or Christian book (i.e. scripture supporting key points). But, I would be remiss to not mention faith in God as central for family health. For most of us, parenting is hard enough to pull off successfully without faith -- the hardships of life, whether dealing with cancer as a mom, or the reality of our personal shortcomings in not knowing how to confront our kid who just broke a window [without screaming]. So, yes, there is a central element at the foundation of this book—that raising a family with God is so much easier, so much more worthwhile, and much more meaningful. For single parents, strained marriages, and worn out parents who seem to be carrying the parenting job like it's a burden—faith in God helps us to thrive, and not just survive.

I have learned that faith in God that includes openness to quantum change experiences elevates family health. In my own journey, I remain profoundly changed after my personal encounter with the love of God. On November 8th, 1997, at the age of 22, on a Saturday night in Bloomington, Minnesota, on the steps of an auditorium at a prayer meeting in a high school, I was intensely transformed by a revelation of God. I was invited to the prayer meeting by my psychology professor, and my first reaction to the idea was "I don't think so." Since we had built up rapport and trust, he encouraged me to just be open to checking it out. There was no pressure at all. I recall him saying "Dan, just trust in God." Rather than head to a dance club (or several) in downtown Minneapolis on that Saturday night, instead, I drove my old Hyundai over to the meeting with curiosity. As the music in the meeting started, all these people put their hands in the air and it felt like the Chicago Stadium (the old one before the United Center Mike built). I realize it was only hundreds of people, but this was how I made sense of the aura of the experience; there was great anticipation and an enthusiasm that captivated me much like those Chicago Bulls games my father, siblings, and I experienced together growing up. Later, I was sitting in the school auditorium watching a scene that night of professional men and women (professionals – teachers, doctors, nurses, lawyers, and millionaire business men) and children of all ages. I couldn't believe my eyes as they began to fall to the ground in front of me after being prayed with.  I was stunned as my eyes were wide open watching this event.  It was a surreal and dreamlike evening that seemed to move in slow motion.  In a response to my skepticism, one fact seared in my memory is a psychologist pointing out the different professional people participating at the prayer meeting, "There's a nuclear engineer, there's a surgeon, there's a nurse, there's a former Miss America contestant."

"What is going on….," I thought to myself as I saw people getting prayed with and being absorbed in God's presence and power. Through the filter of my college acting experience, I actually thought that the people who were falling to the ground was a skit.  I was invited to this meeting by my professor who was my advisor and had a distinguished research agenda – he clearly had credibility in my eyes as I had talked with him about social science and life for many years prior to this meeting.

On aside, years after this astounding night, one of the leaders of this prayer meeting volunteered for me as I practiced working with intelligence tests in my graduate studies.  On a standardized intelligence measure, he performed in the very superior range and in the top 1% of intelligence—with very superior ability in all four intellectual areas: verbal comprehension, perceptual reasoning, working memory, and processing speed. He was very superior in all the following abilities: abstract verbal reasoning, rote verbal memory, word knowledge, arithmetic reasoning, fund of general knowledge, perceptual reasoning, perceptual vigilance, and freedom from distractibility.  So, this obviously wasn't a situation of "low IQ" individuals being moved by emotional catharsis, as is sometimes the unwarranted criticism in academia of "Christian experiences."   What was happening before my eyes was something that could only be called a God thing.

I only learned later that this was a prayer meeting by a charismatic, ecumenical Christian community that was deeply impacted by a movement widely known as the Brownsville Revival in Pensacola, Florida.  To be honest, the cynic in me that night thought, "this skit is stupid," as I reacted to watching people fall to the ground.  I actually have what happened next on video tape, because the videographer had moved the camera in the direction I was headed.  Before I left the building, I remember sitting in my chair thinking that it was time for me to investigate.  So, I walked to the front while stepping over bodies to confront my Catholic psychology professor who invited me to the meeting.  I asked, "what on earth is going on here?"  He shared with me some miracles and healings that had taken place recently but said he could not explain what was happening.  Wisely, he didn't try.  He said, "I can't explain it, it's God."  A few minutes later, after I was prayed with, I had fallen to the floor. While on the floor, I encountered the person of Jesus.  I had experienced a heavenly nearness and a love that pressed on me, but also seemed to make things completely light and free.  I experienced a peace and a joy that I had never felt before.  In psychology, flow is characterized as complete absorption while losing one's sense of space and time.  The video tape shows that I was on the floor for hours but it felt like days.  I had experienced profound healing and forgiveness from my years of wayward choices.  I had experienced wholeness from my brokenness.  Of course, years later, I have learned that more healing has been needed in some areas of my life (we are a work in progress) and repentance is ongoing – my friend likens marriage and children to a crucible, a container that is used to purify metals (as the heat beneath the crucible intensifies, imperfections in the metal rise to the surface, get removed and the metal is purified). Marriage and children produce lots of heat that lead to our greatest weaknesses getting exposed. Pride is just one of many faults that I have had to lay down at the feet of God.

Despite this ongoing crucible in my life and a recognition of my many flaws, that night was a profound and influential beginning. In retrospect, I had gone from despair, pessimism, and cynicism to hope, optimism, and joy in my new-found transformation that was a true conversion in my life. It was an unforgettable experience in my life that set me off on a new course.

My psychology colleagues have traditionally called this type of prayer meeting religious hysteria. Critical theologians label this as emotionally acting out or emotional catharsis that is empty of intellectual critique. On the positive side, terms used in Pentecostal and charismatic Christianity include slaying in the Spirit, falling under the power, resting in the Spirit, or more of the Lord. Other interpretations of these experiences have labeled it an epiphany, a rupture of consciousness, a striking revelation, a religious conversion, or a sudden spiritual breakthrough. Whatever one calls it, I remember walking into my university campus ministry office a few days later and only hearing negative criticism about my experience. I respectfully left the office with my own opinion intact. I had been so profoundly changed that I was going to make up my own mind. I learned quickly that (1) my experience was my own, (2) and I was a brand-new man with a heart after God.

For those who want to examine the experience of "quantum change" through the lens of scientific psychology, read Quantum Change by Miller & Baca. Over the years, I have never forgotten my story and have told it hundreds of times. I have also come to realize that human beings tend to redefine others' experiences, particularly when it is very different from their own experience or different from their religious traditions or ideology. Regardless, I have learned that "Quantum Changes" are best defined by the individual person and can happen in many different ways. Quantum changes are not exclusive to charismatic experiences or quiet meditation in solitude. God can act on a person's life in infinite ways. I have also learned that helping our children be open to quantum changes in God is central to thriving rather than just surviving. In my experience, I knew that I had a life-changing quantum change encounter and became spiritually awakened in my faith life. Since that time, I have worked and lived my family life in the love, peace, and joy that comes from a relationship with God.

I share this story as a backdrop of how I have filtered information and research over the last 20 years. I have been on a mission to read, study, and glean from the best that the field of psychology has to offer – included here in this book are those psychological concepts of parenting excellence that convey truth, love, and, above all, FREEDOM. Although all the concepts in this book are psychological in nature, they are deeply consistent with this life of faith in God.

# Chapter One

## Improving Well-Being with Secure Attachment

*For all of us, life is like the waves of an ocean. The waves of life never stop. Even when we exert conscious control over our emotions, the ups and downs are often felt from the winds and seas of life. Relationships are the wind, the sea, and the oxygen of life. One of my favorite realities of life is that the quality of our lives depends on the quality of our relationships. Navigating these relationships is like engaging in a choreographed dance at the historic Detroit Opera House—only the stage has been transported to a big cargo ship in the middle of the ocean. Like life, the cargo ship can be a little messy, a bit unpredictable, and very challenging. As I've learned since living in Florida, the ocean waves can be dangerous and even staggering at times. Like ocean currents, relationships in life consist of approach and withdrawal, engagement and disengagement, closeness and moving away from, and connections that come together and then come apart—sometimes hard to predict. For some of us, the dance of life is experienced with a calmness of the sea and the movements are as fluid as the New York City Ballet. For some of us, the movements require excessive effort due to the heavy waves. When needs are toxically unmet, life is hard to endure, much less finding the energy to enjoy dancing over the waves.*

The relationships we are exposed to in the beginning of our lives set the stage for how we approach relationships later in life. Some of us perceive others as opportunities for positive experiences in relationships. We have experienced goodness in relationships and developed security as a result of these loving relationships. Others are motivated to avoid, manipulate, use, or distrust. Our experiences in relationships have consisted of pain, distrust, abuse, and negative feelings toward others. The combination of waves like Tsunamis crashing against us and the toxic frustration of unmet needs make for a disastrous combination. As parents, we can influence these experiences in extensive ways. Securely attached children are solid, productive, contributing members of society who make our culture healthier, and make differences in the world. Even if this is difficult for you as a human being, we want to help our children perceive others as opportunities for positive experiences in relationships. We want to bring our children to a place of loving other people.

### Attachment: An Essential Ingredient For Resilience

What is the best way to prepare our children for the adversities that lay ahead? Isn't this the question that we all want to know? Even if they experience good from us, they will get bruised out there. How do we help them respond well to those bruises? Secure attachment is an essential ingredient for preparing our children to face adversity head on. John Bowlby and Mary Ainsworth provided a foundation of thinking for healthy attachment relationships[1]. Ainsworth identified three attachment styles: secure, avoidant, and ambivalent. A fourth attachment style was later identified as disorganized, resulting in four attachment styles that have the potential to influence our interior lives[2]. Each of these styles may have affected you in one relationship or another – your mother and father, relatives, your 8th grade baseball coach, your 12th grade cross country coach, your math teacher that became a mentor or your guidance counselor. Ideally, children are influenced primarily by secure attachment styles. Research suggests that our brains keep track of different types of relationships, thus, maintaining different modes of attachment. Each of these different attachment styles has shaped your interior life and your relationship tendencies.

You may act in different ways and in different settings according to emotions evoked in relationships. These emotional states usually result from either (1) thought patterns or (2) conditioned and implicit reactions. These conditioned and implicit reactions are triggered by others in relationships. Depending on the type of relationship, your primary attachment pattern may become evoked, or your secondary attachment pattern may become awakened. The prevailing thought in the past was that each of us had an attachment style based on early relationships. It is now more accurate to describe relationship tendencies based on primary, secondary, and even tertiary attachment patterns based on current relationships. An understanding of these relationship patterns and insight into our responses in different situations can influence us toward freedom and secure attachment.

Attachment relationships is an essential ingredient for resilience. What is resilience? It is the ability to bounce back following setbacks. We have all known people who appeared to have bounce-back strength. A few years ago, I talked with a first-year college student. Kristin had endured her mother perishing in a house fire. Before Kristin left the house, she had an argument about going out that evening. Upon return, the entire neighborhood was watching the police, EMTs, and the fire department do what they could. As Kristin talked, I was struck by the impression that she had bounce-back strength. She was having college difficulties, working through her loss, and learning how to cope with new friends. It was not easy. Yet, she repeatedly spoke lovingly about her mother and could note her argument on the evening of the fire without generalizing it, letting it weigh her down, and being burdened by guilt. For Kristin, who appeared warm to friends and affectionate with her aunt and uncle, with whom she lived since the tragedy, was resilient because of her attachment relationship history. The degree of resilience prior to a traumatic event will influence whether a person experiences post-traumatic growth versus post-traumatic stress disorder.

Secure Attachment Pattern

Our attachment patterns begin to form at the beginning of life. Let's explore some of these attachment patterns. If you had a relationship with a parent or caregiver who provided consistent soothing, warmth, and unconditional acceptance, then you have a sense of secure attachment. Secure attachment develops over a repeated set of experiences of being cared for and having our emotional needs met. Repeatedly experiencing two moments of warmth per day and having experiences like interpersonal joining facilitated by parents expedites a foundation of secure attachments. Joining involves drawing close to one another both physically and emotionally; when we reach out to our kids and find ways to connect, we are joining. If a baby smiles and receives reciprocal feedback, expresses anger and is soothed, experiences stress and is given consistent attention, then the child grows up viewing the world as a safe place. This is something we all want for our babies, right? These children grow up experiencing emotional integration. They believe that all emotions such as sadness, anger, disgust, fear, and joy are important and work together. The movie *Inside Out* is a good movie for families to watch together and discuss the value of emotions working together. Therapists who work with families all tell me that this has been a great movie for their discussions.

In contrast to the aforementioned examples, if you had a relationship with a parent or caregiver who provided inconsistent soothing, coldness, and conditional acceptance, then you likely suffer from insecure attachment. If you never or rarely had moments of warmth or joining experiences, particularly during stressful moments, then unmet needs have led to being overly dependent or extremely self-sufficient, but insecure. If a baby smiles and does not receive reciprocal feedback, receives limited soothing when expressing anger, and experiences occasional attention, then the child grows up viewing the world as unsafe. Unlike the values of *Inside Out*, the emotions don't work together with children who experience inconsistency and coldness. Children who grow up insecurely attached display disintegrated emotions.

At this point, we should point out chronically poor parenting versus typical parenting. All parents make mistakes, misread facial cues, overreact to minor behavior, exhibit impatience to trivial inconveniences, and magnify problems. Do any of us go through life mistake free? We all carry baggage into the parenting endeavor. It is not parental perfection that reinforces secure attachment, but it is consistent unhealthy parenting that influences insecure attachment. If a child constantly sees an unresponsive face, he or she will feel emotionally deprived. If affection is unpredictable and warmth is conditional, a child's experience may involve feeling deprived of the reassurance he or she yearns for.

Let's look at a more extreme situation on how resilience rises to the surface based on a secure relationship foundation. A few years ago, I had the privilege of getting to know a 26-year-old male veteran named Randall. Randall grew up in a very supportive family, and developed secure attachments. He experienced reassurance, emotional reciprocity, consistent warmth, and reliable love and attention. His parents reinforced with consistency, encouraged boldness and fearlessness, and were there to support him during setbacks. Randall clearly had a secure foundation with secure attachment relationships. After achieving his associates degree, he joined the United States Marine Corps and served four years with two tours in Iraq entailing combat activity and significant war trauma. He lost four close friends, witnessed horrifying IED explosions, endured two close comrades undergo surgical amputation of limbs following mortar attacks, and saw a mother and her child attempt to walk into an area with bombs tied to their chests. He exclaimed, "I experienced horrors that the average American couldn't comprehend." Randall had his Separation Health Assessment, one of the parts of the usual process of separating from active duty. He also was evaluated at the Veteran's Affairs Medical Center. Despite his traumatization, Randall's emotional status fell along the spectrum that was closer to Trauma Growth rather than Post-Traumatic Stress Disorder.[3] Randall's ability to respond with a level of post-traumatic resilience was uniquely inspiring and a tribute to secure attachments in his relationship foundation. He attributed his ability to tolerate, overcome, and be resilient with "the overwhelming support of my family."

---

## WORDS OF WISDOM & STEPS FOR TAKING ACTION

- None of us know the kinds of traumas our children and adolescents will experience one day.

- It is natural based on love and attachment to push any possibilities of significant stress or traumatization happening to our children out of our consciousness.

- The reality is that our secure attachment with consistent soothing, warmth, and unconditional acceptance will be a deeply embedded buffer for future growth, particularly in the face of significant emotional events.

---

Avoidant Attachment Pattern

Another type of attachment results from caregivers who were insensitive and rejected the needs of children. Some children experience their needs rejected or disregarded. Sadly, this is felt deeply when children are hurt or sick. To make matters worse, these insensitive parents discourage crying, but simultaneously neglect comforting the child. When needs are rejected, boys experience disruptions in attachment and tend to develop avoidant patterns that later result in aggressive behavior. Engaged parents sometimes notice that boys' behavior problems come from a place of depressive feelings and or a need to connect in relationship. Symptoms of depression and unmet needs often result in aggressive behaviour, however, disengaged parents are unlikely to make these types of observations.

For girls, aggression may not necessarily occur in later years, but avoidance becomes the unhealthy coping strategy instead. This may involve withdrawing and going inward or seeking unmet needs in other outward and unhealthy ways. However, they have learned that seeking out other people for support is pointless. They have learned that their way of coping with the pain of being rejected depends on self – self-soothing and self -focus. Engaged parents pick up on these behavioral tendencies as well. But, parents that foster this type of attach-

4

ment are disengaged.  They are unlikely to notice these problems and consider strategies to bring changes for girls as well.

Insensitive caregivers during the early years routinely become withdrawn from helping during difficulties and are emotionally unavailable when the children become distressed.  These children would become both physically and emotionally independent of the attachment figure.  Tendencies to avoid became their modus operandi, and have become their neural pathway.  In the same way we drive to a destination on "remote control," the neural pathway of these distressed children is to become more entrenched in emotional independence.

Some teenagers and young adults (e.g. see Matt Damon's character, Will Hunting, in the movie *Good Will Hunting*) develop an avoidant attachment as a way to adapt to relationships.  By the way, *Good Will Hunting* is a great movie for closed off teenagers with talent and loyalty, but closed off to deeper connection and finding purpose.  Over the years, I have referred some clients to this movie. It is a 1997 American drama film starring Matt Damon (who plays Will Hunting) and Robin Williams (who plays a therapist).  The film follows a 20-year-old laborer named Will who is an unrecognized genius but engages in self-defeating behavior like assaulting a police officer.  Through his therapy sessions, Will begins to reflect on his life and make changes as he confronts his past and considers his future. Some people like "Will" experience a breakthrough and gain insight into the reality that life has been lived through an avoidant way of life.  This insight can be empowering and can lead to recognizing that deep inner drive to draw close in connection and relationship with others.  Awareness of these interior signals can lead people to seek out relationships and closeness with others to meet those internal needs.  As this process gets lived out, the avoidant modus operandi transforms, and the non-secure attachment moves toward healthy secure attachment.

Is this you?  Do you tend to be insensitive?  Do you withdraw when things get emotional or hard with the kids?  If you grew up developing avoidant attachment patterns, reflection and hard work can help you overcome this past and remain engaged.  The solution is becoming an engaged parent.  Fathers can become engaged fathers.  In some cases, the following is needed for self-talk – You are not like your Mom.  You are not disengaged like your Dad.  You are emotionally available.  You are an engaged parent!

Ambivalent Attachment Pattern

Another type of attachment results from inconsistency in time, effort, safety, and emotional soothing.  When the parent returns home from work, a child may be unsure about whether she will receive comfort.  When distressed, soothing happens inconsistently.  On some days, Billy experiences soothing.  On other days, Billy does not experience any soothing.  Ambivalence develops because sometimes the parent provides soothing and sometimes not.  Doubt builds but is interrupted with intermittent soothing, an unpredictable frequency of comfort.  The relationship "feels" confusing.  And, normally, a child is unable to put words to their feelings and explain this inconsistency.  A child is not able to say, "Mom, you hugged me when you got home from work yesterday but you did not hug me today."  This observation is just not an age appropriate expectation.  However, a parent may later say, "It never seemed like you needed my comfort or support. You didn't say anything at those times."

The ability to soothe is often dependent on the parent's emotional state. If the mother is happy, she is more likely going to soothe Lisa. If the mother is angry, she is more likely going to ignore Lisa. If the mother is anxious and fearful, she is more likely going to be an unreliable source of support for Lisa.

Unreliable parenting can result in both ambivalence and enmeshment. Vacillating and inconsistent love results in ambivalence—an uncertain reluctance to draw close because 'they' will withdraw. This inconsistency is particularly difficult when daughters experience this from their fathers. Fathers provide a safe place for a daughter to practice being a woman and relating as a woman. As Kiko transitioned into middle school, she was ambivalent toward teachers, reluctant to give them a chance to get to know her. Unreliable fathering and parenting in general can also result in enmeshment because finally, drinking that glass of water after two days without it can feel life giving. Jenny lost herself as she became absorbed in everything her friend Connie did. Her sense of self was absent as she craved the energy she experienced in this relationship. An absent father, either physically and/or emotionally, facilitates this craving. It is particularly troubling when Jenny becomes absorbed in her boyfriend.

A child is unable to distinguish when a parent will support him or her during distress. A child will also have difficulty separating his or her feelings from the feelings of her inconsistent mother. It is in these situations when children may try to predict soothing. Unfortunately, this cycle sometimes leads children to comfort their parents. Rather than parent, inconsistent parents may look to their children for comfort. This becomes prevalent as the children age, particularly for mothers and their daughters.

At this point---in case you are wondering, let me point out that the mother is supposed to find comfort from family members and friends her own age. Mothers are not supposed to look to their daughters for comforting and support. And, yet, this is what's happening during marriage difficulties. This results in a reciprocal effect – struggling marriages often influence inconsistent soothing[4].

There are several terms that describe these problems such as ambivalent attachment, anxious-resistant insecure attachment, or enmeshment attachment, but the term INCONSISTENCY best summarizes this problematic form of parenting. This attachment pattern may emerge or worsen if a struggling marriage results in divorce. In one family following a divorce, when Jerry was a young boy, he experienced inconsistent responsiveness from parents and step-parents. His story was quite moving. Once, when his father picked him up and put him in his car, Jerry repeatedly hit him, expressing discontent and communicating feelings the way a 4-year-old can. If he had words to express at the time, these messages in his expressions of feelings were: "I'm upset at you. Why do you leave me? Why can't you be with me? Don't leave me. This is terrible. I want to be with you always." In this situation, his father did not want the divorce and was concerned about his children but he had no choice. He did everything he could to keep the family together and continue to live with his kids. But, the young boy couldn't process these facts. He didn't understand but the feeling of anger he had when hitting his dad included, "I am so angry at you for not being with me every day." And, the pain and sadness he experienced was also in his hitting. "I feel so much sadness with this neglect. I feel so much pain that you aren't around." Other expressions would be, "I am so confused," and "I don't feel heard." Naturally, it is unreasonable to expect these expressions from a 4-year-old.

In a different situation, Jerry was picked up from his school by his father and together they enjoyed lunch together, walked along a creek together, and picked out their favorite rocks. The experience was settling for Jerry. The affection he experienced was something he had been craving. They held hands, picked and threw rocks and dunked French fries in ketchup. Together, Jerry embraced his time with his dad and didn't want it to end. While tears flowed when the day ended as Jerry was being dropped off, his father spent extensive time making the day special for his son. In contrast, Dad returned Jerry and his two sisters back to the mother's home at the end of a weekend. Highly distressed, the boy ran after his dad's car as he drove away screaming "Dad, don't leave." He was screaming for his father in desperation but was not comforted. While his dad did his best during these difficult transitions, his comfort and soothing was inconsistent due to the divorce, which is typical in these types of family configurations.

As years passed, some kids come to understand how difficult the experience was for both the parent and themselves. In healthy families, they bond over the past experience without letting the past influence their future. To this day, healthy individuals are able to say, "My Dad is a wonderful man," "My Mom is a wonderful woman." Healthy individuals are able to express gratitude for the sacrifices of their parents. On aside, I met Jerry years after these incidents and he says he thanks his dad for everything he has meant to him. "I feel propelled to channel my gratitude toward his significant sacrifice to pay for large portions of my college tuition and housing."

Is this you? Did you grow up experiencing inconsistent soothing?
Did you have a hard time distinguishing when your parent would support you during distress? When you were terribly upset, how were you soothed? Did your parents go through marriage difficulties? Did your parents go through a divorce? Did they have difficulty separating the pain from the marriage problems from their parenting with you? Did you try to predict their soothing and end up comforting your parents? As the oldest daughter, did you become your mother's comforter as a replacement for your mother's husband, your dad?

If your answer is "YES" to any of these questions, it will be important to not let this past influence your future in your own parenting. Consistent emotional soothing when your child is distressed is essential. If you are having relationship problems, it is critical that you separate the ups and downs of your adult relationships from your role as a parent to your child. This boundary is essential in order to prevent your child from becoming your comforter. Seek support elsewhere. Let your child, particularly your daughter, enjoy her childhood. To be more direct, keep your children out of your marriage conflict. Finally, if your child is distressed, put your problems to the side as you emotionally sooth. Be consistent!

<u>Disorganized Attachment Pattern</u>

        A final attachment pattern is disorganized attachment which occurs in a high percentage of at-risk families with trauma and neglect. Children experience disorganization because they simultaneously experience two dichotomous internal events on a routine basis. Whenever a person experiences abuse, the resultant schema is usually mistrust. Those abused grow up and continue to permit abuse as adults, or they become abusers themselves, which is something we see with generational abusers. Or, those abused avoid relationships altogether because they don't trust anyone. Regardless of how they cope, the consistent theme here is distrust. But, how can you distrust your primary caregiver?

When a parent begins screaming and hitting, most children experience terror. When a child experiences terror, the neural circuit activated during sympathetic activity becomes elevated. The fight, freeze, and flight mechanism is triggered and usually means "RUN" for young children. But, confusion in the interior life of the child results. The "Run for your life" system, all too familiar for children growing up in Urban America, conflicts with the attachment system that is also rooted in the limbic system. The "Run" and the "Draw close" choices become confusing. It is too difficult for children to learn how they cannot be close and far away from the same parent. To desire a hug while simultaneously desiring to withdraw results in confusion, mixed feelings, perplexity, and emotional turmoil. In chronic situations, an approach with simultaneous avoidance can lead to fragmented personalities.

        This disorganized model is best illustrated in a therapy client of mine a couple of years ago. As a warning---the following vignette is not a pleasant read. Jenny was a 23-year-old single female. She spent the first five years of her adulthood dancing at a strip club. She was torn by the idea of her mother having custody of her daughter and had difficulty coping with her anxiety disorder. She was typically emotionally labile in sessions with intermittent tearfulness every few minutes. In addition to sadness about her daughter, she desperately missed her abusive boyfriend who treated her terribly. Interestingly, she had enough insight to be able to draw the connection between her attachment with her extremely emotionally and physically abusive mother and her similarly abusive boyfriend. How could you possibly miss him after experiencing so much hurt by him? "It is what I am used to, I guess." However, her affect was not congruent with her thoughts and speech. She appeared broken with a fragmented personality. Her thinking was marked by uncertainty.

        One of the major symptoms that Jenny appeared to be prone to is dissociation – a process of separating different parts of ourselves such as feelings from memories, thoughts from feelings, and thoughts from behavior[5]. The symptom of dissociation may seem like a permanent fog in how information is processed. This affected how Jenny makes decisions and copes with difficulties.

        If this is you, therapy is needed to bring unresolved issues to resolution so love isn't conveyed to your children in conditional or selfish ways. You must do what you can to build up your support system and get the help you need for the good of your children.

<u>Self-Reflection & Self-Understanding</u>

In the context of reviewing these different attachment patterns, self-reflection and self-understanding is essential. The job of the parent has to be identified as a formative process, one in which each parent becomes more mature, more loving, more human – a better human being. None of us comes into parenting fully formed. How many of us knew exactly what was happening when we were in the hospital having our first baby? When I give parenting talks, "Surely Not!" is a common exclamation. In reality, parenting does not work well when men and women are closed to change. Instead, ongoing growth and development is a necessary condition for parenting excellence. The spirit of this book is to encourage reflection.

Daniel Siegel has studied over ten thousand formal attachment interviews—lots of parents like you and me have been interviewed about our attachment tendencies in different situations. He has found that many of us begin to develop an integrated way of making sense of our lives[6]. By reflecting on attachment experiences, people can begin to gain insights about their life. As time is taken to reflect on and understand our relationships, we begin to connect past memories with current experiences. By reflecting on our attachment tendencies, we can begin to establish a connected sense of self in our personal and on-going life narrative. This is not about categorizing ourselves, but gaining insight and becoming reflective.

The field of psychology has brought us a variety of collection tools that bring about insight and opportunities for reflection like the LOT-R that measures optimism or Rotter's Locus of Control scale (a key discussed later in Chapter 5). One such reflection tool that is used in clinical settings is the Adult Attachment Interview available on-line[7]. During the interview, clients are interviewed about their childhood experiences. They describe their relationship with their parents. They are encouraged to choose five adjectives that reflect their relationship with their mother and their relationship with their father. They would describe what they would do when they felt upset during their childhood experience. They would describe those times parents were ever threatening. "Are there any other aspects of your early experiences, that you think might have held your development back, or had a negative effect on the way you turned out?" "When you were hurt, how would your parents respond?" "When you were sad, how would they respond?" "Why do you think your parents behaved as they did during your childhood?" There are several other questions and subsequent reflections on loss, separation, death, and coping. One of my favorite aspects of this interview is that the reflection moves toward our current experiences as a parent. The following are excellent questions for self-reflection. How do you respond now, in terms of feelings, when you separate from your child / children? Upon reflecting on your childhood experiences, what would you hope your child might learn from his/her experiences of being parented by you? If the field of psychology is going to make a difference, an assessment tool like this one is going to speak to our minds and move our hearts as we reflect on our lives.

# REFLECTION TIPS

As a mental health exercise for a retreat, or a two-hour nature meditation, or some get-away time while the kids are in school, I recommend that parents take time to write out (old school) their answers to these questions.

**Questions that invite self-reflection:**

• Are there any ways that you experience healing by parenting differently?

• In what ways do you parent differently than your parents?

• What 5 things would you have wanted your father to say to you growing up that he didn't say? These are the kinds of things that you tell your teenager.

• What are some of the positive aspects of your parents' parenting that you want to incorporate into your parenting?

• How do you encourage dialogue rather than shut the talk down?

• Do you provide choices rather than enforce one way?

• Do you allow negotiation rather than demand? Do you embrace and express affection rather than hit?

• Do you love unconditionally rather than based on convenience or mood?

• Do you abstain from alcohol or use it in moderation with the energy on the family rather than using alcohol as a primary source of time, energy, and expense causing chronic family problems?

• Do you maintain one-on-one conflict with your partner rather than involve your daughter triangulating the conflict? Do you speak well of your children's other parent rather than bad talk him, undermine her, or influence relationship rifts?

• In what ways can you talk to your children about your parenting? Are you able to make comments to your kids like, "Some parents choose to do this and others..." showing rationale behind your decision and openness to learning?

> *Love thrives in the face of all of life's hazards, save one — neglect.*
> — John Dryden

## Parenting Style

A healthy mindset of a young person is a result of secure attachment relationships and three positive factors: (1) He/she experienced a healthy balance of choices and limits communicated with warmth throughout childhood; (2) He/she experienced consistency from their parents, and (3) He/she experienced nurturance and acceptance.

Let's take a step back and review the three traditional views of parenting orientations or prototypes that influence the limits, consistency, and nurturance levels. The traditional views of parental prototypes are best assessed using the Parental Authority Questionnaire developed by John Buri[8], which has now been translated into more than three dozen languages. The questionnaire was developed for measuring Diana Baumrind's permissive, authoritarian, and authoritative parenting styles[9].

The following are some item examples from the Parental Authority Questionnaire that represent permissive parenting ("mother" can be replaced with "father"):

- As I was growing up, my mother did not direct the behaviors, activities, and desires of the children in the family.
- My mother did not view herself as responsible for directing and guiding my behavior as I was growing up.
- As I was growing up, my mother seldom gave me expectations and guidelines for my behavior.

The following are some item examples from the Parental Authority Questionnaire that represent authoritarian parenting:

- As I was growing up, my mother often told me exactly what she wanted me to do and how she expected me to do it.
- Even if her children didn't agree with her, my mother felt that it was for our own good if we were forced to conform to what she thought was right.
- My mother has always felt that more force should be used by parents in order to get their children to behave the way they are supposed to.

The following are some item examples from the Parental Authority Questionnaire that represent authoritative parenting:

- My mother has always encouraged verbal give-and-take whenever I have felt that family rules and restrictions were unreasonable.

11

- My mother gave me direction for my behavior and activities as I was growing up and she expected me to follow her direction, but she was always willing to listen to my concerns and to discuss that direction with me.

- As I was growing up, if my mother made a decision in the family that hurt me, she was willing to discuss that decision with me and to admit it if she had made a mistake.

These examples speak volumes about the differences in parenting styles. Permissive parenting is high in warmth but low in control. There are no expectations, rules, consequences, and limits. "No Curfew?!" Ice cream whenever we want? Yes!!! Authoritarian parenting is low in warmth but high in control. These types of parents were not open to discussions, give and take, negotiating, or an interest in feelings. The "because I said so" comment was communicated often. "When does Mom get home?" "When she gets here." "Why can't I go out and play?" "Because I said so." There is little thought that goes into the responses of the authoritarian parent. Children with average intellectual functioning gradually or eventually perceive that they are getting little effort by their parent. In contrast, authoritative parenting consists of transparent communication with all questions answered and reasons explained. Authoritative parenting is high in both warmth and control. Discipline is based on reasoning and rationale, disagreements are allowed, and feelings are important. For decades, research has pointed to authoritative parenting as being the best approach for young people in measures of academic, relational, vocational or any other measures of success.

Many parents are transitioning from the old "because I said so" phrase to more connecting phrases such as "When...Then..." When you've cleaned your room, then you can go out and play. When you've finished your school homework, then you can play on the computer. And, the "when...then..." is fully negotiable. Another phrase is "Asked and Answered[10]." Children appear to have internal programming that says something like "If I ask 72 times, the parent will change his or her mind." To make things worse, somewhere down the line, we changed our minds on the 28th request to 'end the nagging.' From now on, anytime a child repeats a question that has already been answered, parents can simply say "Asked and Answered." When children whine about a parent's decision to not go to Dairy Queen after soccer practice, explaining the rationale is always more advantageous. When the questions keep coming, a parent might respond with, "Have you heard of 'Asked and Answered?'" Then briefly review the question and answer ("Did you ask me if we could go to DQ?" "What was the answer?") Then the parent may ask, "Do I seem like the kind of parent who would change his mind when you ask over and over?" Following responses entail "Asked and Answered."

This technique is effective for those chronic inquiries when the kid won't give up no matter what. However, I still recommend thoroughly discussing the reasons and the rationale and encouraging the child to agree to disagree. Maintaining an active conversation is more valuable than "Asked and Answered" techniques that might end the discussion.

*It is better to debate a question without settling it than to settle a question without debating it.*
*- Joseph Joubert*

---

## WORDS OF WISDOM & STEPS FOR TAKING ACTION

- The research is clear that authoritative parenting is optimal.

- Provide verbal give-and-take as frequently as needed as children learn to work within family rules and restrictions.

- Apologize for making mistakes.  If you make a parenting mistake, children are empowered by humility when parents admit their mistake.

- Communicate the expectation that your child follow directions, but you as the parents will always be willing to listen to any concerns he or she has.

- Maintain consistent soothing, warmth, and unconditional acceptance.

- Transition from "because I said so" to more connecting phrases such as "When...Then..." or "Asked and Answered."

- Maintain conversation rather than look for ways to end it.

---

Attachment Parenting

Now, let's look at some other types of parenting styles.  In light of the importance of helping young people become securely attached, let's examine this new wave of parenting, often referred to as attachment parenting, also sometimes known as intensive mothering.  These ideas have been studied for 60 years, but have been popularized by Dr. William Sears and his wife Martha Sears, RN in the 1990s.

According to Attachment Parenting International, the eight principles of attachment parenting are: Prepare for pregnancy, birth & parenting; Feed with love and respect; Respond with sensitivity; Use nurturing touch; Ensure safe sleep, physically and emotionally; Provide consistent and loving care; Practice positive discipline: Strive for balance in your personal and family life.
Parents applying the principles consistent with attachment parenting are very concerned about understanding the biological and psychological needs of their child.  They are very concerned about meeting the child's preferences, emotional needs, and desires for affection and love.  Parents who practice attachment

parenting have a strong desire to bond with their child. These parents use re-direction, natural consequences, listening and modeling in their primary parenting toolkit. While boundaries and limits are intended to be age appropriate, they are sometimes delayed or not enforced at all -- no matter what. Co-sleeping is sometimes emphasized. I recently saw a child named Johnny who slept in Mom's bed until the age of 6. I thought this was a big deal until I met an 8-year-old named Miranda a few weeks later who was sleeping with her mother. Research is not conclusive on its long-term advantages. It should be noted that Western culture has emphasized independence in sleeping arrangements, whereas many Japanese children co-sleep with their parents through childhood and 50% co-sleep until the mid teens. Attachment parenting is highly labor intensive, particularly for mothers.

Parenting that depends on attachment parenting theory will not use traditional behavioral interventions. Time-outs and other negative or punitive consequences with clear limits are not incorporated. In theory, this has many advantages: a strong emotional bonding, trust, a robust parent child relationship, affectionate interactions, parental nurturance, and warmth.

When attachment parenting is incorporated in real life parenting of children who test limits, have behavior problems, refuse to go to bed, throw things, have temper tantrums, and may refuse affection [which are common behaviors in children of all ages], attachment parenting has its limitations. The way this can play out with some parents is an unwillingness to say "No" to a child who is refusing to follow a request such as sitting at the dinner table or refusing to go to bed. I worked with a family who allowed their son Billy to wander around playing and the parents who initially attempted to have dinner at the table actually started taking their plates to the toy area in the family room. One might say, no big deal. But, this has consequences. Dinner at the toy table or wherever else Billy chooses can be routine for parents trying to include a 4-year old's wishes. The motivation behind the parents was to encourage the child's needs for attachment and bonding. The disadvantage in this example is that children like Billy are not taught to bond within a parameter orchestrated by the parents; instead, the parameter of affection is orchestrated by the children. Again, this disadvantage can be seen as a positive from the attachment theory perspective. The answer is to allow particular choices within the parameters of the parents' family expectations such as where the child would like to sit at the dinner table or what type of plate she would like to use.

Consider the second example, unwillingness to provide structure at sleep time – a girl named Lisa was encouraged with affection each time she left her bed. Lisa repeatedly came out and dragged her 7:30 p.m. bedtime to 11:00 p.m. or later (on a regular basis). Sleep time can be a draining experience for parents conflicted with an attachment bond but refusing to set limits and boundaries. Parents may never set limits, say no, or implement consequences if a child continues to get out of bed. As you might suspect, this is not an intervention that I recommend and alternative strategies eventually realigned Lisa's sleep habits with her parents. However, from an attachment-parenting viewpoint, parents say that the bond is stronger and more important than learning limits or boundaries.

In reality, the problem with attachment parenting is that it eventually transfers into a permissive parenting approach. One of the long-term consequences of permissive parenting is that negative emotions become intolerable. Consider the reality that if you never experience a "no," one's tolerance of nos is low. This limited tolerance results in fewer opportunities to adjust and cope with unmet preferences. Put simply, it is good for children to experience limits and hear the word "no." Without hearing "no," they don't get to practice coping with disappointment. When children do hear "no," they learn to cope with disappointment. With few limits and subsequently insufficient coping skills, children develop in such a way that they avoid all risks. They avoid risks because they don't know how to cope with discomfort and disappointments.

Emotional Intelligence (EQ) is the ability to manage your own emotions and accept the emotions of others. It generally includes three skills: (1) emotional awareness—the ability to identify your own emotions and the emotions of others; (2) emotional deftness—the ability to harness emotions and apply them to problem solving; (3) emotional management—the ability to regulate one's own emotions as well as cheer up or calm down someone else without attempting to control a person. Similar to intelligence (IQ), emotional intelligence (EQ) isn't a biological set point. EQ can be developed when children learn to feel comfortable with more challenging feelings. When children hear "no," their tolerance threshold for hearing "nos" can increase. A child who avoids all risks never learns to cope with challenging feelings resulting in extremely low or borderline emotional intelligence.

Another long-term consequence of attachment and permissive parents is the development of self-control. Children without limits may have difficulty putting limits on themselves. Consider a dog that will eat dog food in one sitting until he dies. Do any of us have a kid that would keep eating the Halloween candy without limits? Basically, kids need limits. Without them, they don't learn to limit themselves. Individuals raised in permissive households have a higher probability of problems with tobacco use, alcohol use, street drug use, riding a motorcycle without a helmet, drinking or using drugs and driving, driving recklessly, unprotected sex, walking in dangerous areas, and other problems[11].

Reasons behind attachment parenting boils down to three motives: (a) parents wanting to do things differently with their children than they had experienced with their parents, (b) parents wanting to make sure that their children feel "loved" – which can lead people to overdo privileges and underdo restrictions, and (c) simply getting in a pattern of doing whatever is most convenient – there are quite a few people who are not very intentional in their parenting --- it's simply easier to have your child sleep with you than it is to help them sleep on their own.

## REFLECTION TIPS

- If you subscribe to an attachment parenting philosophy, incorporate consistency and limits to make your parenting healthier.

- If dinner ends up at a different location than the dinner table, meals together are better than meals separated. Family togetherness is best facilitated by eating together.

- Parents find bed-time easier when they communicate with consistency around the issue of sleep. A gold standard routine is any routine done consistently.

- Excellent parenting consists of a close to precise balance of privileges and restrictions.

- Be intentional as a parent.

*The most prevalent failure of love is the failure to express it.*
                                                   - Paul E. Johnson

### Conditional Love Parenting

While attachment parenting is based on a thorough set of ideas and philosophy, there are other types of parenting that are not thought through and can lead to problems. How many of us think through our parenting strategies? I was surprised to hear from an unembarrassed and enthusiastic father named Kevin who attended one of my parenting talks. He raised his hand and fervently stated, "I never stop and think. Instead, I rely on my instinct to do the right thing." While most people aren't like Kevin---at least from the standpoint of being curious enough to attend parenting talks, it seems that Kevin speaks for many. Our entertainment age makes it harder and harder to reflect on our lives and many of us do rely on our instincts without reflecting. When we aren't squeezing in diaper changes, soccer practices, and birthday parties, parents appear to make decisions based on its entertainment value. Consider car commercials who now emphasize the movie screens on the back of car seats. Or, a commercial featuring an uncle babysitting his nephews and appearing overwhelmed until he pulls out the tablets. Movies, computer games, television, internet, sports, music, videos, smartphones, smart watches, and the list continues. Do all these products actually make our lives better? Do they just make us more distracted?

One thing that appears clear is that this entertainment doesn't help in the reflectiveness department of our lives. And, in the absence of reflectiveness, the most common methods of instinct are ignoring and anger. These instinct methods are more likely going to pop up during times of stress. Now is a good time to reflect on these methods and rely less on our parenting instinct and more on clear well-thought out parenting ideas. First of all, ignoring doesn't work. And, sometimes ignoring is really "taking a parenting break" and being "apathetic." How many of us want to withdraw when stressed? If we are honest, many of us. Parents who use ignoring fail to attend to a window – an opportunity to teach or listen.

Anger is another method of instinct that doesn't work. Anger is used often, but is usually ineffective as an intervention. Anger sends the message that the parent has lost control. Staying objective and neutral with consequences is an ideal parenting goal. Of course, easier said than done. But, this means that parents are more concerned about teaching and not forcing, or supplying enough pressure to make your children different. Some parents will use anger as a way to supply pressure. "If I only supply enough pressure [using anger], then my child will change her messy bedroom habit." Maintaining poise in the face of distress is more effective than getting angry. "If I only supply enough pressure [using anger], then Johnny will stop talking back." "If I only get angry enough and holler across the house, my child will stop saying 'you're mean!' "If he experiences my anger, he will know that I am in charge." Many parents get in an anger rut. Something happens and anger is the immediate reaction. Composure and grace work much better than anger and pressure.

*Love doesn't sit there like a stone, it has to be made, like bread; remade all the time, made new.*
*– Ursula LeGuin*

Then there are those things that parents do that are not as noticeable. Using ignoring and using anger are very noticeable to the outside observer. Conditional love parenting, which is rooted in the idea that expressions of love are based on the child meeting a set of conditions, occurs in the parent-child dynamics in a very subtle way, not so obvious to those looking in. This subtle strategy that a child needs to meet a set of conditions is a fallacy. When Ted and I were watching our daughters at gymnastics practice, I routinely witnessed Ted say to his youngest son who was a bit disruptive, "If you really loved me, you would do what I want." This conditional love fallacy is a belief that basically gets in the way of the expression of love between parents and children.

## REFLECTION TIPS

**Here are some things that parents may say as an expression of conditional love:**

- "If you really loved me, you would follow my directions."

- "If you really loved me, then you would get dressed like I asked."

- "If you really loved me, then you would practice for your recital more."

- "If you really loved me, then you would not go out with your friends and you would stay here and help with the laundry."

- "If you really loved me, then you would shut up so I can watch the game."

- "If you really loved me, then you would stop crying."

Whenever a parent uses the words "if you really loved me," it is almost always unhealthy. The message that is communicated in the "if you really loved me" messages is that the parent's love is conditional. "I will only love you if you do X." Conditional love parenting patterns emerge in all kinds of family configurations. Conditional love issues tend to occur for adolescents from non-intact families. I worked with a 19-year-old college 1st year student named Amy who endured her parents divorcing when she was 16 years old. She experienced counseling and coped with support from family and friends during 6 painful months. After she began to "feel like she was turning the corner," she realized that she had to endure continued "dysfunctional pulling" by both parents. She found herself in the middle of her parents vying for favoritism, which included the use of money to maintain "control." She subtly experienced manipulation by her mother regarding payments for tuition, which influenced whether she would drop out of her part-time job or not. She felt stuck because time spent on weekends and holidays influenced tuition payments. Amy experienced communication about these matters as subtle and manipulative. What she found most difficult was how love in the areas of listening and expressing affection depended on her mother's perception that she was spending more time with her than her father. Amy began to find the relationship exhausting. "It wasn't just the excessive texts about everyday conversations when I was with Dad trying to pull my attention toward her. It was her moodiness. If I didn't call enough, she would mope and scowl. And if I didn't join her in her gloominess, then it meant I didn't care about her."

One of the major tenets of successful parenting is that parents will love children, teenagers, and young adults no matter what the circumstances are.

18

Love is neither added nor subtracted. There is nothing a child can do to increase a parent's love for them. And, there is nothing a child can do to decrease a parent's love for them. Divorces certainly are messy, but even divorces should not be an antecedent to conditional love. A critical element of healthy parental functioning in non-intact families is for parents to find support from outside of the family, as opposed to leaning on a son or daughter. Amy needed her mother to find support elsewhere so Amy could invest her emotional resources into college life.

Unconditional love parenting can be taught to children early on, and serve as a reminder to us that this is a value to the family. When my youngest son was four, his response to being roughhoused by a sibling or hearing an undesired "no" from a parent was saying, "I don't love you." I sat down and gave my son an alternative expression. In our family, we always love each other and we never say, "I don't love you." Instead, "when you get pinned down by your brother, you can say, "I am angry at you when you hold me down." When you can't have a popsicle before bedtime, you can say, "I am angry at you for saying no." As a family, we can teach our children that love for each other never changes on the whim or by a recent argument or fight. Instead, expressing anger is appropriate, valued, and respected in our family.

> " *Loving can cost a lot but not loving always costs more, and those who fear to love often find that want of love is an emptiness that robs joy from life.* — Merle Shain

### Take Time To Heal

The journey of life is a difficult one. And we all accumulate hurts along the way. Sometimes, these hurts result in blind spots if we aren't aware of them. One of our life jobs is to resolve blind spots from our history in order to prevent conditional love in our parenting. The last thing kids need is conditional love. Yet, this subtle poison comes out in how well the kid performs in her tumbling as part of her gymnastics floor routine or how well he performs in his dance recital. Kids need unconditional love when it comes to performance, behavior in the classroom, or any other area. No matter what kids do, kids need to know that their parents will love them no matter what. Drugs, teenage pregnancy, juvenile detention, not getting Ivy League scholarships, not winning, not breaking records, misspelling on tests or whatever it is that might be perceived as a "disappointment." Love needs to be there throughout life's victories and defeats.

Sometimes unresolved blind spots cause conditional love such as those things that bring on flooding, overgeneralizations ("you always or you never"), visual resentments, or anger problems. Information on the human brain sheds insight here. Up front is the frontal lobe, specifically the prefrontal cortex. When parents are overwhelmed quickly, they may start to flood emotionally; this leads to shutting down, withdrawing, or avoiding an important discussion. It is in the prefrontal cortex where we learn, abstract, inhibit, and reason. These abilities decline in the face of parental stress. Another brain area is the parietal lobe which is where problem solving takes place along with attention and association. When parents say, "you always do that," the overgeneralization is an association problem [what is needed is specifically staying on subject]. The visual process occurs in the occipital lobe—parents who visually replay the criticism, back-talking, and other behavior problems tend to resent their teenagers. Another key area are the temporal lobes which are located on both sides of your head. These lobes deal with word recognition, language, memory and facial recognition. If you struggle with anger, you probably have some hot temporal lobes.

Let me take a moment here to encourage parents who have underlying issues that may lead to conditional love parenting. Most of us would agree that the best environment for a child to thrive is one that is grounded in unconditional love, but resolving blind spots is the best way to accomplish this. We can agree that most parents love their children. Love is likely not an issue for those reading this book. But, sometimes underlying issues get in the way of loving our children unconditionally. If this is you, I recommend seeking therapy to address issues that get in the way of unconditional love between you and your children. The first place to start is to do a self-examination and begin to notice any of your conditional love patterns.

A common blind-spot is in the area of family of origin issues, where you can notice conditional love patterns. On questions related to the mistakes of their own parents, many adults look down on the road of their life and say something like, "My parents did the best that they could." There is little insight and reflectiveness on anything that they would have done differently.

On the other end of the spectrum, some adults say, "I don't want anything to do with my parents." In these situations, some adults are better off not being around their parents due to alcoholism, sexual abuse, physical abuse, or other poisonous behaviors. In other situations, that are safe and not as toxic, adults and their children might benefit from positive experiences but are unable to forgive and forget disappointments. Their recollections of their personal histories consist of unresolved emotional entanglements. Consequently, some kids only hear negative comments about their grandparents and these children are the ones who suffer relationally.

Consider, for example, Harvey, a father of three. I had gotten to know Harvey quite well as a soccer dad—I coached one of his sons for two seasons. He came to a parenting talk Sarah and I gave in Sarasota and desired some time to talk afterwards over coffee. He and his wife Tiffany wanted to talk about a struggle they were having in their family. As the conversation got rolling, Harvey began to talk about his relationship with his dad: "My father was very controlling in my childhood. When I grew up, it always seemed like I could never do anything right. He was always criticizing me and was negative with me all the time. When I didn't advance in the 7th grade spelling bee, he only focused on the words I missed even though I was second in my class. When I made varsity as a sophomore in Track, he criticized my events. Whether academics, sports, or friends, he was Mr. Critical." The background for this discussion was that Harvey's father (and his step-mother) were planning to move down to Sarasota from Ohio and Harvey and Tiffany were discussing its impact on their three children. Harvey was rightly concerned about how "Grandpa" was going to approach being a grandfather. Was Grandpa going to be positive, hopeful, warm, kind, a source of encouragement, and a nurturer of fondness and appreciation? Or, was Grandpa going to be negative, cold, selfish, critical, and a source of discouragement? I suggested to Harvey that "he was going to have to monitor the situation and use his best judgment. Perhaps "Grandpa's time with the kids would initially only be in your house until you could get a good read on his attitude with the kids."

At the heart of the matter was Harvey's forgiveness. I suggested that while he would need to monitor the situation, his desire to be forgiving may go a long way for all of the family relationships. As long as Harvey's father isn't bringing any poisonous behaviors down to Florida, I suggested that "giving it a try" might be a great thing for both "Dad" and Harvey's kids.

Everyone has an opinion on what people should do about past issues. On the one side, advice usually consists of "time to move on," "forgive and forget," "let bygones be bygones," "life is short, put that bad feeling behind you." On the other side, advice consists of "refuse to give attention to people who have hurt you," or "they don't deserve your love." The goal of present resolution that can occur in therapy is that the past doesn't have a grip on one's present. In those situations, where the past truly does affect the present, therapy can help alleviate unresolved hurt and bring some degree of resolution—forgiving, letting go, problem solving, acceptance, and healing— all result from therapy about the past. With success, adults can allow reminiscing on good things to hold more weight than past negatives. And, most importantly, adults can simply emphasize grandchild-grandparent relationships for the good of the kids. I saw Harvey a year later and he reported that his kids' relationships with Grandpa were great. He was surprised and pleased at the stark difference. He also noted that his desire to forgive his dad had made a difference in his openness.

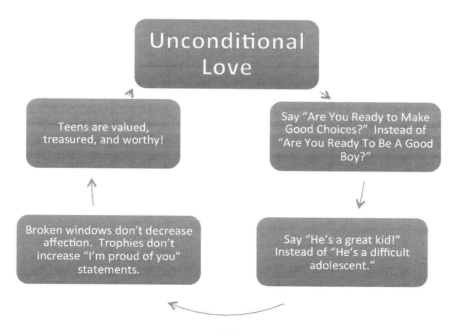

Dying Hard To Inconveniences

Some parents have a hard time adjusting to parenting. And, I'm not just talking about the first year of a couple's first child. I have talked with some parents who had trouble adjusting for 20 years and stayed out of their child's life or were mainly on the sidelines as opposed to being in the game. I call this convenience parenting. They will be involved to a degree, as long as it is convenient.

Dedicated parents invest themselves despite the inconveniences. A classic movie from the past is "Die Hard." The challenges of parenting are very difficult to say the least. The words disheartening and discouraging describes parenting experiences from time to time. When new parents describe parenting difficulties, I am often reminded of John McClain's movie quote (Bruce Willis' character in Die Hard): "Welcome to the party pal."

There are many things about the parenting process that can be summarized by being inconvenienced. Sometimes, during low moments, parents can feel like it is "all" about being inconvenienced. During our high moments, we realize it is all worth it. Excellent parents can tolerate inconveniences with poise. I call the process of repeatedly being inconvenienced with more understanding as increasing the tolerance threshold. The goal isn't to pull up the boot straps and force ourselves through yet "another difficulty." Instead, the growth of our tolerance threshold should bring us to a place of being able to nurture fondness more effectively, cultivate an attitude of gratitude more regularly, and genuinely express good-hearted positivity.

Considering the inconvenience possibilities are endless:

Finally getting a chance to read the book you've steadily had to put off (after cleaning the floor), your toddler wakes up from a nap.

You are unable to do your scheduled workout because your kid is sick and you have to take him to a doctor.

Trying a new recipe for dinner gets repeatedly interrupted by sibling rivalry.

Your bubble bath gets cold as you get ready, because your third grader keeps coming out of her bedroom (after bedtime) and reminding you of her homework that she forgot.

Car rides and drives to practices for your teenage soccer player.

Preparing lunches, washing a preferred outfit at the last minute, and the list goes on and on.

In Die Hard, there is a good period of time when the character gets blamed even when he is doing all he can to defeat the terrorists. As funny as the metaphor is, there are some similarities in parenting. There is a good period of time

> *The greatest weapon against stress is our ability to choose one thought over another.*   - William James

in parenting when the job is thankless.  A parent continues to address his child but the child is sent home from Kindergarten because he won't stop throwing his crayons.  A parent leaves extra early from home to avoid the 5th tardy in a row, but gets a flat tire.  A parent receives criticism at work because she is constantly needing to pick up the sick kid from school or the kid who is aggressive and sent home.   Parenting is a highly thankless job.  How thankful are children when we ask them to responsibly participate in family chores?  How thankful are children when we say no to an unreasonable request?  How thankful are children when we identify dinner-time as a phone-free zone and remind them that "we don't check for texts."

A lot of parenting is about dying hard for the good of the child's and adolescent's future.  Parenting consists of a lot of sacrifice for the good of children, but rarely (if at all) is it helpful to communicate how difficult things are.  Parenting is best when selflessness is the goal.  Thus, parents need to refrain from reminding their teenagers how difficult they are, how inconvenient or "how many changes they are causing for my schedule."  These comments simply do not earn points and "jewels on their crown," and are unhelpful for any parent-child relationship.  "Do you know how much that costs?"  "Do you know what you are doing to me?"  "Do you know how much of an inconvenience you are to me right now?"   Make a commitment to keep these thoughts unspoken, work to change these thoughts, and keep selflessness as the goal.

Then there are those serious life disruptions that make small inconveniences appear unimportant.  There are those life changing interferences that make heartbroken parents want to be inconvenienced with bubble bath interruptions, sibling arguments, and car rides to basketball practice.  Inconveniences are relative, as colds, diarrhea, ear infections, pinkeye, and food poisoning pale compared to life altering events, medical illness, and death.  The Johnsons faithfully drove their 8-year-old daughter Louise for her regular chemotherapy appointments to treat her acute lymphocytic leukemia.  Jackie tearfully drove her son upon his return to school after the combined funeral of her daughter (Billy's sister) and her husband (Billy's father) who were lost in a major car accident three weeks ago.   The reality of illness or death bring parents to a place of desperately missing those minor inconveniences.

One of the remedies to being inconvenienced is recognizing the value and power of humility.  Parenting is an imperfect job.  And, it's guaranteed that you as a parent will come up short.  Kids need to hear that we are all flawed.  Every one of us has shortcomings.  All parents make a lot of mistakes.  The antidote to our flaws is acknowledging that we are flawed.  Humility is such an attractive trait and essential to learning to tolerate being inconvenienced.  Humility and the 3 Cs help parents maintain poise when being inconvenienced.

**Calm under pressure**
    **Compassion** – kind-heartedness and warmth
    **Consistency** – addressing problems consistently

In addition to humility, another remedy to being inconvenienced is elevating gratitude. Humility helps increase our tolerance for being inconvenienced. Humility is like an aroma that is dispersed from a beautiful garden. Have you ever disliked being around someone who conveyed genuine humility? It would be a rarity. Most people thoroughly enjoy the company of humility. Gratitude is the psychological quality that conveys similar positive feelings. Have you felt better when you deliberately identified things, experiences, blessings you are grateful for?

## REFLECTION EXERCISE

Gratitude is a cousin of humility. Reflecting on minor inconveniences pales in comparison to life-altering heartbreaking experiences. One of the more meaningful exercises we can do as parents is increase our gratitude. Our perspective broadens with Gratitude Exercises.

**Identify three things you are grateful for with each child:**

1_____

2_____

3_____

> *On entering upon family life, he (she) saw at every step that it was utterly different from what he (she) had imagined.  At every step, he (she) experienced what a man (woman) would experience who, after admiring the smooth, happy course of a little boat on a lake, should get into that little boat.  He (she) saw that it was not all sitting still, floating smoothly; that one had to think too, not for an instant to forget where one was floating; and that there was water under one, and that one must row; and that his (her) unaccustomed hands would be sore; and that it was only to look at it that was easy; but that doing it, though very delightful, was very difficult.*
>
> - Leo Tolstoy

## Shutting the Door on Shame

There are a range of problems that can develop from permissive parenting, authoritarian parenting, conditional love parenting, and convenience parenting.  And, we have analyzed the advantages and disadvantages of attachment parenting.  In contrast, healthy parenting consists of a precise balance of choices and limits with steady privileges and restrictions; consistency in all areas; and unconditional love with nurturance and acceptance.  Healthy parenting also involves working one's way toward reducing SHAMING and increasing JOINING.  SHAME is that awful emotion that sets in when our youth internalize the belief "I am not good enough" or "I'm not enough."   Isn't "Shame" something we want to keep away from our children?   Shame can stick like glue.  Whenever I used glue as a child growing up, that sticky stuff would get between my fingers and become sticky and messy and sometimes harden.  It was a nuisance that sometimes stayed on all day.  It also tasted nasty if I went to bite my nails and forgot that I hadn't washed yet.  I can still remember that taste from elementary school.  Shame has that same kind of effect.

When it comes to shaming, examining our use of words is critical.  A lot of the words and phrases we use and speak in our everyday life is culturally based.  Some of these phrases need to get updated with current psychological understanding.  Parents will say, "Are you ready to be a good girl or good boy?"  "Be a good girl today."  This "good girl," "bad girl," "good boy," and "bad boy" language is a shame-based problem.  This language is so ingrained that it is continuously passed down.  Several years ago, my son threw a simple toy at our baby sitter's face and wrote a letter of regret and communicated his apology. They embraced and she graciously forgave him and then said, "You're going to be a good boy today now."

Parents will say "You're such a good boy" after they demonstrate appropriate behavior (i.e. well-mannered at church or a restaurant).  It is very common for parents to use this language.   The underlying message is that when you exhibit appropriate behavior or desired behavior, you are good.  When you do not do those appropriate behaviors, you are not good. This simple language sets the mentality for that child that their goodness, who they are, is impacted by what they do. It is critical to understand that children are not the sum total of their behavior. This is contrary to famous quotes and philosophies that say – you are what you do. This mantra is now a guide for how we approach parenting. Instead, a child's specialness, uniqueness, and loveliness is in who they are, even if they don't act lovely from time to time.

Good girl, good boy language sets the stage for shame. Shame is destructive emotion and distinct from guilt. Shame is a feeling I have when I do something wrong and I think there is something wrong with me. Shame results when I believe that I'm a bad person, that I am unworthy of love, that I am unworthy of connection. Shame is loudest when I view myself as being defective. There is something about me that people don't want to be around because I'm defective. Using "good girl, good boy" language after behavior sets up a destructive pattern. The language suggests that children are not good because of their behavior. Their goodness is inherent. No matter what, they are good boys and good girls.

What we want to do instead is use language such as "Good job carrying your plate to the counter," not good girl or good boy. "Are you ready to be a good boy in church?" Instead, the better question is, "Are you ready to make good choices?" "Are you ready to meet standards of behavior?" That might sound formulaic but it moves the child's focus toward their behavior. "Are you ready to maintain appropriate and polite behavior?" Or on simple things…… "Are you ready to sit still?" "Are you ready to be quiet when somebody else is talking?" This sounds much better than, "Are you ready to be a good girl when someone is talking?" When kids do a really nice job in the restaurant – appropriate, inside voice, polite; parents may say "You were such a good girl in the restaurant." The more specific the communication is, the better the parenting. "You did such a good job sitting in your seat in the restaurant." "Thank you for not running all over the restaurant." These comments are more precise and move the child away from shaming.

Is this really necessary? Aren't we talking semantics here? No, this distinction is critical because the language we use is influenced by our attitude toward our children. The bottom line is that children are already good. There is no child who is a bad child. Children are inherently good. All children are lovable. All children are worthy of our love. The main idea here regarding coaching our kids is specifying behavior. It is one very small correction that goes a long way in brightening our view of how we see children in our lives and makes a big difference for children.

Let's consider other types of shame-based parenting. "I am so disappointed in you!" "I am so ashamed of you!" "What is wrong with me for you to turn out like this?" "You are a disgrace!" "How dare you embarrass me like that!" These shame-based tactics work the same way because they chip away at the child's sense of lovableness. These comments pulverize a child's sense of self-worth. What's a few comments here and there? It's a gradual chipping away at your son's (daughter's) sense of self. Eventually, these comments send the message that your child is bad, unlovable, and worthless.

As teenagers progress toward young adulthood, the message is the same.

Teenagers are inherently good.  Our kids are worth it.  They have worth, significance, and loveliness.  Our teenagers have dignity and worth does not depend
on what they do.  Many parents approach day to day attitudes toward their kids
that attaches "good" and "bad" to who their kids are.  Consider the following
thoughts:  when kids do their chores and follow directions, they are good kids;
when my adolescent becomes noncompliant, withdrawn, or selfish, she's a bad
kid.  Beyond behavior, when teens score well on exams, they are good kids.  When
adolescents struggle in math and exhibit poor study habits, they are lousy kids.
"Jimmy's such a bad kid right now, he quit the baseball team and has no purpose
right now."  "Tomeka keeps quitting her jobs, I don't understand her."

After volunteering at a summer camp, I talked with a mom who was worried about her teenage son, Aaron, who seemed rebellious, was obsessed about
rap music, and was becoming "very different" as a teenager. She was surprised
to hear the words, "He's such a great kid" and appeared to disagree a bit looking dazed and confused.  While many parents like to brag, and put honor roll
bumper stickers on their cars, the overwhelmed parents will prefer to categorize
their teens as "difficult adolescents."  Aaron's mom said, "You just don't know him
like I do!"  I responded, "I don't, but I know he's a great kid!"   There should be
nothing that can make our kids inherently good.

One of the best ways our coaches, mentors, teachers, counselors, and
most importantly, parents can touch the lives of our teens—is genuinely believing in them and their potential to be contributing members of society, make our
culture healthier, and be world changers.  This starts with seeing our teenagers as
inherently good.  Teens are valued, treasured, and worthy.  All are worthy of our
love.  This unconditional love shuts the door on shame.

## WORDS OF WISDOM & STEPS FOR TAKING ACTION

- Eliminate "good girl" – "bad girl" and "good boy" – "bad boy" language based on the principle that children are inherently good.

- Emphasize specific behavior praising, evaluating, and providing
  feedback on specific actions.

- Recognize defectiveness and that subsequent shame results from
  conditional love.

- Live and parent by the primary principle that unconditional love
  guides all parenting.  Broken windows don't decrease affection and
  trophies don't increase "I'm proud of you" statements.

Interpersonal Joining

Interpersonal joining is doing those things that say to your child that you are with them no matter what. Joining behaviors send the message of we-ness, solidarity, and togetherness. While it's helpful for parents to be language sensitive to reduce shaming and seeing our kids as inherently good, it is just as important for parents to be passionate about joining. A concern that several professional clinicians have when working with parents is that joining efforts occur following their child's achievements, but coldness and rejection emerge after failures. Interpersonal joining consists of connecting at those moments of hardship and failure.

It is critical for each of the three parenting tenets to be embedded with joining behaviors. The three major tenets of excellent parenting are (1) authoritative parenting—transparent communication with choices and limits, (2) consistency, the ability to respond in words and interventions with consistency, and (3) nurturance and acceptance – an all too important skill that helps young people feel supported and loved.

> " *Time is too slow for those who wait, too swift for those who fear, too long for those who grieve, too short for those who rejoice, but for those who love, time is eternity.*
> - Henry van Dyke

At the heart of joining with nurturance is warmth. Parents who express warmth display unconditional acceptance of their children. High achieving parents may display conditional acceptance, which then leads to feelings of rejection. Parents ignore, stay distracted, disengage, and find reasons to avoid attending dance recitals, theatre performances, or basketball games. "Sometimes rejection" occurs in nasty comments such as "You'll never amount to anything" or "What good are you?"

When parents express joining warmth, it makes a significant difference for children of all ages. Sometimes, a hug in the middle of behavioral interventions prioritizes what is most important for the child. And, this is a good measure for parents to see if they can stay neutral despite the "frustration." I recently worked with a family who was overwhelmed by their son's behavior (i.e. yelling, hitting, noncompliance). I recommended that the son express "I need a hug" whenever he felt disconnected or stressed. Now, this technique doesn't work for some kids and family configurations, but it seems to be a good fit for this child. This small modification made a difference as the boy repeatedly expressed "I need a hug" and it was encouraged to give regardless of what happened. At first, his mother Judy was against this technique and brainstormed reasons why it wouldn't work. "I don't think this is a good idea. He's going to confuse the two-both aggression and affection." "The affection will encourage the behavior problems." As she threw out excuses, it occurred to me that Judy couldn't hug when she was angry at Matthew. As a result, it seemed that the intervention was important for both mom and son. This emotional expression improves understanding and bonding. Judy learned to hug first, then address the behavior after the affection. She found that Matthew was more cooperative after the hug. She also found that several behavioral spirals were nipped in the bud.

Besides the "in the moment" experiences, I recommend explicitly planning on two moments of warmth per child for each day. Eye gazing, being present, speaking good words into their kids' life, sincere praise for effort, expressions of goodness, strength finding, engagement with the son or daughter, intentional listening, physical closeness, hand-holding, extended fist bumping, handshake creation, explicitly expressing "I love you so much," directly stating "I am so proud of who you are," warmly embracing and the joining list continues.

> *We think sometimes that poverty is only being hungry, naked and homeless. The poverty of being unwanted, unloved and uncared for is the greatest poverty. We must start in our own homes to remedy this kind of poverty.* - Mother Theresa

Joining is a unique way to show love and express warmth. In addition to excellent parenting, unconditional acceptance, and warm moments, joining is best shown when parents back up their kids. Parents can model "I have your back" from early on. And, never is this more critical than in difficult situations involving other people. Consider the following example. The Lee family is at a baseball game and the dad engages with the kids with some low-level roughhousing in their seats at the ball park. The dad's watch gets accidentally broken. After the game, the dad brings the child to the store to get his watch fixed. Mr. Lee calls out his son by explaining to the employee that my son did this to me, "We were at a baseball game and my son broke my watch." The dad was receptive to my suggestion that he should never have called out his son. His goal should have been protecting his son in the process of joining with him. On a side note, joining is not a helicopter example of over-protectiveness. There are plenty of opportunities in life where the man's son will get to take chances without his dad's protection. And, it will come at age appropriate times. No, in this example, a father wants to look for those opportunities to join with his son. A father should say "I broke my watch" as a way of joining with his son. A kid shouldn't be embarrassed as a result of his father's venting. Instead, a parent protects his boy.

When a family is at a restaurant, and the daughter spills her lemonade, her mother may inform the waitress that "Lucy spilled her lemonade. Could we have another lemonade?" In contrast, "I spilled the lemonade" is better. Or, "We spilled the lemonade." But, the parent saying, "I spilled our water pitcher" to the waiter at the restaurant simply provides better family traction. When a young teenage son makes a mistake, and purchases the wrong part at the hardware store, sometimes forming a team and strengthening solidarity is more important than teaching a lesson. A joining dad might say, "I told my son the wrong part before he purchased this" at the hardware store. A father can look larger in his son's (daughter's) eyes during the process of joining behaviors. Joining in this context of "having your kids' back" is a small way to show love to your children and strengthen the family. This starts when the Dad (or Mom) stops being embarrassed and starts being the family protector.

---

## WORDS OF WISDOM & STEPS FOR TAKING ACTION

- Excellent parenting consists of three factors: (1) A healthy balance of choices and limits communicated with warmth, (2) Implementing Interventions with Consistency, and (3) Nurturance and acceptance

- Secure parents work hard to protect their children and prevent any embarrassment of their children.

- Joining involves the parent "standing in the gap" for their son or daughter.

- Explicitly plan on two moments of warmth per child for each day.

---

# Chapter Two

## Minimizing Reinforcement Errors

*If you go against your reinforcement history, you are in for a fight.*
- John Buri, Ph.D.

*We talked about how navigating life's relationships is like engaging in a choreographed dance at the historic Detroit Opera House—only the house has been moved to a big cargo ship in the middle of the ocean. Sometimes, the waves are calm and other times they are heavy. Despite the ups and downs of waves that so accurately match life's experiences, there are things we can do to help make our child's dance more fluid. And, there are things we can do as parents that disrupt the fluidity of the ballet experience. These ballet disruptions are reinforcement errors. Some are minor and others can be detrimental.*

While attachment is the first parenting step, the next step closely behind is reinforcement. Reinforcement is a consequence that will increase the likelihood of the behavior happening again. One of the keys to helping our children become solid, productive, contributing members of society, make the culture healthier, and improve the world is influenced by their reinforcement history. Each of our reinforcement histories are the accumulated experience of healthy reinforcement, attachment styles, and shaping. Our reinforcement history is also influenced by reinforcement errors. A reinforcement error is a mistake parents make when they reinforce unwanted behavior. Reinforcement errors are those parenting decisions that reinforce negative behaviors for society, reduce the health of our culture, and don't do much to improve the world. Reinforcement errors are those parenting moments that reinforce and subsequently encourage defiance, argumentativeness, social isolation, unhealthy coping strategies, unhealthy anger reactions, manipulation, and disrespectful behaviors to name some of the most common.

Healthy reinforcement should begin right at the start of toddlerhood. At the very start of toddlerhood, parents should establish a precedent of following directions as an expectation. Permitting the "testing" with humor is a mistake. "Oh, he is so cute when he expresses disobedience." That doesn't work. Toddlers as young as two can learn to negotiate when they disagree. Two-year olds can learn 1-2-3 Magic: "Johnny, come to Dad when I call you. Johnny 1, Johnny 2, Johnny 3;" these little ones can learn to respond prior to the parent counting to 3[1]. When kids cry, parents can teach children appropriate times to cry. In the same way, we don't want to get bent out of shape over spilled milk, we want to teach our children that crying over not getting candy before bed time is not worthy of crying. Smashing our head or falling on our stomach is worthy of crying, but not getting what we want isn't. The alternative option is negotiating. Teaching our children to negotiate for their needs and preferences can start as early as two and is a skill that can be worked on through childhood and adolescence. Healthy parents send the message that disagreement is allowed when done respectfully. Reinforcement errors occur in these circumstances when a child's crying over a sweet treat is reinforced by "giving in" to stop the crying. Or, the reinforcement error occurs when kids learn to withdraw because their communication is stifled and negotiation isn't encouraged.

### Sensitivity and Communication

One of the ways parents can prevent reinforcement errors is by intentionally being sensitive to how they reinforce. A sensitive parent is perceptive, insightful, responsive, and fully aware of how they communicate with their children. Sensitive parents refrain from being on "automatic" with their kids, but instead are intentional about how they communicate and how they instruct and interact. Sensitive parents teach communication skills at an early age. As a toddler enters early childhood, sensitive and responsive parents consistently communicate that children are expected to either follow directions or negotiate. As children in early childhood transition into middle childhood, sensitive and responsive parents set the expectation that disagreements are valued and encouraged.

This point has been hard for parents to accept. When we give parenting talks, it is common for parents to react to this idea. I remember one mom who stood up and spoke with confidence at a parenting talk. She insisted that "disagreeing means disrespect in our household." I was startled but impressed by her boldness. "I am not going to allow my kids to fight and bicker and you certainly don't talk back. That's not how I was raised. And, that's not how I'm going to raise my children!" I thanked her for her contribution to the discussion and decided it would be best for us to break down these concepts during the seminar. What do we mean by saying that disagreements are valued and encouraged?

First, parents should teach young children to say, "I will follow directions but I disagree" and reward these statements when they are used properly. It is helpful for kids when parents develop reward structures for doing those two things at the same time—following directions and stating a disagreement. But let's be clear, this is not the child screaming "Fine," then slamming the door prior to reluctantly cleaning up the bedroom. Instead, expressing disagreement respectfully, with an appropriate tone, maintaining poise, using an inside the house voice, and speaking politely and considerately. These are the goals of learning how to disagree without being disagreeable.

## ALLOWING DISAGREEMENT

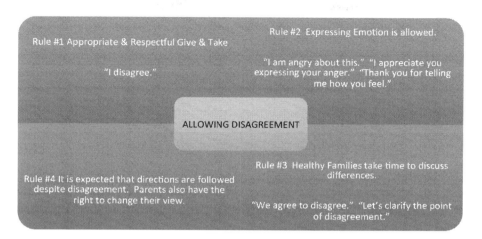

Rule #1 Appropriate & Respectful Give & Take

"I disagree."

Rule #2 Expressing Emotion is allowed.

"I am angry about this." "I appreciate you expressing your anger." "Thank you for telling me how you feel."

ALLOWING DISAGREEMENT

Rule #4 It is expected that directions are followed despite disagreement. Parents also have the right to change their view.

Rule #3 Healthy Families take time to discuss differences.

"We agree to disagree." "Let's clarify the point of disagreement."

Parents sensitive to reinforcement encourage negotiation. As kids get older, parents help children by inviting them to negotiate with politeness and respect. In these situations, parents balance out changing their mind and not changing their mind. It's a case by case basis but parents are careful not to develop a pattern of giving in. Clear thinking, problem solving, and reinforcement sensitivity is applied. After negotiations, family meetings are great times to discuss any negotiations that occurred over the last week.

One of the skills that kids can learn in their sibling rivalry is to learn the difference between petty arguments and purposeful arguments. Petty fights are the size of pizza or who is better at meaningless activities. These happen in every family. When they become a chronic problem—bickering over chairs at dinner, fighting over toys, unnecessary aggressive behavior, a barrage of telling on each other, yells of "stop," "quit," "go away," "you always," "you never," and other disconnecting comments; this is when a solution is needed. Problem solve specific arguments by having each child take turns holding a straw. Kids take turns holding the straw [or some other object] one minute at a time. Whoever holds the straw is the one who shares their side of the story. During conflict resolution, the kids learn to listen, clarify their side, agree to disagree, say "I was wrong," express "I appreciate your perspective," seek the truth in a problem, and be solution-oriented.

Most of the time, kids need to be asked whether this is a petty fight or a purposeful fight. And, they will be asked to defend why they believe it is purposeful. Arguing "order of bathroom use" or "who changed the channel" is not purposeful. Purposeful fights include healthy debates on important topics: (a) the amount of television permitted by a family, (b) the amount of time to spend with neighbors who are negative or have a questionable influence, (c) the # of books to read each week to be successful.

## WORDS OF WISDOM & STEPS FOR TAKING ACTION

- At an early age, consistently communicate that children are expected to either "follow directions or negotiate."

- Throughout childhood and adolescence, set the expectation that disagreements are valued and encouraged.

- In the process of valuing and encouraging disagreement, educate children on clarifying petty arguments from purposeful/important arguments. Example of petty fight: "My popsicle is bigger than yours," "No it's not." Examples of purposeful fights: (a) the family pet should be a dog or a cat; (b) where the family should give its money, (c) where the family goes on vacation.

- Communicate conclusions such as "agree to disagree," "I was wrong," "I appreciate your perspective," & other flexible statements.

- Facilitate practicing disagreements between siblings and parent-child relationships on an issue, staying on point, and respecting other's opinion in the category of purposeful / important arguments.

### Sensitivity to Reinforcement

Emotionally intelligent (high EQ) parents have reinforcement sensitivity. As toddlers grow, these EQ parents are sensitive to how they reinforce and teach their children. With the idea of this sensitivity in mind, let's review the fundamentals of reinforcement with some parenting logic. Consider Javion, a 7-year-old boy I saw in my psychology practice. Javion gets limited attention when he reads, draws a picture, or helps take out the trash, but receives a lot of attention (even if it's negative) when he hits his brother. When this happens, Javion is more likely to get aggressive in his future behavior. In some ways, this is the origin of bullying – Javion learns that negative attention gives him his identity. The age-old wisdom in this example is how his mother can make a difference for Javion by learning to reverse her reinforcement bias. By reversing her reinforcement bias and fixing her attention on what she wants for Javion rather than what she doesn't want from him, she is able to reinforce something better that will improve his world and the world's future.

On another example, consider if Javion sees his mom get angry whenever there is conflict. If the anger is disturbing (i.e. involves yelling, screaming, or hitting), then Javion may learn that it is unwise to push Mom's buttons. We will revisit the "buttons" later during Javion's teenage years. For now, he has learned that conflict is not allowed. In this example, Javion learns to avoid conflict rather than to successfully disagree. He learns that the best approach to conflict is anger and behavioral disturbance.

A benign stimulus such as a candy bar to silence the temper tantrum actually causes long-term problems. A gummy bear to stop the crying actually teaches and encourages temper tantrums. As a result of this reinforcement, children will require immediate gratification, and sugar, to make things worse, in order to regulate their physiological arousal. In addition to awareness of sensitivity, understanding that reinforcement occurs at multiple layers is critical.

*Listening is not merely not talking, though even that is beyond most of our powers; it means taking a vigorous, human interest in what is being said.* - Alice Duer Miller

A high EQ parent who is reinforcement sensitive will find time to give attention, and give effort (even when exhausted) to conflict and allow for differing opinions. Parents help their children most long-term when they enforce rules and consequences, but allowing children to disagree and expressing that disagreement in an appropriate way is empowering. Permitting conflict with appropriate and respectful give and take communication sets up Javion to succeed. In my work with Javion, this is something I set up with his mother and it worked very effectively. They began to practice appropriate and respectful give and take interactions. Additionally, Javion needed to learn that anger is a natural and normal emotion. This was carried out by incorporating statements for Mom that allowed Javion to be angry ("I appreciate you expressing your anger." "Thank you for telling me how you feel.") This was critical for Javion and his family, because when anger is used to manipulate and control relationships, it is destructive. A key mantra here --- healthy conflict is appropriate and allowed in healthy families. Or some healthy families have the mantra: kids are allowed to disagree, and expressions of feelings are encouraged; however, it is expected that directions are followed despite disagreement.

High EQ parents are in tune with how they reinforce, and know that their tendencies and their own behavior reinforce their children. There is simultaneously a modeling and reinforcement effect. When parents reinforce inconsistently, I call this low EQ behavior. Inconsistent reinforcement often results in inconsistent behavior.

## WORDS OF WISDOM & STEPS FOR TAKING ACTION

- Recognize the power of reinforcement sensitivity in all parenting decisions.

- Explicitly discuss reinforcement errors after they have occurred.

- Identify both subtle and big reinforcement errors and work against these errors on an active basis.

- Specifically review areas of your parenting. Intentionally look for ways you can be more consistent as a parent.

*Honest disagreement is often a good sign of progress.*
- Mahatma Gandhi

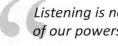

*Listening is not merely not talking, though even that is beyond most of our powers; it means taking a vigorous, human interest in what is being said.* *- Alice Duer Miller*

Reinforcement Sensitivity Requires Consequence Consistency: WE-NESS

I met a gentleman named Jim at a Sarasota parenting talk. He was married and a very successful business owner with three children. He was articulate and logical and wanted an additional perspective on things at home so we began to process family stressors. As I listened to Jim, I thought: "Oh no, I've heard this hundreds of times." In this case, he and his wife had staying power after being married for 10 years, and were supporting each other in their respective careers. Yet, their communication about their kid was a problem.

As Jim went on, it became clear that this was a complicated communication problem. Jim described his wife Kara's interactions with their 5-year old, "She will say to him 'if you do that again, you are going to go to bed.' He would then do it again. She once again says 'If you do that again you are going to bed.' She will say this to our son five or six times but never follows through. If I ever try to intervene, she turns and yells at me. I've learned to choose my battles."

I wish I could say that Jim and Kara's situation is unique—that very few parents approach parenting from different angles. But unfortunately, I can't; it's

36

so common that some parents appear to come from different planets and their attempts to resolve their differences have built up layers of emotional barriers – yelling, anger, hostility, and resentment. Clearly, some marriages require lots of emotional medicine – patience, kindness, love, dates, compassion, and various strategies of attending to the relationship.

From the perspective of parenting, I recommend that couples like Jim and his wife sit down and discuss parenting issues once a week, even for 15 minutes. "She is unable to approach it logically," Jim despairs. Despite Jim's early reluctance, his son required his parents to sit and discuss a plan that would be consistent and would allow them both to follow through. The weekly parenting meetings were not easy at first but they stuck with it. As Kara began to realize that Jim appreciated her perspective, she became more open to making some changes in how she approached their son. As Jim realized that Kara was thankful for his suggestions, he became aware of Kara's creativity. Gratitude for each other appeared to help both parents open up to each other's ideas. I have found that when parents express gratitude and appreciation, it helps moves them toward parenting solutions regardless of how complicated the misbehavior is (or how difficult other parts of the marriage is). We-ness was the goal for Jim and Kara and consequence consistency is the change children need.

### Exceptions Need Not Change Our Sensitivity to Reinforcement

There is virtually an exception to every parenting rule. Recently, I was walking with my family in the parking lot at a store. A mother was walking well ahead of her son, who appeared to be crying and exhibiting whining behavior. At first glance, the child was probably being noncompliant and the mother was intentionally walking ahead so the child was forced to follow. Depending on some factors, this parenting technique can work as long as there are no issues about safety. The problem was that this intervention was being done in the parking lot. I was extremely concerned about the boy's safety.

Let's fast forward to some teenager examples that can further clarify the need for high EQ parents to remain reinforcement sensitive. Consider defiant adolescents, who are very difficult for mental health therapists to work with (and parents, too). I recently sat with a 17-year-old named Larry who had recently exhibited screaming and heavy criticism of his own mother in a library. She was right there with him during the appointment and had the courage to face the challenging parenting head on without avoidance due to embarrassment. Defiant teenagers often seek confrontations in which they push the buttons of authority figures to gain control over situations. Defiant teenagers make terrible comments to their parents or teachers, "I hate you," "You suck as a teacher," "You are a lousy mother, so don't tell me what to do." These comments are manipulative by intent. They often paralyze or frustrate the teacher or parent into doing whatever the adolescent wants. The "take responsibility" or "who's responsible for your behavior" discussion fails in these situations because extremely skillful teenagers are unwilling to back down. Parents report that these comments start early: "I hate you!" "You are a terrible mother!" "I wish you weren't my mother!" These comments start as early as three or four years old depending on the development of verbal skills.

The best approach is nipping these statements in the bud. Parents can set a precedent by addressing these statements directly when they first begin. Here are examples of what a parent can say: "We don't say 'I hate you' comments in this family." "You don't talk that way to your mother. It is unacceptable to say your mother is terrible." "When you say, 'I wish you weren't my mother,' you are being manipulative. Instead, in our family, you are expected to express your feelings." "In our family, we don't manipulate; we talk specifically about the problem."

These comments clarify expectations for the children. They also teach children to stop avoiding and instead, express what the problem is. "Instead of saying 'I hate you,' I expect you to say, 'I am angry because we decided to not go out for dinner.'" Teaching children to extinguish these comments is critical.

*A few strong instincts and a few plain rules suffice us.*
– Ralph Waldo Emerson

The solution here for Larry is being consistent and enforcing rules and consequences. But, the emotional entanglement from the hot buttons pushed by the teenager can cause the parent to become confused. Emotional reasoning can set in, leading parents to question their parenting effectiveness. "Oh, my goodness. What am I doing? I am incompetent. I don't know what to do." "I am a terrible mother because my child hates me." Parents of defiant children become overwhelmed by the button-pushing skills on display. Instead, the parents need to be like an eagle and rise up to take perspective of the situation.

Consider another 13-year-old boy that I worked with named Kevin. His mother reported that he frequently lost his temper and hit other children in the classroom or in the neighborhood. His mother was convinced that the boy's problem was a chemical imbalance that prevented him from controlling his temper. The problem had worsened over the years and he had seen many different psychiatrists. Clearly, the boy and the family needed help. To start, defining the problem as a chemical imbalance needed to be changed to defining the problem as changeable and in the control of the parents and the boy. It is important to reframe many problem behaviors as solvable through parental intervention. This is even more important nowadays with over 8 million kids on psychiatric meds.

The best strategy for Kevin was outlining clear rules and enforcing effective consequences. The unfortunate thing here is that behavioral interventions are now thought of as the exception to the rule. The new rule and standard is medications first, behavioral interventions second. To break down the 8 million kids further—It is an unfortunate reality that physicians are prescribing Ritalin and other psychostimulants to children as early as two to five years old and as early as 0-1 years of age in recent years. Believe it or not, according to a vendor of U.S. physicians prescribing data in 2014, 1,422 children 0-1 years old were prescribed ADHD medications. Furthermore, 26,406 children 0-1 years of age were prescribed antidepressants, 654 children aged 0-1 years of age were prescribed antipsychotics, and 227,132 children aged 0-1 years were prescribed anti-anxiety medication. Why are all these babies on psychotropic medication? I've discussed this with psychiatric nurses, psychiatrists, and physician colleagues and they remain bewildered by the news. We have over four million kids on ADHD drugs, over two million on antidepressants, and over two million on anti-anxiety meds. One in 13 US schoolkids are taking a psychiatric medication. 2,723,126 U.S. children aged 6-12 are prescribed ADHD children—the age range where reinforcement sensitivity is critically needed. Houston—we have a problem!

Back to Kevin, if an adolescent is moody, depressed or distant, it may be due to several factors: (1) A normal developmental need for autonomy; (2) Sleep deprivation; (3) Hunger as a growing boy; (4) Just moodiness without reflection; (5) A negative reaction to an overprotective parent; (6) Or a result of drug or alcohol use, negative peer relationships, gang involvement, or some other glaring negative in the young person's life.

For each of these solutions, there is a solution and an exception depending on the kid. If it's autonomy, generally, the answer is warmth. This is particularly critical for the father. But, if you are a type A parent, or a rules oriented person, an achiever, or an ambitious person, it is helpful to continually stop to foster tenderness and warmth. If the adolescent is exhibiting a reaction to a level of overprotectiveness, the solution may be less protectiveness. The common reaction is for parents to discount the teenager's needs based on his or her developmental level and maturity. This was the issue for Kevin who shared with his previous counselor that he was never allowed to make choices at home. This change was implemented at home as a first step. So, while outlining clear rules and enforcing effective consequences established parameters in his life, he was encouraged to express his needs and preferences and his mother agreed to give him choices. This included discussing fair consequences for his behavior.

What if it's a glaring negative in your adolescent's life? This is relevant in Kevin's life—there was clearly a negative situation in his life. If the reaction of moodiness, depressed feelings or distancing behavior is in response to a negative situation, then healthy (high EQ) parents problem solve with their child. The most common sense problem solving method is the following 5-step method:

- What is the problem?
- What are all the things that I could do about it?
- What will probably happen if I do those things?
- Which solution do I think will work best?
- After I have tried it with my best effort, how did I do?

This problem-solving method is a basic set of questions to obtain clarity. A more advanced method is processing through the barriers in the family that prevent problem solving discussions. Identifying barriers to processing family issues is critical for a healthy family. What distractions are in the way of sitting down and having family meetings? Sometimes, pride is in the way of sitting down, being humble, and desiring connection over "being right." Sometimes, mobile devices are in the way of processing family issues. The American Association of Pediatrics recommends screen free zones in the house for healthy families[2]. Screen free zones are ideal for family dinners and processing family issues. When a family can sit down and process family issues, ideally, parents have some things that they have thought about prior to the meeting. Here is a set of questions that can facilitate the discussion.

- What are some things in our family that would be helpful to discuss?
- Are there any family rules that would be helpful to adjust?
- Are there any points of conflict that remain unresolved?

## 8 Rs of Successful Consequences

Family meetings and problem solving strategies work much more effectively when families establish clear rules and enforce effective consequences with consistency. Following through is critical. The essence of a reinforcement error is when a parent doesn't follow through. The following 8 Rs of consequences make a difference for families:

**Release the need for perfection**

Your family will be late for church. Thanksgiving will not be perfect. Kids will say something inappropriate to Grandma. Lots of things will go wrong. Many things will go right too. Often, parents will want the perfect Christmas; but Tony dives into the gifts and the tree falls, or the slow gift unwrapping experience is actually a compulsive race to see what's inside.

**Realistic expectations; kids will test and learn**

Some parents want to be the best hosts for a dinner party. They will expect the kids to deliver – with polite conversation and appropriate behavior. It is helpful when parents lower their expectations.

**Respond, don't react**

Be relaxed, not angry. Explaining to Elijah his consequence for shooting a hole through the neighbor's window with his BB gun can be done with a relaxed tone. "Look Elijah, you will work off the payment by doing additional jobs around the house and you will go without your video game for a month. In addition, you must demonstrate understanding of BB gun safety by writing an essay and giving a speech to the neighbor and this family." Parents can even invite Elijah to provide input on the consequence. "What do you think would be an appropriate consequence?" The bottom line is that anger doesn't work. Stay relaxed and calm.

**Respectful, not shameful**

Most misbehavior simply requires a parent-child discussion. When parents teach, shape, instruct, inspire, and encourage, conveying respect is critical. Eye rolling, sighing, making comments like "How can you be so stupid?" "You're acting like such a baby," or "What good are you?" elicit feelings of shame. When a child experiences shame, they view themselves as "bad" and "deficient." We want to inspire and encourage behavior that is self-disciplined and honorable and it's best done when we convey respect.

**Related to the misbehavior**

Lessons are best learned when the consequence is closely aligned to the misbehavior. Consider cleaning your baseboards, a time-consuming, but worthwhile house-cleaning task. Teaching this job to children is best done with the idea of encouraging responsibility, contributing to house cleaning, and fostering discipline. But, cleaning baseboards as a penalty for homework laziness is misdirected. Instead, a homework schedule with set times to improve preparation is the antidote. Consequences work best when they are related to the misbehavior. If you leave a mess in the car, then you wash the car. If you leave wrappers on the floor, then you sweep and mop the kitchen. If you leave excess clothes on the bedroom floor, then you participate in folding clothes during laundry time.

**Reasonable in duration, not permanent**

It doesn't make sense to tell Billy, a 3-year old, "You'll be in trouble when Daddy gets home." Billy may not even remember what it's about at the end of the day. In the same way, Billy needs an immediate consequence, and being grounded for the entire summer is obviously unreasonable. Consequences need to be reasonable in duration based on age, maturity, and degree of problem.

**Revealed in advance; child knows prior to behavior**

One of the keys to healthy consequences is that parents communicate in advance what the expectations are and what will happen if misbehavior occurs. There should be no surprises. If the Johnson family have a planned outing to Dairy Queen and suddenly, Jake hits his sister, loss of a Buster Bar or a Blizzard seems spontaneous. Did Jake know in advance that aggression during a special outing results in the loss of the treat?

**Restated back to you, showing hearing & listening**

One of the goals of parent-child discussions is building communication skills. Encourage children to hear, listen, and restate the communicated consequence. Ask Ellie to explain in her own words what will happen if she calls her brother an unkind name again.

## 8 R s OF CONSEQUENCES

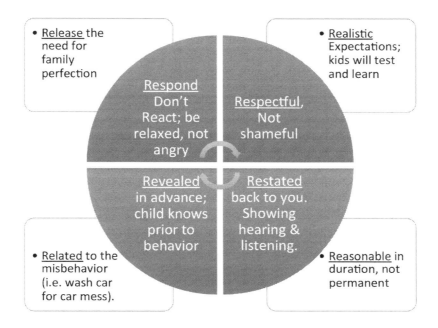

## WORDS OF WISDOM & STEPS FOR TAKING ACTION

**A.** Outline clear rules and enforce effective consequences with consistent follow through.

- Recognize exceptions to each of the parenting solutions.

- Outline clear rules and enforce effective consequences with consistent follow through.

- Three of these solutions are warmth [especially for fathers], reducing overprotectiveness, and processing negative situations in your child's life.

- Facilitate opportunities for processing family issues in screen free zones.

**B.** Implement the 8 Rs of Consequences

- Release the need for family perfection.

- Realistic expectations; kids will test and learn.

- Respond, don't react; be relaxed, not angry.

- Respectful, not shameful.

- Related to the misbehavior (i.e. wash car for car mess).

- Reasonable in duration, not permanent.

- Revealed in advance: child knows prior to behavior.

- Restated back to you. Showing, hearing & listening.

## Manipulation

Reinforcement sensitivity is best illustrated in how much parents are aware of manipulation behaviors by themselves and their children. Have you ever heard the statement, "Every family is dysfunctional?" It's true. But, as we reflect on family troubles, some families are more dysfunctional than others. Perhaps a spectrum of dysfunction reflects family life. My favorite description of dysfunctional families is John Buri[3] equating it to psychological, spiritual, relational, and emotional bacteria. "Some families parcel out mild forms of these bacteria, whereas others act as a veritable petri dish." None of us are free of parenting mistakes.

*Growth begins when we start to admit our own weaknesses.*
- Jean Vanier

The first step for parents is recognizing their own tendency to manipulate. Self-insight is power. The second step is recognizing manipulation tendencies and behaviors with all family members. There are active and intentional things that families can do to reduce unhealthy behaviors, essentially reducing our dispersed bacteria. And, one of those is doing what you can to stop manipulation. Remember, if Lisa exclaims "I hate you," don't take it personally at all; instead see it as a teaching opportunity. Nipping manipulation in the bud is a critical component of healthy relationships in families. At this point, we should do a quick reality check on manipulation because it is easy for parents to conclude "not in our family." It is easy to assume that manipulators are those "defiant kids" or those "other parents with personality disorders." The reality check is that manipulation occurs at some point in all families.

Manipulation is an unhealthy and dysfunctional form of getting what you want. Manipulation is not an effective intervention for parenting but is often attempted by overwhelmed parents. Sometimes, attempts to manipulate by parents are experienced as passive aggressiveness. "After all I've done for you, why can't you just put your clothes away?" "You make me so mad." "I am going to do this for you right now because you aren't acting like your sister." "I'm not going to drive you to your friend's house because of your attitude over dinner." These manipulative and passive aggressive comments teach youth poor relational skills. When parents can't be assertive and communicate their needs, they may let anger and resentment build, relying on passive-aggressive behavior such as resisting things for no reason (i.e. refusing to drive kids places, delaying grocery shopping or cooking, avoiding expressing...).

The solutions to these problems are assertiveness training and directly discussing needs. Rather than using the phrase, "after all I've done for you," parents simply request that the kids put their clothes away. Likewise, parents directly discuss the problem or the disagreement rather than say, "You make me so mad." This is every day (or weekly) language for some parents but the manipulation is making children responsible for the parent's emotional state. The problem isn't expressing feelings. The problem is saying your child has control over your emotions and you are mad at him for that. Rather than put one's feelings on a child, say directly, "When you tell me about needing school supplies just as we are walking out the door to school, it is a problem." "It is unacceptable to demand clothes to be washed without putting them in the hamper."

As another example, rather than "not driving Lilliana to her friend's house" because of an "attitude," name the specific attitude directly. "What is bothering you?" If the teen is closed to talking, giving her space may be what's needed. However, having a family dinner and expecting Lilliana to come to the dinner table is direct communication. Reminders of specific behaviors and family standards like politeness, kindliness, and everyone talks at the dinner table is a healthy approach.

Parents often find that their children will withhold affection when the kids/teens don't get what they want. On another occasion, when Lilliana couldn't go to her friend's house because the family dinner was the priority, she withdrew and conveyed coldness and resentment. A healthy parent will communicate this issue directly – "We don't withhold affection when we're upset. Instead, express how you feel. Say 'I am angry because I couldn't go to my friend's house.'"
When parents recognize their own dysfunctional behavior here, insight encourages parents to be more effective. Parents need to directly confront their own behavior by parenting with courage and assertiveness. Doing things directly is the best way to raise young people into healthy adults.

Sometimes, healthy parenting interventions are confused with manipulation. But, a negative consequence that follows a negative behavior is not manipulation, but your basic and traditional form of discipline (i.e. loss of iPad/tablet privileges for lying). Additionally, rewards or positive reinforcers such as praise or a pack of gum for doing extra chores around the house is not manipulation. Penalties and rewards are not manipulative, but healthy responses to educate, instruct, and curb decisions. In our current society with psychologizing and over-emphasizing self-esteem, this logic is traditionally called common sense.

In contrast to normal and healthy parental give and take, a range of behaviors are manipulative: lying, guilt tripping, shaming, intimidation using anger, and bribing are forms of manipulation. Children use manipulation early in childhood and if the strategy is not addressed, they can develop this strategy into a nasty communication habit. This requires parents to be alert and address these manipulation behaviors. Even in healthy families, these types of behaviors occur on a frequent basis. Consider a 5-year old who says, "If you don't play this game with me, then I am not going to share my crayons." What parents need to do here is name the manipulation in a direct manner with courage and assertiveness. Here is an example of how a parent would want to address this manipulation: "You are manipulating when you say that you won't share if you won't get your way." In addition to naming the manipulation, it is important for parents to provide an alternative statement by (1) expressing your feeling, (2) communicating your preference, and (3) accepting the outcome. So, a parent can provide this statement as an alternative: "I <u>feel disappointed</u> that you won't play this game with me. I <u>strongly prefer</u> that you play the game with me but I <u>accept</u> your reasons." The comment, "I accept but I still disagree" can also be added since "accepting" comments will take time.

Sometimes, specific methods are needed in order to enforce communication and consistency when facing manipulation. A method to enforce expectations is the "oven timer" strategy. I worked with the Johnson family who routinely had their two teenagers withhold love and shut down; their parents' first and primary step was to name the manipulation and encourage discussion. If shutting down continued which it did (i.e. being quiet, withholding love and communication...), then the following enforcer was rehearsed and spoken: "I'm going to keep track of the oven timer and for every minute you refuse to engage toward problem solving, it's going to be five minutes taken from your use of your iPhone and earlier bed time." In these situations, which worked effectively for the Johnsons, parents can restrict what is most important to their children - phone, TV, video games, times with friends, computer activity - and then it is up to the parents to follow through to make the strategy ultimately effective.

## STOPPING MANIPULATION

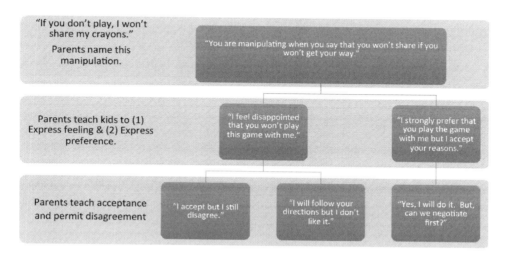

A 15-year old may shut down and use silence as a form of manipulation. In a passive-aggressive way, Phillip may resist things for no reason (i.e. refusing family outings, delaying chores...). Similarly, his sister Lisa may refuse to do something like clean her room in order to retaliate. The retaliation, like shutting down, is another form of manipulation. As calmly as possible in order to avoid a power struggle, healthy parenting involves communicating to your teen that this kind of behavior is not acceptable. Again, this is done in a courageous and assertive manner. If Lisa persists, it's time, once again, to reinforce that there is a consequence for such behavior.

There are four <u>rules to follow</u> that enhance the process of naming and reducing manipulation:
- Be calm and stay neutral.
- Be consistent; don't neglect, instead, express unconditional love.
- Don't overly critique or control.
- Reinforce well and be engaged - intentional engagement.

## WORDS OF WISDOM & STEPS FOR TAKING ACTION

- Parent with courage and assertiveness without getting sucked into passive-aggressive tendencies.

- Identify manipulation in direct ways by naming the manipulation (i.e. "You are manipulating. There is a better way to communicate: (1) Express your feeling, (2) Be direct with your preference, & (3) Accept the outcome but acknowledge it's ok to disagree.

- Enforce consequences for manipulation, if disengagement continues. As calmly as possible, let your teen know that this kind of behavior is not acceptable. If she persists, it's time, once again, to reinforce that there is a consequence for such behavior. It is expected that you problem-solve.

- The earlier a parent names manipulation, the better long-term.

### Minor Reinforcement Errors Can Become Long-Term Pests

There are minor reinforcement errors that result in long term learning annoyances. Minor errors include responding to interruptions without addressing the social expectation. Ignoring the interruption but attending to the child's stated point reinforces interruptive behavior. In a family therapy session last year, Fred turned toward his son's interruption without indicating the need to wait until Mom was finished with her point. Fred was working hard to attend to his son, which was a request of his wife Kathy. Unfortunately, this misguided effort to make a wrong right reinforced interruptive and rude behavior. I asked the family if it is usually the case that parents engage in conversations with children reinforcing simultaneous conversations. It turns out that Kathy was the culprit. From her perspective, she was compensating for Fred's lack of attention toward their son. However, interruptive behavior was a chronic problem in the family.

We clarified that the solution for the father-son relationship was more time together. The solution for the interruptive patterns was clarifying expectations of one person talking at a time. As a rule, consistency when communicating this expectation upon interruptions is critical. When the child is young, this should serve as a consistent teaching moment. Practice rehearsals are effective—"When we are talking, this is what I want you to do: say 'excuse me' and wait patiently." Older children and teenagers do need reminders, particularly from the aspect of learning how to communicate professionally. As we reinforce maturity and professionalism, this is behavior to address every time. The larger goal is to reinforce patience, professional communication skills, and valuing points and perspectives. This obvious but subtle regular occurrence is experienced in most families but can be distinguished with consistent effort.

Another way to reduce minor reinforcement errors in parenting is to implement the idea of BTNs – Building a Tolerance of Nos and being able to handle it. Simply put, children don't like "Nos," and have figured out how to get parents to say "Yes" more often. Parents end up avoiding saying "No." Many parents have developed patterns of thinking within the minds of their children that constitute a lack of "Nos," similar to what we discussed with attachment parenting. In fact, parents avoid saying "No" because of an intolerance of a child's reaction when they hear "No." The antidote is the gradual strengthening of the tolerance threshold of the child. In other words, say "No." In addition to poor reinforcement and weakening the No tolerance threshold, a parent can build the emotional skills of the child by discussing what happened when Lisa heard Mom say "NO." If Lisa exhibited inappropriate behavior, parents can have the child re-do or act out (in more positive ways), and discuss how they might respond more effectively when she hears "NO." By discussing expectations and "redoing" the behavior, children gradually learn.

## REFLECTION TIPS

The following minor reinforcement errors are susceptible to becoming major reinforcement problems:

- Laughing off talking back behavior

- Ignoring mild aggression between siblings

- Giving in to avoid entanglements

- Withdrawing love and guidance

- Withholding corrections

## REFLECTION TIPS

The following techniques diffuse temper tantrums, over-reactions, and explosive behavior:

- HALT: Remember the acronym, Hungry, Angry, Lonely, Tired; As parents, these emotions make us more susceptible to overreact during behavior episodes.

- Stay CALM: Calmly breathe, Attend to the present, Let go of perfections, Mindful of the moment.

- Name the behavior and communicate the expected behavior: "Please use a respectful tone." "Please don't roll your eyes, that is rude."

- Do not dismiss or send the child away: Engage the child/teenager despite disagreement. Value the disagreement without avoidance.

- Be CLEAR: Clarify, Listen, Evaluate, Address differences, and Reinforce carefully & specifically in Conversation. Use as few words as possible to make your point. Youth tune out.

### Major Reinforcement Error: Undermining Intrinsic Motivation

Minor reinforcement errors become long-term pests, but they're easier to undo and alter learned behavior. Major reinforcement errors are those things we do that undermine our basic parenting goals and have more severe consequences. When a parent informs a defiant child refusing to go to bed that "If he doesn't return to bed, he will miss the family movie tomorrow night," Mom will need to follow through. Unfortunately, Kevin continued to defiantly get out of bed. As tomorrow comes and the teacher gives a nice report, Dad comes home from a business trip, and the family is excited to have a fun night together, so guess what usually happens? Parents will argue flexibility and making adjustments. The problem is that Mom's word is undermined. Bed-time refusal is reinforced. Buying Larry a new watch after he intentionally breaks his third watch teaches irresponsible behavior. Giving Lisa a pop to entice her to get on the van reinforces noncompliance for future van rides. Lisa may think, 'Why immediately get in the van when I received a pop for waiting last time?'

These reinforcement errors cause long-term problems. Laughing after the child runs out of her bedroom for the third time reinforces delays at bedtime. Ignoring name calling without correction reinforces parental disrespect or sibling hostility. Giving soda after a child demands the drink reinforces poor communi-

48

cation.  However, despite these pests, the most significant reinforcement error is rewarding activities that the child already enjoys with money and gifts.  When parents reward reading, piano playing, soccer, violin, math and virtually any other activity that the child already enjoys with money and gifts, their interest in that activity decreases.  A simple Stanford study gave markers to three groups of kids.[4] One group of kids, referred to as the "expected-reward condition" were told that they would receive a reward for partaking in an activity that they already intrinsically enjoyed.  The second group of kids was given an award unexpectedly, without being told of the reward until after the activity.  The third group of children was not rewarded.

In the next phase of the study, researchers observed the activities of the children.  Only the kids in the "expected-reward condition" had become less interested in their activities because of the rewards.  There was no change in the interest of the second group because they didn't know about the reward, therefore their interest and enjoyment was because of the activity, not a reward.  Finally, the third group also maintained their same intrinsic motivation because their interest and enjoyment of an activity was not poisoned by a reward.

This social psychology is explained by the over justification effect, kids who look at extrinsic rewards have their interest undermined.  The critical error in this reinforcement is that parents undermine the intrinsic motivation of their children by rewarding activity they already enjoy.  Intrinsic motivation to participate in soccer, math, or reading decreases after getting an external incentive.  Remember the Book It program that started in 1985?  Basically, kids who read books were rewarded with personal pan pizzas.  I went to their website and was surprised to see that the program continues.  Nutritionists question the idea of earning unhealthy pizza as a reward for reading.  From a social psychology perspective, research shows that this type of program is susceptible to decreasing reading interest. The bottom line is that parents should reward with attention and praise effort, grit, determination, and not giving up, but avoid rewarding with money and gifts.

## WORDS OF WISDOM & STEPS FOR TAKING ACTION

- At the heart of reinforcement sensitivity is encouraging activities the child enjoys.

- Encouragement consists of offering kids/teens choices and allowing personal satisfaction without pressure.

- Parents should withhold tendencies to reinforce any activities that children already enjoy with external rewards.

## Praise Has Both Advantages and Disadvantages

We should pause for a moment on the genuine need for young people to experience being lifted up. Countless studies have shown the importance of self-esteem and self-efficacy as it relates to their achievements and accomplishments. A key tenet of praise is that it needs to be sincere. Engaged and caring parents are absolutely their kids' biggest cheerleaders, but we are also prone to be their biggest critics. As we dance this routine, from praising to criticizing, parents are apt to lack sincerity in their praise. When parents reflect on their own interactions with their children, especially their teenagers, criticism is a significant blow and needs to end. John Gottman's research on the four horsemen in relationships: defensiveness, contempt, stonewalling, and criticism also applies to our roles as parents. Criticism is a big one, especially with teenagers. I recently worked with a 71-year-old woman named Kate who was having issues with depression, anxiety, and disordered eating. In a heartbreaking disclosure, she tearfully talked about never having children because of her immense fear related to her body changing. Her father's attention, criticism, and praise revolved around her body size, body image, weight gain, and eating. To this day (55-60 years later), she continues to struggle with diet issues. Criticism has a long-term detrimental effect.

Praise can be channeled poorly such as with Kate. Insincere praise can also be packaged as underlying criticism. It doesn't take significant insight for teenagers to read their parents and recognize poorly packaged praise and criticism. The following are examples of insincere praise:

**Comparison praise**: "Very good, that was just like your brother." "That's pretty good. You're getting better at the violin; soon, you may be getting close to your sister."
**The truth is**: Each child wants to be loved for who they are and respected for their own individual path. Children do not want to be compared to other children, particularly cousins or siblings. Comparisons have a negative effect on the parent-child relationship. Avoid comparing at all costs!

**Excessive praise**: "That is a great piece of art" when it clearly isn't. "You played a terrific game" after the kid made three fielding errors.
**The truth is**: Little kids as young as three know a nice building from a poorly constructed building when playing with blocks. Too much positive ignores the truth. Teens will accept "bouncing back," "sticktoitiveness," "praise for grit," and "emphasizing not giving up." They will reject being controlled and anything that doesn't allow them to feel bad after a loss, a setback, or a poor performance.

**Sarcasm praise**: Saying a sarcastic biting comment, "That went really well." While using vocal inflections, the father sarcastically says, "I can't wait for another Christmas gift list." Speaking with ridicule, "Wow, you actually cleaned up your entire room. It's like you're a whole different person now."
**The truth is**: Sarcasm, by nature, is insincere. Many young children don't understand that what is said is the opposite of what is meant. Children pick up on body language and facial expressions but become confused with messages lead-

ing to doubt and emotional insecurity. Sarcasm creates feelings of insecurity and squashes joy. What children do need is a sense of belonging and a sense of security. This happens when parents are sincere and show empathy. The more we show empathy, the more it teaches our children to show empathy when we make mistakes.

Our children need sincerity[5]. Sincerity builds a foundation of joyfulness. The most positive effect of praise is when it is conveyed with sincerity. There are key themes in the literature that describe what is needed for praise to be meaningful including perceived sincerity, performance attributions, emphasizing autonomy and standards.[6]

## REFLECTION TIPS

The following are conversation starters as strategies to build up kids, praise with specificity and sincerity, and strengthen personalities, even for resistant teenagers:

- Direct Praise: "I liked the way you didn't give up on that task." [Building self-esteem by praising effort. Research has shown that praising effort rather than outcomes has long term advantages.]

- Growth Praise: "If you could do it again, how would you do it differently?" [This encourages learning and provides opportunities to encourage and praise reflection.]

- Solution-Focused Praise: "What worked the last time you had this problem?" "I just love the way you are approaching this problem – cool, calm, and collected." [Praise reinforces the focus of your child/teenager on solutions, rather than the problems.]

- Strategic Praise: "What's your plan in getting ready for the practice schedule?" "I appreciate your strategy." [Praise reinforces strategic thinking and planning.]

- Encouragement of Expression: "What was the best part of your day?" "What were the highlights of this past week?" "What were the lowlights of this past week?" [Bonding and connection results from great interest in kids' lives.]

Praise also requires a lack of predictability. Some 8-year olds have already heard "Mom's story" 15 times. Some parents may sound like a broken record without any originality. Certainly, hearing the reasons why we turn lights off when nobody is using them (i.e. "so you won't waste electricity," "so the power won't go off," "so you won't run up the electric bill," "costs money," etc.) naturally comes with the parenting territory. Each family will have their own repeated statements on why people brush their teeth and why people should eat vegetables. But, the originality that is necessary prevents teenagers from hearing "blah, blah, blah" (see, Charlie Brown's teacher). Unique praise requires parents to consistently learn, self-reflect, read, stay curious and open, and learn to offer original ideas and communicate praise that taps into what is important to teenagers.

## That is a Reinforcement Error, Not a Personality Trait

One of the most common and significant reinforcement errors that occur is when parents classify behavior problems as personality traits. The two sort of get meshed together quite frequently in our culture and society. When parents get together and discuss academics, sports achievements, science fairs, traveling soccer teams, and service projects, behavior inevitably emerges. Of course, unique behavioral characteristics are "so cute" when children are very young. As they get older, the "cuteness" wears out and is viewed differently in these conversations. Consider the following statements I heard spoken by parents on the sidelines of basketball and soccer games or during school events in the hallways. "My daughter Erika's personality is difficult; she has a unique way of always talking back whenever I tell her to do something, she is just like her Dad!" "Johnny is probably going to be a great wrestler, he is so aggressive with his brother and there is nothing that I can do about it." "Laura's personality is strong-willed which leads her to often be belligerent with things I ask and I just don't ask her a second time."

While the context of each of these discussions consisted of normal discussions of child development, interests and activities, I couldn't help but notice the way personality is so entangled with behavior. I'm all in for normalizing and empathizing parenting challenges (i.e. "yes, that sounds like a tough one"). However, when parents connect personality with behavior, it renders the parent helpless to the behavior. In the three aforementioned quotes, the mentioned behavior problems are back-talking, aggression, and belligerence. One of the solutions to these problems is distinguishing them from personality traits and naming them for what they actually are- behavior problems. By clarifying this distinction, parents reverse their helplessness (i.e. "there is nothing I can do about it"), and feel more empowered.

> *If we take people as they are, we make them worse. If we treat them as if they were what they ought to be, we help them become what they are capable of becoming.*
> - Johann von Goethe

Big Five Personality Traits

In the context of this issue of blaming everything on personality or simply overemphasizing personality traits, without being aware of reinforcement errors, let's take a moment here to discuss a key question. What is personality? First of all, it should absolutely be pointed out that the Myers Briggs Type Indicator is an absolute myth and not supported by research. Despite being used by 89 of the Fortune 100 companies, it lacks the science to be credible. While not as popular, the science is behind the Big Five personality traits. Its science, accumulated over 5 decades, shows high reliability with genetics and biology and yields high credibility in neuroscience. As a sample, increased conscientiousness correlates with volume in the middle frontal gyrus in the left lateral prefrontal cortex, a region of the brain involved in planning and controlling behavior. High levels of neuroticism have reduced volume in the dorsomedial prefrontal cortex with increased volume in the mid-singulate gyrus. Extraverts have a larger medial orbitofrontal cortex.

What are the five factors? First, Openness to experience - curious to cautious. Kids fall along the spectrum of being curious to being more cautious. Openness reflects the degree of intellectual curiosity, creativity, and a preference for novelty. This trait describes the preference for a variety of activities versus preferring a strict routine. Second, Conscientiousness – personalities tend to be more organized to more easy going. Conscientiousness reflects the degree of being organized, dependable, and self-disciplined. This trait describes the preference for planning activities versus spontaneity. Third, Extraversion – outgoing to solitary (i.e. introversion). Extraversion reflects the degree of sociability and the tendency to seek stimulation in the company of others. This trait describes the level of assertiveness, energy, and talkativeness versus a tendency toward being reserved and social reticence. Fourth, Agreeableness – compassionate to analytical. Agreeableness reflects the degree of compassion and cooperativeness versus suspicion and antagonistic toward others. This trait describes the degree of how trusting a person is. Finally, Neuroticism – nervous to confident. Neuroticism reflects the tendency to experience anger, anxiety, depression or vulnerability fairly easily. Dimensions such as emotionally unstable versus emotional stability or insecure versus secure are explained by this trait.

Now that we've briefly addressed personality in terms of the literature, let me give you an example of something that can be helpful for families. Essentially, we want parents to view their kids from a growth model perspective as opposed to a fixed model perspective. Growth and development is the goal but emphasizing personality traits stymies this growth perspective and can lock children in to fixed traits. So, yes, there are personality traits and tendencies and it is important for parents to acknowledge these differences among kids. At the same time, accepting personality traits while simultaneously taking a growth model perspective is the fun balancing act. Excellent parents perform this trait-growth balancing act well.

The Johnsons family provide an example of this trait-growth balancing act in action. The parents came in to their son's first psychology appointment and described their son as inhibited socially due to his anxiety. As I asked for examples, specific incidents gave me a chance to talk with Ryan about things going through his mind. On one incident, Ryan's mom described him unwilling to talk to the server at a restaurant during a family outing. "I asked the children to make their orders. Ryan's sister, who is much more outgoing, easily made her order smiling and articulating what she wanted. When it was Ryan's turn, he just looked down. I was so embarrassed." As Ryan's mom told the story, her anguish was evident. I asked her, "What did you do then?" "I told the server that he is just a shy introvert and told her 'he'll have the same thing as his sister.'" I continued in helping Ryan tolerate his anxiety, overcome fears, and build his social skills in talk therapy.

After a session, I was able to give Mom some feedback about things. The problem with classifying Ryan as a "shy introvert" is that it potentially locks in this set trait. Let me stop and say that there is no doubt that there are going to be personality differences between our children. Every parent with multiple children sees these amazing differences, and many of these are captured by the Big Five and by different intellectual capabilities. Ryan's sister may indeed be more outgoing than her brother – she may be more people pleasing or extraverted. Intellectually, her strengths may be her verbal skills, her fund of knowledge and communication of that knowledge, and her processing speed; in contrast, her brother's strengths may be his working memory and his spatial awareness and perceptual skills. On aside, birth order is not supported by science, with some exceptions when it comes to the oldest child. Regardless of differences among children, if parents approach this situation from a growth model, they can expect Ryan to develop his social skills and use them at the restaurant—good eye contact with the server, smiling and being polite, speaking loudly and intelligibly, and articulating his food order. These skills have nothing to do with personality traits. These are skills that can be reinforced, but the error of overemphasizing personality traits can get in the way.

> *Of all knowledge, the wise and good seek most to know themselves.*
> *– William Shakespeare*

Eliminating Tendencies Toward Using Love as a Reward or a Consequence

We have highlighted the reinforcement errors of undermining intrinsic motivation and disengaging from the parenting process by classifying problem behavior as "personality traits." Another critical reinforcement error is the use of love in how parenting is sometimes carried out, particularly during moments of disappointment.

It is common for parents to become inaccessible when they feel disappointed. One of the greatest treasures parents can give their children is access into their own emotional lives. So, if parents feel disappointed, it is ideal for the family relationships and the vitality in the family that they remain accessible and express disappointment. This is done when parents express their emotional states. If parents feel sad, they should express those feelings. If parents are disappointed by life circumstances, it is helpful that they express this experience. If Dad loses his job, it is healthy to express his disappointment, as opposed to reacting angrily to perceived slights or unclean rooms. Parents need to avoid becoming emotionally unreachable in response to the ups and downs of life. Life is like the waves of an ocean, and the waves never stop. The ups and downs are continuous. If things are calm now, the waves are coming. And if you are in a storm, calm often follows. With all that life throws at us, parents who are emotionally available to their children set them up for success in all areas. Of course, what is shared is delivered in age appropriate doses.

Besides the things life throws at us, parents' emotions are affected by their children. And, this includes behavior. If it's not Jello thrown at the dinner table, it's a baseball thrown through the window. It could be Jill screaming, "You are a terrible mother." It could be Lisa finding ways to cope with her power struggles with her parents and ending up with an eating disorder. All these behaviors are enough to make parents pull their own hair out. In the face of these behaviors, excellent parents remain true to their word, model selflessness, continue to nurture fondness and appreciation, and cultivate an attitude of gratitude.

> *He who stops being better stops being good.*
> *- Oliver Cromwell*

Some parents may become displeased and withhold love when Johnny misspells spelling words on Friday's test. This is a mistake when we do this! A healthy psychological attitude is believing that there is nothing children can do to increase their parent's love for them – this includes achievements, accomplishments, or appropriate behavior. Lenny shouldn't be hugged more because he gets less timeouts. Cindy shouldn't lose her mother-daughter time because of recent noncompliance. A good parenting motto is that pre-planned special experiences and relationship affection are untouchable to disciplinary measures.

> *If you want to bring happiness to the whole world, go home and love your family.*
> *-Mother Teresa*

There is nothing children can do to decrease their parents' love for them. Parents shouldn't withhold love. At the heart of loving children is unconditional love. Love is Not a Reward. Love Is Not a Consequence. Love is unconditional. And love should not be determined by behavior, addiction, disorder, defiance, opposition, noncompliance, depression, or successes, achievements, compliance, and convenience to name a few. When parents withhold love, they engage in manipulation. No parent would want their child to model this level of relationship manipulation.

## WORDS OF WISDOM & STEPS FOR TAKING ACTION

- Empowered parents distinguish behavior problems from personality traits with clarity. For the most part, stop saying, "Oh, that is just his personality" when you notice a problem behavior.

- Empowered parents also recognize personality traits. For example, impulsivity, the most common diagnostic criteria in the DSM-V behind subjective distress, may be a part of one's personality. But impulsively punching people when angry is a behavior that needs to change. It is the expression of this impulsivity that requires change.

- Parents assume nothing, communicate everything, ignore nothing, and reverse helplessness by naming behavior problems.

- Healthy parents commit to the notion that love is not used as a reward or a consequence.

*It is easy to love the people far away. It is not always easy to love those close to us. Bring love into your home, for this is where our love for each other must start.*
*Mother Teresa*

# Chapter Three

## Reinforcing the Character Strength of Boldness

*Performing a choreographed dance at the historic Detroit Opera House that was moved to a big cargo ship is scary! This is particularly fear inducing if there are heavy waves. Just like the waves of life, the waves of an ocean never stop. While the dance can seem effortless during quiet times, these raging seas can require excessive effort on the part of the dancer during the stressful events on life's journey. A ballet during a storm requires boldness. Setbacks are typical during storms, and your child may find herself thrown right off her feet. What age-old wisdom have we learned about responding to setbacks from generation to generation? Getting back on the horse is the answer. Getting back on the bike is the answer. After a teenager feels like he had a speaking setback in class, returning and speaking in front of the class again is the best way to erase doubt. Teens overcoming social, sports, and academic setbacks requires boldness. Engaging in life in the face of ups and downs requires boldness.*

Now that we've established an attachment parenting foundation and discussed the essential action of reinforcement, let's take a closer look at one of the key psychological principles to reinforce in childhood. Chapter 3 focuses on boldness--the primary solution to fearfulness. There are many fears young people face that requires boldness. Tornado drills have always been a normal drill in elementary school, particularly if you grew up in the Midwest. Now, school shooting drills is a normal school activity. Other fears are rampant for kids-- first jobs, reactions to parents' divorce, navigating social circles, steering through the layers of social media[1], stages of personal development, the challenges of psychosexual maturation, and each transition and phase through school grades. There are a range of stressors forced upon young people today – social media pressures, cyberbullying, overscheduling, standardized testing and the subsequent removal of recess, busy parents, excessive smartphone use reducing social interaction, and the list continues. The solution to these fears and stressors is boldness. To buffer youth, boldness needs to be emphasized as the key antidote. There is a psychological quality in boldness training that elevates fearlessness and endures through the ups and downs of childhood and adolescence. This chapter identifies some of the key strategies, both subtle and direct, that parents can incorporate into their parenting style to address fears.

*We become just by the practice of just actions, self-controlled by exercising self-control, and courageous by performing acts of courage.*
- Aristotle

The boldness worth reinforcing is obviously categorically distinct from high-risk behavior common among adolescents (e.g. "Who has the balls to damage others' property").  We aren't talking about risky behavior such as binge drinking, street drug and opiate use, excessive promiscuity, theft crimes or other illegal behavior that peer pressure can coach kids into.  Nor are we talking about risks to gain respect like hazing rituals in college fraternities and sororities.  Rather, boldness to say no to negative influences and remain positive is an uphill battle and the goal of most parents and all caring professionals for young people.  Reinforcing this level of true boldness starts early in the building of a young person's foundation.

**Confidence in the Face of Bullying**

One of the early steps children face is their first encounters with mean children.  It is common for young girls to begin fickle behavior – nice one day and the cold shoulder the next day.  Boldness in the face of fickleness or meanness does not mean being nasty.  And, it does not mean defending yourself by fighting.  Teaching our kids, especially girls, to be consistent friends despite fickleness is the best buffer we can give them in elementary school.

When I was a kid growing up, I was repeatedly called names like digger (for picking my nose in class) and experienced my share of bullying.  One time, I turned to Harvey and said, "If you call me that again, I'll kick your ass after school."  Unfortunately, I said that next to Richard who went on to tell the whole school.  When I got off the bus, Harvey and hundreds of kids were waiting, including Richard hyping up the fight.  Unfortunately, I succumbed to the social pressures and engaged in a fistfight.  For those keeping score, as the fight came to an end, needless to say, I was not announced the winner.

Fathers debate on boldness when it comes to bullying.  Some still maintain that throwing fists remains the way to stand up for oneself.  Young people have to be careful with the threat of weapons and teenagers fighting on school premises who are being arrested and charged for battery.  I've worked with teenagers in Minneapolis, Detroit, and St. Petersburg, and fighting in these schools and neighborhoods results in legal records, juvenile jail, and weapon threats. Fathers against fighting argue that fighting is an old-fashioned strategy that is dead and people need to use their brains nowadays.  Mothers also fall on different sides of the spectrum.  Boldness is not rudeness.  Boldness is not meanness.  Rather, boldness involves wisdom to uniquely debate points, wisely choosing moments when to confront, prioritizing decisions, and being courageous.

As you could probably guess, this section will emphasize the psychology of boldness in the face of threat – which can involve social situations or tennis tryouts.  When it comes to social confrontations, some kids pull hair, kick, beat up on, and engage in other aggressive behaviors.  In some situations, anti-social behavior is more subtle, discrete, manipulative, and nonverbal nowadays.  Yes, you have your verbal bullying such as criticism, negative comments, judgments based on appearance (i.e. "You are so fat"), and negative evaluations ("You have the coordination of your great grandmother.")  Times have changed.  More often, kids are confronted with nonverbal behavior problems – isolating, manipulating, ostracizing, ignoring, and excluding others. Sometimes, boys tend to be more about punching a kid's arm or worse. Sometimes, girls may be more apt to ostracize, or use non-verbals to lower another kid's perceived value in a friendship circle. Of course, each kid is different, and is influenced by culture and a range of variables. As kids get older, the next level of bullying finds its way on social media. Negative comments often find their place on social media websites making it difficult to confront and challenge. Many kids find the trouble that accompanies social media disheartening—the challenges never go away, conflict continues into the night (as opposed to leaving it at school like kids did in the past), and layers of distress accompany Instagram and Twitter.

> *If you don't understand, they feel frustrated. If you don't try to understand, they feel hurt.* – Mark Goulston

In the past 15 years, cyberbullying has taken on a dreadful experience for many young people. In 2008, Jessica Logan was an 18-year-old Sycamore High School senior who sent a nude photo of herself to her boyfriend; it was then sent to hundreds of teenagers in at least seven Cincinnati-area high schools after the couple broke up. Jessica hung herself. In 2009, Hope Sitwell hung herself after a picture of her breasts that she sexted were shared amongst students at six different schools. There are no easy answers to the level of embarrassment Hope experienced. We all have compassion for her family after a terrible tragedy. No words can heal the pain in the hearts of Jessica's or Hope's parents. In situations like these, as the years go by, parents find some degree of solace in thinking about ways this would never happen to other children. What would a bold response look like in this situation? Besides a safe use of technology, a bold response (albeit a very difficult one) would be to battle the suicide thoughts and face this embarrassment head on. Obtaining a counselor, finding support with knowledge of the situation, and overcoming fear of embarrassment.

One of the answers and first steps to these examples of cyberbullying is a safe use of technology. Internet safety tips include (1) Never posting personal information or your location on mobile apps like Snapchat or Instagram, (2) Never sharing passwords with anyone, (3) Using the privacy settings of social networking sites, (4) Children talk with their parents whenever they feel uncomfortable online, while gaming or when using their cell phones. See our resources for information on Internet Safety for children and teenagers.

The essential answer is open communication in the family with both smart tech and responding to bullying. The key principle with children is that parents teach their children—Don't bully and don't let yourself be bullied. Even with safe technology, some of it is out of kids' control. Now kids are using a person's face and photo-shopping a nude body and sending the picture out; thus, you have cyberbullying with the use of nude pics without the victim's participation via messaging. Sending out these pictures with naked bodies makes it appear that sexting occurred when it didn't. These incidents are scaring parents. Despite this bullying reality, we want children to feel like they will be completely supported if they ever become a victim of any type of bullying. We also want young people to develop confidence in the face of different kinds of bullying, whether it is explicit or subtle. And, both explicit and subtle moments of disconnection and isolation are hurtful of others. One of the ways to address these issues is for parents to address these issues head on. Assume nothing and communicate everything. The cruel reality of cyberbullying may be unavoidable for some, even if teens have kept safety a priority.

---

## WORDS OF WISDOM & STEPS FOR TAKING ACTION

- With family dinners a priority, establish regular conversations about bullying: physical bullying, emotional bullying, cyber-bullying.

- Provide hypothetical bullying examples during family meetings and discuss solutions if this were to happen to one of your children or a friend. Dialogue – "How would you handle this scenario?"

- Increase interpersonal self-efficacy by consistent dialogue about the kinds of things "you would do if you witnessed bullying of another kid."

- Engage in conversations about strategies in advance when faced with bullying.

- Continue to educate family on technology safety.

---

### Helping Your Child or Teen Cope with Anxiety- Talking, School, Sleeping...

Boldness takes on a new meaning when we are discussing the challenge of overcoming fears. Empowered parents are comfortable talking about anxiety with their children. The word "Anxiety" is not a curse word to avoid nor is it "poisoning" our children. Consider the following words relevant to the experience of children and adolescents: nervous, tense, anxious, angst, apprehension, concern, disquiet, doubt, dread, jitters, panic, restlessness, uneasiness, butterflies, creeps, distress, fidgetiness, disquiet, worry, foreboding, and emotional alarm among many others.

Many parents are afraid to talk about their child's anxiety with them. Discussing a list of words (1) Desensitizes anxiety by making it easier to open up to parents, (2) Destigmatizes the process of actually getting help for anxiety, (3) And begins to elevate the dialogue by using language to explain experiences. If you have a child with anxiety, removing the language barrier is like taking the helium out of the balloon. It really does zap the power that language has, and anxiety is no longer something to be afraid of. Parents can do a lot to help with anxiety by not being afraid to talk about it.

I see a lot of individuals with anxiety disorders. Most of the children, teens and adults have a common theme: anxiety was never discussed in their childhood or is currently being discussed in adolescence. The topic of "Anxiety" was and remains taboo. There are several things that parents can do for their children to encourage bold honesty with themselves and others.

First, teach self-soothing strategies besides TV, iPad, mobile phone game apps, and unhealthy foods like excessive potato chip consumption. Distraction techniques are ok but it is better to rely on internal things and healthy habits – like reading, drawing, Plato, or painting, and subject changes from worries to engaging in talking about play – soccer or unique strategies for hide and go seek. With mature children and teenagers, identifying a list of healthy self-soothing strategies (SSSs) and tension reduction behaviors (TRBs) helps normalize tension and builds a tool kit that's available and accessible.

## REFLECTION EXERCISE

Identifying a healthy set of Self-Soothing Strategies (SSSs) and Tension Reduction Behaviors (TRBs) using the five senses decreases anxiety and increases parasympathetic activity:

**VISION**

Look at old pictures

Read old letters

Notice the nature walking

Gaze at art

Draw

**TOUCH**

Take a bubble bath

Get a massage

Use a favorite lotion

Use a Rumbleroller®

**HEARING**

Listening to the birds

Pandora® or favorite music

Use a sound machine

Sing, call a friend

**SMELL**

Light a candle

Bake cookies

Use essential oils for aroma

Smell of flowers

**TASTE**

Eat dark chocolate very slowly and mindfully [superfood]

Drink a cup of tea; green tea is full of antioxidants

Savoring, or mindful eating, slowly consuming berries: blueberries, blackberries, cranberries, raspberries, and strawberries.

Enjoy the satisfaction of slowly swallowing honey in your mouth. Honey helps to inhibit the growth of bacteria, yeast, fungi, and viruses and has significant levels of antioxidants.

A second helpful element of anxiety alleviation is gradual exposure in time increments.  So, for a simple example, if a child is anxious to play hide and go seek alone, (1) the first step may be hiding with another, (2) followed by hiding by themselves for 5 seconds, (3) then gradually increase the time until they can count on their own.  On a more serious example that is highly prevalent, counselors and school professionals experience high stress facing the dilemma of children refusing to go to school and the avoidance occasionally reinforced by the parents.  In those complicated situations, sometimes parents need education on potential steps to bringing about change.  Education on how encouraging the child's school avoidance actually increases the child's anxiety is critical.  Once the parent is on the same page, the following is a common set of steps for a child with social anxiety who avoids school.  The following actions are sometimes best facilitated by a school counselor.  One of the first steps that some parents can do include (1) taking the child to school and being at the school when no students are present, such as a Saturday (i.e. even if it's just school grounds).  As a next step, parents can try to (2) arrange it so the child can spend time with her teacher in the classroom when no students are there.  The next steps might be (3) staying in class for a ½ day then allowed to stay home, (4) staying in class the entire day but allowed to call home, (5) staying in class for a ½ day but not allowed to call home, and (6) staying in class the entire day and not allowed to call.  These steps normally don't work out in order and require adjustments.

> *I believe half the unhappiness in life comes from people being afraid to go straight at things.*   – William J. Lock

Another big one for young children with anxiety is to move them along incrementally to sleeping in their own bed.  Developmentally, it is best when 8-year olds (or 3-year olds) don't sleep with Mommy.  Gradual exposure with reinforcement is the goal here.  The hierarchy here works in a similar way as the "go to school" process.  Parents establish individualized steps with reinforcement.  I have found that precise incremental steps are less important than parents establishing a principle of "separate beds make for optimal sleep."

## WORDS OF WISDOM & STEPS FOR TAKING ACTION

- Bold exposure occurs in small steps, starting with the least distressing step first.

- Recognize that a classic negative reinforcement example is permitting avoidance of school. Avoidance Locks in School Fears. The goal is to prevent "Locks", so even a phone call home, which is suggested in the list of steps, may be negatively reinforcing.

- Boldness as a psychological strength is the opposite of avoidance.

### Enabling Avoidance is Not Love

One of the most important aspects of anxiety management combined with reinforcement is eliminating those unhealthy strategies that reinforce anxiety – and one of those is enabling. The essential truth of enabling is that it is not love. If your son falls off a bike or gets hit by a car while riding, he will definitely be afraid of riding his bike. The best thing to do is get your son back on the bike for the next family bike ride. It is during this process that boldness is reinforced. If done well, praise for overcoming the fear can be a signature strength builder, a momentum swinger, a significant emotional event, and an anchor point that will strengthen the child to take risks, try out for things, pursue things even with uncertainty, and leave their comfort zone. As time passes, specific praise like overcoming the feelings and riding the bike anyway can translate to generalized comments such as, "Whenever you have come face to face with fears, you seem to not back down. That is really impressive Donald."

*The way you help heal the world is that you start with your own family.* - Mother Teresa

In contrast, many parents will be fine not having the child ride his bike again. They will just put attention on other things "not wanting to put pressure on him" and saying, "We don't have to go on the bike ride." "I understand, what you went through was very hard." That is compassionate counseling. But, what the kid (who will be unhappy) needs to do is get on the bike and get riding. The child's feelings need to be validated. The parents need to avoid pressuring the child.

What's the difference?   The difference is that the goal is to reinforce boldness – finding unique ways to get riding again.  Similar to the child who stays home from school, avoidance locks in the sympathetic activity at the time of the emotional event.   Consider emotional scaling. When a person experiences a 9 or 10 on the scale of 0 (completely relaxed) to 10 (maximum anxiety), the sympathetic activity gets locked in on the anxiety scale at a 9 or a 10.  The best strategy for specific fears is to nip them in the bud, face them head on, and help young people overcome them by engaging in previously enjoyed activities so the anxiety doesn't get locked in.  Bike riding is a common activity that can result in a negative experience.  With boldness and courage, this can be reversed.

When I was a child, I was afraid of heights on our travels in the mountains. I was permitted to stay in the car or stay away from sightseeing areas.  On the one hand, I experienced niceness as opposed to forcefulness.  On the other hand, my avoidance was encouraged.  When avoidance is encouraged, this could result in a long-term problem.  In my case, as time passed, my fear was extinguished through various exposure opportunities.  What I needed was initial exposure to facing my fears head on.  In addition to exposure, I needed my catastrophic thoughts of the worst-case scenario 'decastrophized.' The problem with avoidance that is encouraged in scenarios with children like in my example is the fact that enabling fears is not love.  Facing the fears – sleeping alone, hiding alone, riding your bike again, these are examples of love (and building boldness).

The primary goal for parents is to eliminate enabling, encourage kids to confront their fears, and reduce avoidance.  The way this is done is approaching our children with empathy and compassion, not with forcefulness.  When your child is afraid, whether age 5 or age 16, approaching fears with respect goes a long way.  It is helpful for parents to keep themselves from talking the child out of being afraid.  Rather, saying "I'm afraid" is honest, authentic, and empowering. When parents stay calm and maintain poise, it has a calming effect because how we talk to children about fears is more important than what we say.  Remember that at least 65% of communication is nonverbal[2].  In the process of confronting fears, it is helpful to find out what works, is comfortable for the child, and to go at their own pace.  However, don't let the child off the hook because avoidance strengthens anxiety.  Encouraging coping responses like drawing, deep breathing techniques, distraction techniques and providing rewards that are both small and bigger helps further the process along.

---

## REFLECTION TIPS

The following are strategies for parents to approach fears with respect. The following inquiries increase mindfulness of emotions for older children and teenagers:

- What feelings can you name or identify?

- Did you identify the trigger that elicited the emotion?

- What thoughts did you notice as you felt the emotion?

- Were you able to notice where the emotion showed up in your body?

- What did you do with distracting thoughts? What did you do to stay in the present?

- What did you observe in the moment?

- Did you experience any kind of appreciation?

---

### How to Raise Two Marshmallow Children? Five Strategies

In 1968, a four-year old boy at Bing School at Stanford University was shown some marshmallows[3]. He was then told that when a supervisor returns from running an errand after 15 minutes, he could have two marshmallows. But, if he can't wait, he could have one marshmallow. One marshmallow now or two marshmallows in 15 minutes. Children are faced with these types of scenarios and confronted with the following questions – Do I delay gratification, or do I give in to what I desire in the immediate moment? Will I maintain self-control with a focus on the long-term goal, or will I yield to pleasure now? Will I succumb to immediate satisfaction, or do I persist in my efforts to persevere for something better?

This same scenario was given to 635 children from 1968 to 1974. Most of the children failed to delay gratification. These same children as adolescents showed stark differences in their emotional intelligence. Those who could delay gratification were more likely able to delay gratification as teenagers and young adults. Two-marshmallow individuals had better self-mastery – they were able to exert control over life circumstances, were better planners with an eye on long-term goals, and were better at adjusting to life's problems. They had better academic scores, better relationships, and functioned better in their day-to-day living.

Children that chose the one marshmallow without waiting for the second had poor stress management skills, became easily rattled under pressure, avoided challenges, and were not dependable in relationships. They lacked self-confidence and continued to make decisions for their immediate gratification.

So, every parent wants to know, how can you make your child a two-marshmallow individual? It does take work to reinforce children who embrace challenges, pursue challenging tasks in the face of difficulties, learn to become self-reliant, manage their frustration without quitting, and maintain poise on the balance beam of life. Here are five strategies that parents can implement to facilitate two-marshmallow thinking.

Reinforce Gratification Delay as early as possible to facilitate patience and strength in this area. Practically, start children young by practicing marshmallow tests on a regular basis. Of course, this is best generalized to other things, and healthier food choices if possible.

Emphasize how much better things are by waiting in discussions and family meetings. It is helpful to let this play out in practical life. We can undercut ourselves – you can have that shirt when you save enough money. But we get that shirt the next time we are at the store when a kid is begging for it. That undercuts our initial plan. Motivated parents are mindful of delaying gratification in multiple ways for their children. Play challenge games that involve waiting & patience. For example, a family goes to Dairy Queen and sits on tables waiting 10 minutes before they order. It is clearly communicated that the "wait time" is not a punishment, but rather, a reminder of learning to delay gratification. Youth can get annoyed but are easily swayed with humor. If parents turn these types of things into games, it turns fun fast! As examples: parents can incorporate spelling games with prizes during wait times; or, on the 4th Saturday of the month, every five minutes of waiting can increase the size of the Blizzard.

Implement Behavioral Rehearsals that involve practicing Re-Dos for all impatient acts or activities that involve rushing. Families implement rehearsals as a way to engage in alternative behavior choices. Rehearsals accomplish two things: (1) teaches that behavior is a choice, (2) mistakes are allowed, (3) re-dos are permitted. As an example, Cindy was rushing to the car and elbowed her four-year-old brother Max while getting into the van. Her mother, a colleague who shared the story, smartly didn't listen to her own tendency to rush too. Instead, she stopped everything and addressed the behavior. She laughed during her story telling, "Our family was already 10 minutes late to church, what's the difference if we were 14 minutes late?" Mom asked Cindy and Max to get out of the van and engage in a rehearsal. Max was repositioned and Cindy was invited to wait patiently and get in the van cooperatively rather than trampling and elbowing her brother. This "Re-Do" encourages patience, particularly when Mom models it. Discuss the all-important concepts of consequences and time. The goal is to help children develop their understanding of consequences and time. "To get what I want in the long term, I'll do what I don't want now." When kids save their money, do they want 10 little $1 store items, one item per week for 10 consecutive weeks or a $10 Target store toy. Parents are engaged in the moment but speak about being mindful "like a Jedi" of making decisions on what is best long-term.

> *"Never worry about numbers. Help one at a time, and always start with those nearest you."* - Mother Teresa

## FACILITATING TWO-MARSHMALLOW THINKING

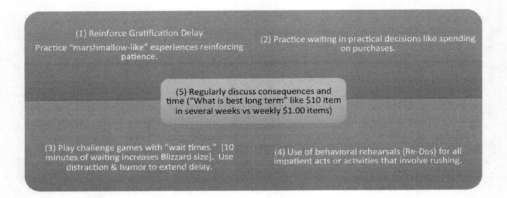

(1) Reinforce Gratification Delay
Practice "marshmallow-like" experiences reinforcing patience.

(2) Practice waiting in practical decisions like spending on purchases.

(5) Regularly discuss consequences and time ("What is best long term" like $10 item in several weeks vs weekly $1.00 items)

(3) Play challenge games with "wait times." [10 minutes of waiting increases Blizzard size]. Use distraction & humor to extend delay.

(4) Use of behavioral rehearsals (Re-Dos) for all impatient acts or activities that involve rushing.

### Eliminating All Characteristics of Child-Like Parenting

The number one way to encourage BOLDNESS is for a parent to reflect this trait in the quality of their own life. Reflecting boldness involves being bold. This could mean doing a "mud run" or "warrior dash," giving speeches at toastmasters for the first time, or going shark hunting at midnight. Diving off cliffs, running marathons, and leaving one's comfortable job for another challenging one are typical examples of boldness. Certainly, overcoming our own fears goes a long way in raising bold and fearless children. Modeling boldness influences our kids to be willing to leave their comfort zone. Remember, everything we say and do is observed. And, parents can't say "Do what I say, but don't do what I do." To be consistent, what we say and do reflects what we want. We speak out of what we do. Consistency in all areas of our life is reflective of mature parenting that reinforces boldness.

Boldness is required for those accomplishments—pull up and push up cross fit training, long distance running, or a job change. But the deeper requirement for mature parenting is boldness in self-examination. I want to take a moment here and identify one area of consistency that is key to mature parenting. Bold self-examination can result in emotional integration—the process of experiencing genuine healing from past hurts. Some parents let the past dictate how they react in the present.

Self-examining may involve dealing with the anger from the past to prevent current anger overreactions. In my own personal work, I grew up in a family where anger was unpredictable. As a result, this is something that I had to learn to curb in my life as a parent. I established a program with my kids that if I am firm, it needs to be for a legitimate reason.  Thus, if back-talking showed its ugly head or aggression between siblings emerged, Dad was going to be firm and this was expected.  However, if I overreacted based on a misperception, then we identified that as inappropriately firm.  That's right!  We categorized firm parenting as appropriately firm and inappropriately firm.  If I was inappropriately firm, I would explain myself, apologize for my mistake, and do 20 push-ups as a consequence.  Sometimes, self-examining involves dealing with fears or feelings of abandonment.  I am a big believer of ruthlessly doing the personal work to prevent walls between parents and their children.  One of the fruits of doing personal work is emotional integration, which is different from emotional release or catharsis that have to do with expressing emotions.  Emotional integration requires emotional honesty—working through tough stuff from the past.  A key feature of personal work is recognizing that old issues don't permanently disappear.  It's a lifetime journey of starving the negative and reinforcing the positive.  Feeding the anger monster or letting it starve is a lifelong journey.  The same can be said about narcissism, an exaggerated sense of self-importance and a hypersensitivity to the potential criticism of others, or interpersonal avoidance—having an intense fear of negative evaluations by others leading to avoiding social situations.  These deeper issues of anger, narcissism, or interpersonal avoidance, or behaviors such as drinking, gambling, or pornography require a bold self-examination.

Parents who do little reflection tend to engage in what I call childlike parenting.  Childlike parents are fearful, anxious, and often play a childlike role.  They often leave the caretaking or parenting to children, robbing children of their youth and childhood.   In some ways, it is the Michael Jackson phenomenon.  He even sang a beautiful song, "Have you seen my Childhood?"  Some of the lyrics include "People say I'm not okay.  Cause I love such elementary things.  It's been my fate to compensate for the childhood I've never known."  Some of this might be a self-fulfilling prophesy for Michael since he reflected on this so well and sang about it.  But, putting Michael to the side, his lyrics reflect many parental characteristics.

Now, someone who becomes famous at such a young age is an extreme example.  Many of us did not lose our childhood.  But, we are all susceptible to regressing to child-like parenting characteristics.  Some parents take life by its horns and continually engage in self-reflection and self-examination.  Some parents are terrified and anxious. I'm not referring to that initial scariness and unknown at childbirth when we become parents for the first time.  Rather, chronic fearfulness leads to unhealthy neural pathways and results in child-like parenting.  The following are examples of emotional bombs that parents use to dump on their kids for various reasons, and these usually come out of child-like parenting.  Rather than engaging in mature parenting that involves a reflective life and self-examination, these parents regress to child-like characteristics that involve throwing out these emotional bombs.

## Anxious Paranoia Bomb
Consider the anxious mom who won't sign a permission slip for her daughter's field trip out of fear something bad will happen.  This level of fear is emotionally crippling for children.  The mother puts her fear onto the child and it

stunts the emotional growth of children and keeps them stuck in anxiety and fear.

## Guilt Bomb

There are immature parents who engage in child-like parenting by controlling others through guilt. For example, if a father has an anger eruption, he may use the language, "See you made me angry." "What you did made me angry." This deferring responsibility is sometimes motivated to increase guilt in children. The truth is, "I felt angry after hearing what you did" is more accurate. Unfortunately, these types of patterns are chronic emotional bombs.

*A man who listens because he has nothing to say can hardly be a source of inspiration. The only listening that counts is that of the talker who alternatively absorbs and expresses ideas.*
- Agnes Repplier

## Manipulation Bomb

Parents can subtly manipulate their children, as discussed earlier. Parents will manipulate by not being direct and using emotions to enforce behavior. "I am so disappointed" in you is a common emotional bomb dumped on the kid. With this emotional bomb, parents aren't separating emotions from behavior and choices. Parents will hold disappointment over their children.

*The way to love anything is to realize that it might be lost.*
- G. K. Chesterton

## Concerned About What Others Think Bomb

Concern about what others think is a prominent problem in our culture today. Something happens around the pre-teen stage where kids go from giving speeches in elementary school to now requiring accommodations for social anxiety in middle onward to high school. What happened? One possibility is that they have become more adept at reading the anxiety in their parents. Many parents make decisions with their children due to fear of embarrassment and their anxiety influences their parenting. Social perception influences poor reinforcement. Would Tammy give in if she was the only one in the store facing the temper tantrum? Probably not.

## AVOID THESE EMOTIONAL BOMBS

| | |
|---|---|
| **Anxious Paranoia Bomb**<br><br>Won't sign field trip permission slip ("something bad will happen.") | **Guilt Bomb**<br><br>Induce guilt by blaming ("You made me angry!") |
| **Manipulation Bomb**<br><br>Not being direct and using emotions to enforce behavior ("I am so disappointed.") | **Concerned about what others think Bomb**<br><br>Easily embarrassed or makes decisions based on social perception. |

The problem with these emotional bombs is that they become routines and the neural pathways get established. To reverse these neural pathways, ADULT parenting which involves continually reflecting, takes on the following elements. First and foremost, a parent accepts that their job is to raise a child. This involves being high in control and high in warmth. An element of being high in control doesn't mean not offering choices. Rather, choices are offered and emphasized. "I think this is a good consequence, what do you think? What do you suggest?" This choice technique made a significant difference for Javion and his mother. Within three weeks, his problem behaviors decreased as he felt more empowered by his mother's initiative to engage in give-and-take conversation.

Second, an adult parent is not a friend, but a parent. It is in this relationship dynamic where parents miss their calling. And this is the heart of permissive parenting, the emphasis is on friendship rather than raising a child. Parents mistakenly look to their children for affection to make up for insecurities in their own life. Secure parents are determined to raise their child with unconditional love without needing anything from them. When parents love without a need for affection, they are unselfishly seeing things beyond the moment and raising adult-like rather than child-like characteristics. I was inspired by a subtle action on Lisa's part one day. Lisa was a client of mine seeking therapy for depression. She was a single mom working hard to parent two teenagers and manage her full-time job. She shared a moment with me when she was feeling lonely and went to her daughter's room for emotional support. Her daughter, lost in her own world of relationships and hormone changes, was uninterested in connecting. She didn't even want a hug. Lisa, unfazed, did not hold resentment or feel sorry for herself; instead, she was able to tell her daughter, "I'm here if you need anything." Lisa's story was a real-life genuine story reflective of mature parenting.

Third, an engaged adult parent instructs their child engaging in patterns of talking, teaching, correcting, and fully taking part in a give and take relationship. An engaged adult parent studies ideas on how to approach things from different angles. An engaged parent imparts ideas, philosophies, and knowledge into their child. When a child says, "You're mean" at a time when there isn't objectively mean behavior occurring, then an engaged parent teaches the child about emotions and gives them statements to say such as, "I felt angry when you wouldn't stop cooking and help me." An engaged parent will say something like, "Thank you for sharing. Your feelings are very important to me."

Fourth, an engaged parent who has outgrown childlike parenting tendencies is direct and firm when he or she needs to be. But, not abusive, not perfectionistic, not anxiously paranoid, not manipulative, and does not do things to induce guilt. Engaged parents don't throw emotional bombs, instead they live a reflective and engaged life.

Finally, an engaged adult parent seeks healthy ways to mature, grow up, and find support from other parents. Positive parenting support is particularly needed for young parents. Neuropsychological and neurological research has shown that the brain hasn't fully developed until the age of 25. There is a lot spinning around in the head for young parents – nuggets of wisdom and getting others' perspectives can be a sense of stability. The ultimate treasure in a parent is a strong motivation to be a good parent. These parents talk with others, read books, and engage in self-reflection about their parenting skills.

---

## WORDS OF WISDOM & STEPS FOR TAKING ACTION

- A basic assumption of excellent parenting is eliminating child-like parenting characteristics.

- An adult parent exercises a balance of control and warmth, not solely a friend.

- An engaged parent facilitates a 3-F environment: Fun, Fair, and Firm.

## 6 Steps to Replacing Fear of Embarrassment With Boldness

Children and adolescents have a deep need to connect in relationships. But fear of embarrassment becomes an interior barrier and blocks this need to connect. Many kids struggle with embarrassment. At its essence, embarrassment is fear of rejection. The fear of rejection influences an underlying set of thoughts in which kids question their own social abilities. When adolescents experience self-doubt, they often suffer from negative comparisons. They compare themselves to others, lose in the comparison and the cost is decreased confidence. This further buries hopes for connection and increases fear of rejection. This of course distances them from the goal of making a difference in their culture.

There are steps that can be taken to nip this process in the bud. The first step is to discuss not being afraid of others' opinions and others' perceptions. One of the empirically supported treatment methods to decreasing social anxiety is social mishap exposure therapy. Essentially, practicing mishaps to feel less anxiety around mistakes in front of others. When working with adults, I may invite them to stand in front of a restaurant and ask for directions to that restaurant. Practicing mistakes helps normalize the fact that everybody makes mistakes, and helps to take the helium out of the balloon of having made a mistake. Socially non-anxious adolescents and college students in their social psychology classes love to practice social mishaps. They find it thrilling to repeatedly almost get off on the wrong floor of a crowded elevator. For some kids, mistakes are highly anxiety producing. Practicing social mishaps with intention and focus can begin to reverse barriers toward accepting mistakes. Practicing social mishaps leads people to realize that "it isn't a big deal" and they can cope and tolerate with mishaps. Some parents will trip on the bleachers, look around, and then get up and then say to their kid, "Does it matter that I just fell? Do I care about others perceiving me as clumsy? No, because I am not clumsy. Do I care that others might perceive me as careless? No, because I try not to be... Should I be concerned that others think I make mistakes? No, not at all! I should not be concerned that others think that because it is true. I do make mistakes. Everybody does."

*Genius...means little more than the faculty of perceiving in an unhabitual way.* -William James

So, Step #1 – Discuss with the child about being unafraid of others' opinions.

The second step is to routinely use extreme examples to expose kids to "worst case scenarios." These are those embarrassing moments that involve elevated emotional arousal and lead people to say, "I wish that didn't happen." Googling "embarrassing moments for kids" is good exposure for kids. But, not just for its own sake. It is important to link these moments of avoidance to key questions – could you tolerate this situation? Could you cope? In what ways would you tolerate this scenario?

Consider the following scenarios. A college student was running to class in the middle of an icy and cold winter day. While running across an intersection, he tripped and fell on his face sliding head first on the ice in the middle of the street. Many students and drivers at the red light saw the entire slide. Consider a 7th grader who rebounded a basket on a one and one foul shot in a basketball game. When the shooter missed the free throw, the 7th grader was the only one to leave the lane and rebound the ball. The other players were thinking that it was a "shooting two scenario." After the rebound, he missed three layups as the other players were wondering what he was doing. He then turned and said, "Come on boys, let's play basketball." As he exclaimed the words, he took some steps and was whistled for traveling. 600 fans laughed in unison at the young man. Or consider the father who ripped the entire back of his pants at a father daughter dance and his entire underwear was easily viewable all the way down. Every person has some of these stories. These stories are not unique. What is unique is sharing these stories. It is recommended that stories are solicited from guests who visit families' homes. This gives children an opportunity to hear about those times when "others feel like the world's most embarrassed." Families who discuss social mishaps desensitize kids to exhibiting abreactions to socially awkward experiences. Lots of discussions on embarrassing stories increase the tolerance threshold of kids.

Going a step further beyond exposure to these stories, it is helpful to connect these stories with tolerance. Key questions for children when hearing stories of embarrassment. Could you tolerate these experiences? In what ways would you tolerate this scenario? Could you laugh at yourself? Ok, what if the kid says no? "I'm not saying you could easily laugh at yourself, but, hypothetically if you could, what would be some ways you could find amusement?
Step #2 – Expose kids to worst case scenarios.

The third step is to directly discuss with kids about trying to never be embarrassed. There is a unique nuance with this goal. Rather than avoid embarrassment, the actual goal is to not be afraid of embarrassment if and when it actually happens. Children can freeze themselves in social situations because of being deathly afraid of the Big E in the room. Some children worry about being embarrassed, and their uneasiness is reinforced by constantly worrying about some bad outcome in the future. This future concern can be alleviated with processing possible scenarios. The sting can be taken out in advance of most social situations by practicing not being afraid of being embarrassed.

---

**REFLECTION TIPS**

- The following questions for kids increase thoughtfulness about the issue of embarrassment:

- What are the worst possible and most embarrassing moments?

- Can you come up with a list of most embarrassing moments?

- What would you do in those situations?

- What could you do to not be embarrassed?

- How would you cope with that situation?

---

Step #3- Directly discuss with kids about trying to never be embarrassed and/or being unafraid of embarrassment.

The 4th step is to directly discuss with children about being able to laugh at yourself, especially around other people. This, of course, only works when parents are able to laugh at themselves when they miss their mouth and put juice over their shirt. When I work with anxious children, I have successfully developed strategies for families to increase laughter within their homes. This of course works if the parents are flexible and receptive to trying new things. This is difficult at times because a child's anxiety is influenced by the family history of anxiety. But, an example of an intervention that increases family laughter is the mother setting up a situation where she can spill juice on her lap at dinner time. Anxiety often results from high levels of control in family systems. At the same time, families looking to bring changes and healing are open to incorporating flexibility in their routines.

A key distinction here is differentiating kids who laugh in mean ways, kids who target, and bully by mean behavior while laughing at kids, versus all kids who laugh. Asking kids the difference between mean laughter versus funny laughter when laughing can be a good discussion at dinner-time. Sometimes, it is called laughing at versus laughing with. But, routine conversations about the difference are helpful because it increases understanding. And, teaching kids to laugh at themselves can actually be confidence building.

Step #4 – Directly discuss with children about being able to laugh at ourselves, especially around other people.

Step 5 is directly discussing ways kids can laugh with other kids. Some of this occurs naturally in the development of relationships, and feels good to parents when their kids are around "nice kids." The problem is that sometimes kids are not around polite and respectable children. When I was at Jane Addams Middle School in Bolingbrook, IL, I used to facilitate cut down fights between friends.

Cut down fights was our artistic form of verbal debates. We would score each other based on who could "cut down" or criticize the other person in the most creative way. During one incident (in the middle of English class), I was in charge of scoring points between two friends based on the degree of their respective cut downs, or creativity used in saying the worst thing about one's mother. For those of us who need reminders, here are some of the more positively natured "your mama" jokes: Your mom is so stupid she sold her car for gas money. Your mama is so fat she stepped on a scale and it said, 'to be continued.' Your mom is so stupid that when I said, "drinks on the house," she got a ladder. Your mom's breath is so bad she walked by a clock and it said, "tic tac." Your mom is so stupid it takes her two hours to watch 60 Minutes. Your mom is so short she ties her shoes standing up. Your Momma is so old, her Social Security Number is 6. Your momma is so stupid that she got hit by a parked car. Your mama is so ugly she made a blind kid cry. Alright, you got the point. Essentially, the goal of the contest was to cut down the person fully. And, the aforementioned examples were scored low compared to the negative and heavily critical examples.

Upon reflection, most of the cut downs were not humorous or based in wit or creativity. There was nothing positive or intelligent about most of them. Some of the examples given here are well thought out and creative. But, most gutter humor was based on ignorance. And, I question whether people walked away with more positive attitudes, more loving feelings, and more respectful views of friends' families as well as one's own family. I suspect that these criticisms diminished perspectives rather than enlarged empathy and compassion for others.

This reminds us that there are standards to humor. Many good-natured parents know that humor should build up, not put down. Humor should bring life, not tear down. Humor should not be exclusive, ideally all are invited to laugh. I routinely encourage my kids to look for a child who is alone and invite them to play. Invite them in. The same approach can be taken with humor. Laughter is contagious and the best medicine.

Step 5 is directly discussing ways kids can laugh with other kids using inclusive humor that builds up others.

Step #6 – Boldly Take Risks

Let's take some time to define the different aspects of boldness. Our dic-
*I've missed more than 9000 shots in my career. I've lost almost 300 games. 26 times, I've been trusted to take the game winning shot and missed. I've failed over and over and over again in my life. And that is why I succeed.* - Michael Jordan

tionary defines boldness as not hesitating or fearful in the face of actual or possible danger. A decisive analysis of this definition would include acknowledging that a child boldly standing up for another kid being bullied may involve fearfulness. Boldness, or bravery, is doing what needs to be done despite fear. Is fearlessness realistic? When we encourage children to "be fearless," is that actually possible? Being fearless is based on the classic saying, "Do not be afraid." Related to the root of the word courage is encouragement, which means to give support, confidence, or hope to someone. When we encourage youth to be fearless or to not be afraid, this is at the heart of our encouragement. Every child needs our encouragement and the number one thing an adult can do for youth is to encourage. Part of that is encouraging people to be unafraid.

However, the reality of human beings is that those of us with intact nervous systems, which includes the sympathetic nervous system, experience fear. Boldness, or bravery, is acting regardless of the fear. African American children helped desegregate schools in the south. This no doubt was courageous behavior despite fear. The young Unknown Rebel known as "Tank Man" stood his ground against an army tank during the Tiananmen Square Massacre. We can logically conclude that he acted boldly despite fear.

When teenagers resist peer pressure to cheat on an exam, they often have to segregate their physiology from the rest of themselves. Some fear is very frequently experienced in performance situations, unless apathy is an issue. Spelling bees, choir performances, championship football games, ACT/SAT examinations, talent shows, performing arts, and cross country meets to name a few. Success in these performances usually results from a combination of practice, talent, poise despite pressure and the right balance of arousal[4]. The Yerkes – Dodson Law of Arousal speaks to the importance of a "right" balanced level of arousal. Too little arousal, and apathy and low energy settle in. Low arousal is one of the issues that leads to indifference. With low arousal, individuals tend to have poor performance. Too much arousal results in impaired performance. When a person has too much arousal, this tends to affect performance anxiety. Overwhelm impacts skills. There is an optimal level of arousal that leads to optimal performance.

I worked with a 16-year-old male named Gus. He was excelling in school and was particularly bright in math and computers. He got a little exercise at home but wasn't very athletic. His extracurricular activities included band. His social circle was limited. He had trouble making friends not because he was bullied. He had a stuttering problem that was primarily anxiety related. However, when he was discussing music and future band experiences, he lit up like a Christmas tree. When kids asked him about computers or math, he happily shared his knowledge and engaged in tutoring. However, outside of these knowledge areas, he felt limited. He avoided situations due to anxiety in groups. He worried about panicking in front of others. He became preoccupied with concerns about being embarrassed. He came in for therapy and we engaged in a standard protocol of cognitive-behavioral therapy with social skills training, relaxation training, improving his self-talk, and social exposures – courageously talk with other students in unfamiliar environments. After 10 weeks, the boldness that was most impressive about Gus was his willingness to ask questions, show interest in others, and begin to engage in conversations about topics that he wasn't interested in for the sake of relationships. The phrases "arise and shine" and "stand up and stand out" truly reflected Gus' boldness. It should be noted that he would be the first to say that overcoming some barriers occurred despite his fear, not due to a lack of fear.

## WORDS OF WISDOM & STEPS FOR TAKING ACTION

Implement the Six Steps to Replacing Fear of Embarrassment with Boldness

- Discuss with the child about being unafraid of others' opinions.

- Directly discuss with kids about trying to never be embarrassed and/or being unafraid of embarrassment.

- Expose kids to conversations about worst case scenarios.

- Directly discuss with children about being able to laugh at ourselves, especially around other people.

- Directly discussing ways kids can laugh with other kids using inclusive humor that builds up others.

**SIX STEPS TO REPLACING FEAR OF EMBARRASSMENT WITH BOLDNESS**

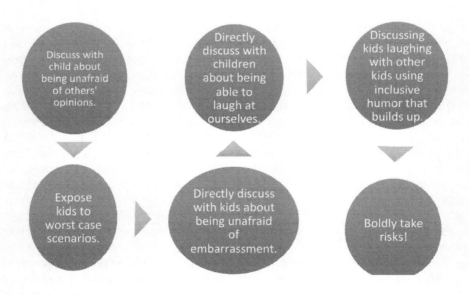

**<u>Modeling Brave Behaviors</u>**

I am a youth sports coach in soccer, basketball, and baseball. In a recent season, I had a parent who reinforced fear of lightning. The rubbing of the shoulder, telling the child he would be O.K., and removing him from soccer practice appeared to be too much in the context of some flash of lightning several miles away. In contrast, hundreds of other kids and parents remained on the soccer field because the lightning was clearly too far away to be a scary factor.

It is important to not make fun, ignore the problem, or minimize the child's feelings. Comments like, "Don't be so babyish" are invalidating and unhelpful. It's extremely helpful to take the fears seriously (i.e. acknowledging the seriousness of lightning in SW FL is important), listen and validate, and model brave behaviors. One family experienced their son breaking his arm when he was hit by a car while riding his bike. Several months later, the kid was highly distraught when the family was going for a bike ride. The child was encouraged to come along since "this is what the family is doing." Despite the distress, the child came along with significant reluctance. But, soon, the biking was fun, the fear and anxiety was extinguished, and the memory was in the past. Johnny was riding his bike up and down the neighborhood with boyish aggression and joy and seemed unfazed by his prior fear. In contrast, a parent in another family may say, "It's ok Johnny, you don't have to ride the bike." As a result, the child might never ride his bike again, which maintains the fear frozen at the time of the experience.

## Boldness in the Face of Meanness

Boldness comes in all flavors. For some, the five strategies to building emotional intelligence and gratification delay [two-marshmallow thinking] and the six steps to eliminating embarrassment elevates boldness in the life of the child or teen. For some kids, applying these steps may take some time after phases of emotional development and maturation. Before that happens, boldness may involve just getting through the day.

As an example, I spoke with Lenny, a single father with full custody of his 11-year-old daughter. His daughter Kelly was having difficulty with depressed moods and had an uncontrollable crying episode while washing the dishes the other day. Lenny was concerned about her feelings as excessive crying and an unusually increased amount of hugging had been occurring lately. "She hugs me many times each day." From all angles, it appears that Lenny is a responsive father. To add to the difficulty is her poor sleep. Kelly averages at least five awakenings during the night. Some of these include recurrent episodes of incomplete awakening from sleep accompanied by sleepwalking. "She is hard to wake up and will come into my bedroom talking and rambling on in the middle of the night." Kelly is receiving psychiatric medication, psychological counseling, and support from a behavioral sleep specialist.

She was a bit nervous about seeing a counselor and I was able to encourage her. "The counselor will be like a FBI agent, and will protect your information like it's secret government information. Your personal secrets will be protected and your support team will be 'metaphorically like secret agents on your success team in helping you get through middle school.'" Kelly laughed a little and smiled as we talked about how finding support can be both helpful for she and her dad. My reframe seemed to reduce some of the pressure she was feeling about counseling.  No doubt it can be intimidating.

Big picture – Kelly is starting middle school and doesn't have a mother in the picture.  She is experiencing loneliness and depression.  Intellectually and academically, she is doing fine but she is regularly trying to fend off nastiness among the 6th grade girls.  One of her goals seems to be finding ways to respond well to the jerks and the jerkettes.  During my discussion with Lenny and Kelly, I suggested that she continue to find support from her secret agent support team – her counselor, teacher, father, aunt and uncle, and close friends.  So how does one find this pot of gold in the 6th grade?  How do you find pearls in the midst of social turmoil?

There are many things that Kelly needs as she navigates the school year.  Boldness for Kelly may not be joining the debate team or the middle school cross country team.  It could—middle school is often a time where significant maturation occurs and extracurricular activities may facilitate skills, confidence and friendships.  But, boldness for Kelly may just involve getting to school each day and strategically befriending those nice kids with consistent kindness.  Very often, bold kindness defeats meanness and nastiness.

## Boldness by Being Friendly

Children and adolescents with social anxiety need three things: (1) Coping skills to regulate increased anxiety and uncomfortable bodily sensations, (2) Boldness to face people and social situations rather than avoid them, and (3) People skills.  Social deftness and the ability to talk to people takes time to develop.  Developing our kids' communication skills are critical because in this day and age, with all the social media and faces 'permanently' glued on their handhelds, interpersonal skills appear to be deteriorating, or at least being delayed in their development.  I have talked with several psychologists who work in college counseling centers and the excessive use of social media is a major factor that limits social experiences.  One psychologist at a Big 10 counseling center stated, "Our young ones have rewired brains caused by excessive use of social media that renders them emotionally dysregulated, less empathetic and socially inept. Thin skinned hardly captures the enormity of the problem. The impact of chronic stress must be contextualized within the digital native population."

Even parents without socially anxious adolescents are concerned about their teenagers' abilities to interact with relatives, interview for jobs, communicate questions to their athletic coaches, and meet new friends.  Families describe concerns when cousins get together at a family reunion and sit across from each other texting, rather than talking.  A concerned mother asked me, "How will my son interview for a job when he can't use his elaborate social networking skills?"  A witty social worker at a recent seminar that I taught quipped, "He won't have to interview.  Everything is online.  His limitations will only stop him from maintaining a job."  Sociological studies suggest that humans are hard-wired to seek and make friends in ways we have always done in the past, regardless of new social network opportunities such as Facebook, Twitter, Snapchat, and Tumblr.  In an analysis of college students and Hadza hunter-gatherers of Tanzania, teenagers and young adults have hard-wired similarities.  Networks consist of one or two best friends, friendships in a "friend group" of five to six close friends, and placed within a broader group of approximately 150 people.[5]

While the communication methods between friends has changed, the development of friend networks appears to have remained similar through history. However, the issue that most parents remain concerned about is that the new communication methods among millennials cannot be generalized to real life situations such as professional interviews or developing real life relationships.

Perhaps the most pressing issue is future relationships. Countless studies have shown the impact of limited intimacy skills on long-term relationship health. The ability to maintain a healthy relationship goes well beyond the skills required in the "hook up" culture. Prominent family and relationship experts liken gender differences to more girls than not growing up developing intimacy skills and closeness in relationships, and more boys than not growing up with less intimacy skills.[6] Certainly, many boys grow up with the ability to relate adequately in relationships. However, it may seem a bit easier for women than men who generally have more relationship skills based on their relationship history. While men can certainly catch up, our goal as parents is to raise boys on par with girls that they consistently demonstrate an ability to process and articulate, express compassion and problem solve, and communicate with closeness in relationships. The concern for all young people is that by overemphasizing texting, video games usage, and social media, the ability for digital natives to develop needed social skills is delayed.

One of the most successful treatment strategies for high school and college students with anxiety is the four-level intervention.[7] The four-level intervention consists of three phases of treatment: (1) Education, (2) Reflection, and (3) Practice and Implementation. First, clients are educated on the four levels of communication. Second, teenagers are invited to identify times in the past week recalling when they communicated each of the four levels. Finally, individuals are encouraged to practice and implement each of the four levels of communication in different contexts.

How does this relate to youth? How can we use the four-level intervention to build the social skills of our kids? Do we as parents even have time to apply these steps? So often, we are just getting by.

The four-level intervention is one of the laser beam solutions for individuals with social anxiety, digital natives, individuals who grew up without developing their intimacy skills, and millennials. Learning about the four levels, reflecting on the past week, and practicing the four levels of communication are fairly easy to implement.

First, let's identify the four levels of communication. Level I communication consists of small talk: "How are you doing?" "What's up?" This is the type of conversation that is important in all levels of relationships. Small talk is helpful after soldiers run into the arms of their spouse after a tour. Small talk is important at family reunions. Level I conversation including weather talk and chit-chat helps maintain the politeness at the gas station, the grocery store, and the mailman. Whether small town or big city life, these conversations add flavor to the richness of life. Of course, we need to go deeper than just level I, but there is no doubt that the reality of weather talk and chit chat makes life much better and enriching.

Level II communication consists of talk about people, places, and things. Conversation about our children is one of the more common Level II discussions. These often consist of achievements we are excited about which leads to a typical Facebook post (i.e. a victory in wrestling), challenges we are working through (i.e. being fitted for braces), and goals we are working on such as visiting colleges. Places include places of travel, family vacations, and "where you're from." In Florida, everybody is a transplant. In nursing facilities, a significantly high percentage of residents are from the east, northeast, or midwest. Finally, things you do include hobbies, interests, sports, strategies for studying and the list continues. People, places, and things consist of who you know, where you've been, and things you do.

Level III communication is related to what people reveal about their attitudes, values, and beliefs. This has to do with disclosing personal information about who we are, what's important to us, and what we really care about. When we touch upon this level, we reveal what we believe and what we value. Level III is clearly a deeper level of conversation and entails fearless honesty at times, deliberate personal reflection to figure out who we are, and an actively reflective life to continue to wrestle with what we believe and what we care about. It was Socrates who said, "The unexamined life is not worth living."

Level IV communication is even more personal and deep. In this level, we begin to share with someone the impact circumstances and events are having on us personally. Of course, this is much deeper than using emoticons on text messages. In some ways, reviewing a list of emotion words lacks the depth that Level IV entails. How we experience life and the circumstances that affect us, change us, and influence our interpretations and relationships. Life impacts us and sharing the impact is the deepest form of disclosure. This is Level IV communication.

## FOUR LEVELS OF COMMUNICATION

Level I: Small Talk
Weather talk

Level II: People, Places, Things
Who you know, where you've been, what you do.

Level III: Beliefs
Disclosing who we are, what's important to us, and what we really care about.

Level IV: Personally Impacted
Impact circumstances have on us personally. Deepest sharing about how we are affected by experiences.

This chapter closes on communication because the fruit of boldness is improved relationships. Learning and practicing these four levels is at the center of fostering boldness in our children. Something that I have always believed wholeheartedly is in the quality of our lives is dependent on the quality of our relationships. Likewise, the quality of our children's relationships will depend on the quality of their communication. Bold communication skills, as opposed to passive, is key in every life area: intimacy and marriage, handling conflict well, cooperating with supervisors and colleagues in the workplace, and deepening friendships to name a few.

*The greatest use of a life is to spend it on something that will outlast it.* -William James

## REFLECTION TIPS

- Recognize that the developmental process consists of a learning curve for acquiring communication skills. Extraverts may find it easier than introverts. More important than personality types is the value of practice.

- Developing the communication skills that are similar for socially anxious individuals, digital natives, shy and inhibited individuals and millennials. The goals are the same: exposure, practice, and learning what to say.

- Teach young people the power of the QUESTION and learning how to show interest in other people.

- Use the four levels as a way to practice. The three phases are a good way to practice the four levels of communication.

- After learning the four levels of communication from surface talk to increasing depth, identifying opportunities from the past week helps teens apply their experience. Next, practicing over the next week helps with further application. (1) Education, (2) Reflection – what levels did I implement in the past week? And (3) Practice and Implementation of the four levels.

# Chapter Four

## Promoting the Reflective Life – An Interior Optimism

*Most youth will find calm waves enjoyable and heavy and shaky waves uncomfortable on the cargo ship of life. For most young people, jumping into the choreographed dance of life will be accompanied with performance anxiety. The calm waves can add to the pleasant experience or the heavy waves can be an additional threat that raises angst. There is no doubt that society has changed with young people raised in a culture where they learn to maximize pleasures and avoid pains. Some argue that hedonism has been a battle for young people since the 1960s. The pleasure-pain principle has become even more intensified with the advancement of technology and the impulse toward immediate gratifications. Many teenagers have significant difficulty when putting down their smartphone. But smartphone technology doesn't bring down the size of the heavy waves of life. Texting and social media can be temporary distractions but they're not what helps us get through the tough times compared to the psychological strength of optimism. One of the keys to healthy child raising is helping our children learn to be optimistic when those waves are heavy and shaking up the cargo ship, even disrupting life's performances.*

One of the keys to helping our children become solid, productive, contributing members of society, make our culture healthier, and improve our world starts with how they learn to interpret stressors in their life. Becoming reflective and optimistic is not a random result. It requires intentional parenting in this area. Reflection -- Thinking about how we think -- is a critical component to develop in our children. The other half is optimism.

Problem of Positive Thinking

Over 60 years ago, Norman Vincent Peale (1952) wrote a very influential book that has impacted many people, *The Power of Positive Thinking*[1]. My father, a philosophy professor at the University of St. Thomas and one who encouraged me to reflect, gave me the book during the summer of 1994 and I was positively influenced like so many others. This is a self-help book that proposes methods on how people can develop "positive thinking." The book aims at helping readers achieve a constructive and optimistic attitude through positive conscious thought by using affirmations and visualizations. Basically, individuals who read this book felt greatly empowered about their life by thinking more positively, finding solutions for their problems, and feeling better overall. Criticism of the book included a lack of citations and references in the book, a lack of empirical evidence to support its ideas, and a lack of replicable scientific activity. Speaking plainly, when part of the philosophical thinking is applied to parenting, it can become problematic. For example, an overemphasis on positive thinking can get in the way of positive reinforcement. Consider Jan, a single mom who had difficulty figuring out how to calm her rambunctious son. At a mall, she was doing an errand and her child asked for a yellow frosted cookie at the cookie business. It was dinner-time and she was rushing to drive back home to feed the family. Jan shared one of her thoughts, "Maybe Kevin's appetite won't get ruined this time." Applied positive thinking, right? The first problem in this scenario is that the purchase reinforces undesired behavior. "If I'm inappropriate, I will get a cookie." Secondly, it reinforces sugar before dinner. Additionally, impulsive decision-making is also reinforced.

An overemphasis on positive thinking also diminishes achievement. When a 4-year old builds a Lincoln log house, saying it is a magnificent house when it's a lousy house lowers the standard. Regarding praise, being realistic and honest with specifics moves children along more effectively. For years, it was the self-esteem movement, with an emphasis on feelings that reduced motivation for true achievement. Feelings were emphasized in place of achievements. It is healthier for parents to view self-esteem as a bi-product, as an effect of achievement. Research suggests self-control, not self-esteem leads to success. Speaking plainly, youth have higher self-esteem by focusing on achievements than they would by focusing on feelings and positive thinking [2].

A more realistic and healthier modality of thinking compared to "positive thinking" is optimism. Both positive thinking and optimism is expecting the best possible outcome from any given situation. Both positive thinking and optimism reflects a belief that future situations will work out for the best. But optimism also acknowledges the problems and adversity that comes our way beyond positive thinking. Optimism consists of valuing negative emotions in order to learn life lessons and flourish under pressure. Positive thinking is a mistake in some situations – like the pilot deciding he doesn't need to de-ice the wings of the plane or a partygoer believing he can drive. As Martin Seligman states, positive thinking is a problem in these situations. Additionally, positive thinking is very often a problem when applied to parenting. In contrast, the field of positive psychology emphasizes the empirical study of learned optimism with dispositional optimism and the value of the attributional style[3]. Our teenagers' tendencies to react in a particular way in the face of adversity can be molded into a pattern that will be most effective for them long term. But, it requires cultivating an optimistic outlook on failure.

The Rejection of the 3 Ps for Optimistic Teenagers

One way we can help our children learn to reflect and increase their optimism is by helping our kids learn how optimistic kids see problems. Thus, we can teach our kids how to approach problems in the same way. Optimistic teenagers see all problems as temporary, not Permanent. Optimistic teenagers see all problems as specific to one area, not Pervasive, affecting all areas. Optimistic teenagers are empowered by adversity, rather than Personalizing it negatively. In contrast, pessimists Personalize, blaming themselves for things out of their control.

Let's expound on these three main points of optimism. Optimistic people believe bad events are temporary, not permanent. The pain from a relationship breakup is temporary. Optimists tend to have quicker recoveries following emotional hurts in life. Getting cut from the volleyball team, not accepted into a

85

college, a lower than expected score on the SAT. Seeing these as temporary is optimistic. They also believe good things happen for reasons that are more permanent, rather than based on luck. Pessimistic people see problems as permanent and have a harder time recovering from a relationship breakup or a failed biology lab. Optimists are more likely to exclaim, "It's just a temporary setback."

Second, optimistic people see problems as specific, <u>not pervasive</u>. When Darryl got cut from his 8th grade baseball team during tryouts, the disappointment from the failure is specific for an optimist, and a disappointment in just one of many areas in his life. This set of thinking is sometimes hard to accomplish with teenagers. A typical interest repertoire of three things: math, chess, and baseball, for example, is typical. And a hit in one of these areas often leads to disappointment and frustration.

Third, optimists see bad events as empowering, <u>not personal or pathological</u>. Consequently, optimists are more confident and can consciously challenge negative self-talk to feel empowered. They are healthier, and less prone to health problems and depression like pessimists.

## ENDING SHAMING FOR OPTIMISTIC TEENAGERS

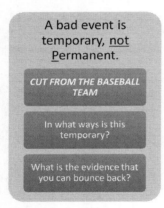
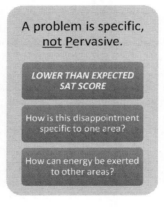
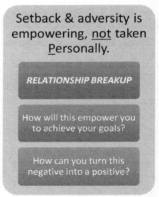

# WORDS OF WISDOM & STEPS FOR TAKING ACTION

- Parents can increase optimism in their children by applying the principles of optimism in the face of adversity.

- Acknowledge normal emotions following bad news. For example, sadness is normal after a failure like getting cut from try-outs.

- Parents build optimism by warmly exploring questions that help explain bad events without permanence, pervasiveness, and personalization. The following is a 5-Step Plan for Building Optimism when a bad event occurs.

- [Please say in your words to avoid formulaic speak]

  1. Warmly express compassion.

  2. Ask in your own words -- What is the evidence that suggests that this setback is permanent? In what ways is this setback temporary? What is the evidence that you can bounce back from this setback?

  3. Ask in your own words – What is the evidence that this disappointment is specific to one area? What are some ways that energy can be exerted in other areas?

  4. Ask in your words – What is the evidence that this will empower you to achieve your goals? In what ways can you turn this negative into a positive?

  5. What positive words could you use to describe this disappointment? This step involves associating "good words" to the setback experience. In future discussions, these words are used when recollecting this experience.

*"Failure is only permanent where resiliency fails to exist."*

*"The spirit of resiliency defeats all trials and tribulations."*
**- Edmond Mbiaka**

*"Great people are made in the crucible of experiences."*
**- Osho Samuel Adetunji**

*"All things which greatly hurt me greatly teach me."*
**- Karen Salmansohn**

*"Having high resilience does not mean it doesn't sometimes sting."*
**- Aisha Mirza**

Sucking Lemons, Doing Handstands, and Icing Feet

One of my experiences as a parent and in my observation of other parents is that optimism is best modeled in the day to day grind of being inconvenienced. One of the things that all of us parents have in common is being inconvenienced. And, it is during moments of being inconvenienced when pessimism is the easiest and showing optimism is the hardest.

When my wife Sarah graduated with her Ph.D., it was a triumph of high achievement. We painfully accomplished the goal together raising children, driving long distances to school [150 miles each day], and optimizing a balancing act that was far from perfect. But we did it! And Sarah was nothing short of amazing in her grit. She has accomplished a number of things; she shook President Clinton's hand as valedictorian of her blue ribbon high school; she played college soccer and ran cross country while studying as a pre-med student; she moved to China after college and got off the plane without knowing one word of Mandarin and was able to fully engage in conversations one year later. In China, she went from no words when she started there and struggled by herself with no friends or contacts. Despite being closely monitored by the communist party, she slowly found her place and left surrounded by a great community of dear friends (and a new language). Additionally, she ran a couple marathons, one with a foot injury, which may have miraculously healed right before the race. She also had three very difficult C-sections -- complications and struggles that many women can identify with.

Upon her Ph.D. graduation, her grit was best summarized in her willingness to suck lemons, do handstands, and ice feet. In order to stay awake at 3:00 am on many nights of graduate school while writing, researching, and studying, she did what it took to stay awake including sucking lemons, doing handstands, or icing her feet. Of course, this was not like college as she had children running in to see her at 6:30 am. No rest for the weary.

Sarah's efforts remind me of the hard work parents do day in and day out for 18+ years. I've had thousands of conversations in my psychologist office, and I've come up with a major conclusion regarding parenting inconveniences. Parenting is all about sucking lemons, doing handstands, and icing feet.

- When kids break their arms, parents are there to hold their child in the hospital.
- When kids are vomiting at 3:00 am, parents are there at the toilet with their son.
- When Lisa can't stick her gymnastics vault landing and is in tears, Mom is there. When Johnny gets cut from the team, a father who is engaged in his son's life is there to put his arm around him.
- When Tommy drags the garbage bag rather than lift and carry, ripping it open and spreading egg yolk leftovers across the driveway, his father is patient in his instruction.
- When Maria complains about her ankle for the 100th time in the last month and her doctor says there is no swelling, no persistent pain (just intermittent), and no redness, her parents recognize her very low pain tolerance threshold but maintain a soft-spoken quality of voice.
- When Amy raises her voice and screams over her mother's corrections, her mother unwearyingly reminds Amy that she values her opinion and deescalates the intensity with a gentle voice. She endures Amy's overreactions and

reminds her it is OK to disagree. After some time passes, she gives her a hug and reminds her that the relationship is most important.

- When Joe is suspended for cheating on his test, his parents discuss values, but expend the most communication energy on being behind him 100%. "We wholeheartedly believe in your ability to honestly prepare for future tests."
- When Melissa, 16 years of age, finds out she is pregnant, her parents communicate empathy, compassion, and a willingness to be there for her no matter what.

All these examples remind me of the grit and sticktoitiveness that I see in parents. And a standout principle to me is the importance of parents saying, "I am with you no matter what." Parents being side by side no matter the bad, no matter the good, no matter what large waves knock them down.

The bottom line about "being inconvenienced" is not about how much we can endure with grit. Many parents clench their teeth and press forward in life without taking a big picture perspective. The sacrifices we make as parents are less about us and more about how and what we desire for our children. Our hope is that our sacrifices and life lessons will accomplish these three major objectives:

- That our children become solid, productive, contributing members of society.
- That because they have been alive, our world will be a much better place in which to live.
- That as a result of their lives, our culture will be healthier.

Being inconvenienced a lot is an absolute certainty. Rather than clenching teeth and pressing forward, establishing a goal of conveying optimism is a great way to move our kids toward the reflective and optimistic life. When kids see Mom or Dad viewing these inconveniences as temporary, not permanent, specific, not pervasive, and empowering, not personal or pathological, it's long term fruit is evident.

Is Intelligence Fixed?

The approach to fostering a reflective life and a high degree of optimism emerges in how we as parents reflect and approach adversity optimistically. Developing our kids with a growth mindset is positively linked with reflectiveness and optimism.

Brain is like a muscle. The more you use it, the more it grows. Studies at Stanford point to two types of mindsets when it comes to learning: fixed or growth.[4] A fixed mindset is the belief that an individual's intelligence is based on biological and genetic factors. A growth mindset is the belief that an individual's abilities can be developed through dedication and hard work. A growth mindset consists of not just "brains," but includes the powerful combination of intelligence, love of learning, and resilience that leads to accomplishment.

Consider Randall, a sophomore in HS who is now flourishing in his adopted family. As an 8th grader, he was a high scorer on his basketball team but floundering in his academics. At the time, he was living in his fourth foster home with no stability in sight. Basketball, one of his coaches, and a concerned teacher appeared to be the primary factors that kept him off the streets. Although he stayed out of legal problems, his academic abilities developed a fixed mindset based on what he had learned about his parents. His birth mother never got past the 6th grade in school. She became pregnant as a teenager and was murdered in a bad drug deal. Randall's father didn't complete the 10th grade before roaming the streets and is currently incarcerated for life. He believed his only hope was in basketball but his view of his capability and academic self-efficacy was fixed.

Research shows that in the right environment, IQ scores can improve by one standard deviation[5]. During the summer before Randall's sophomore year, a welcoming and supportive family of five adopted him. It turns out that this family was related to Randall's eighth grade basketball coach and had discussed the possibility for one year and finalized the legal documents near the end of his freshman year. While there were certainly adjustments for all family members, there was an immediate change that Randall noticed about what he thought he was capable of. In addition to feeling unconditional love and support for the first time in his life, his way of explaining his circumstances was how "their positivity had rubbed off on me." After a series of conversations with his adopted parents, and experiencing the "positive flow" and "positive exchanges" within the family relationships, Randall now believed something new about himself. A few months into his sophomore season, he was now flourishing in his academics and experiencing a love for learning that he had never known before. It was not easy, but the parents made a concerted effort to engage in one-hour conversations every night including weekends, instilling hope and belief into Randall's mindset. One way to conceptualize a key change in Randall influenced by his adoptive family was a transition from a fixed mindset toward a growth mindset.

What did his parents say during all those conversations every night that was so helpful? They persistently expressed belief in Randall's ability. They told him "his doubt was temporary" in as many different ways that they could think of. They reminded him that "the struggle was worth it" and encouraged him to "be patient." They reinforced a "love for learning" that Randall had never known before. They also taught him how to have a "positive attitude when doing something difficult."

Valuing Failure with a Growth Mindset

People with growth mindsets believe that capability and intelligence can be grown through effort, struggle and failure. One of my favorite emotional building exercises that strengthens emotional intelligence, reflectiveness, and resilience, is discussing one's top 10 failures. These can be divided into two categories: individual mistakes and external barriers (i.e. job termination, relationship break-up, cut from the baseball team). When parents have reflected on their own shortcomings and life mistakes, it gives them perspective to draw upon for future moments with their children and adolescents. Most people rarely reflect on such things. And, while 10 or a top 10 isn't necessarily a magic number, reflecting on the key instrumental mistakes in life builds a repertoire of understanding for adolescents and young adults going through hard times.

The purpose of this level of reflectiveness is developing and instilling a growth mindset. We have learned valuable lessons but the best nuggets come from our failures. We all have them. When we saved studying for the test until the last night and the all-nighter caused us to sleep during the class. Or, how about the time we tried out for a sport rather than taking the path of least resistance but failing anyway. Or, the mistake of taking our car in its last moments and appearing desperate driving it into the car dealership. Or, the time we spent our only $50 on a ridiculous outfit only to regret it the next day. Some of these may not be top 10. We may realize that some of these are trivial. It gets closer to home when pride got the best of us and we burned a bridge at a job. Or, when we ended a relationship too soon.

A second valuable result of this level of reflectiveness is vulnerability. The presence of vulnerability brings connection. The absence of vulnerability combined with "preachy" parents leads to eye rolls. There are few things more important than honest failure talk. Let me say that the key to failure talk is not self-pity or to draw attention away from a teenager. Instead, failure talk is more about bouncing back, gathered life lessons, and building optimism.

<u>Valuing Failure as Energy Toward Resilience</u>

I recall the day when I played my last one-on-one basketball game against my dad right before he moved to St. Paul, Minnesota in 1989. I was 14 years old when my father took a philosophy professor position at the University of St. Thomas. My dream of playing ball at his college started that night. In many ways, I couldn't wait to go to the university where my father went and now taught. Over the years, my dream of college basketball strengthened when my dad mailed me newspaper clippings of the university's All American, Brent Longval, coming through in clutch moments.

I grew up in Bolingbrook, Illinois, at my mother's home as my primary residence, and at my father's home in St. Charles, Illinois. These locations were near Warrenville, Illinois where my mother grew up and West Chicago where my father grew up. I have fond memories of my grandparents' homes that enriched my life experience. Despite my parents' divorce during my early childhood, I grew up with a very reliable and consistent schedule. From as early as I can remember until the age of 14, my sisters and I spent every other weekend at my Dad's house and had dinner out every other Friday night. My stable schedule growing up in a divorced home was critical for my development. Divorces are messy and can be extremely difficult on children. A key piece of the ideal solution following a divorce is a predictable calendar. Consistency without an exception that I can remember served as a relationship foundation.

Things were not always smooth growing up. But, one thing that seemed to be a unifier was basketball, at least from my young vantage point. Both my father and my step-father played and loved basketball. As an adolescent, basketball was my refuge and a place where I began to dream. I'll never forget winning a Midwestern Illinois free throw contest with my dad and my step-dad watching. Another key moment was winning the 8th grade conference championship at Jane Addams Middle School, led by our star, Randall Crutcher, who went on to become a great college and professional player and remains a good friend.

While my love for the game rivaled anybody, I became only an average point guard on a bad high school team. While my dream drove me early in college, it didn't end well. In 1995, I sat in a hospital bed recovering from pneumonia with the realization that my dream of playing college basketball was over. My father had just informed me that I was cut from the University of St. Thomas basketball team for the second consecutive year. I had to accept that my "identity in who I was" was no more. As a 20-year old, I had deeply hoped that I was good enough. Here I was, sitting in the hospital after years of devotion to the game. Looking back at that heartbreaking moment, I was able to bond with my dad in the midst of the tough circumstances of a failed dream.

The Power of Story-Telling

---

## REFLECTION EXERCISE

Have you ever taken the time to reflect on your failures? This isn't a dreaded over-emphasis on the past. This isn't a "dig the skeletons out of the closet" type of exercise. Rather, this is a refreshing exercise that builds optimism. However, it takes some work, it may feel both pleasant and unpleasant, and requires times to deeply reflect. What are those setbacks that made you stronger? These include those times when you almost gave up or lessons learned when you did.

10 _____

9 _____

8 _____

7 _____

6 _____

5 _____

4 _____

3 _____

2 _____

1 _____

---

The purpose of this failure reflective exercise is to identify those lessons learned, failures experienced, and key significant moments. Children growing up want all their parents' histories – the good and the bad. Of course, the time to start this is before it's too late. Once story telling is established, then stories are filed for the right time. The power of a parent's top 10 failures comes in the opportunities to share those stories in detail at the right times.

I recently worked with a father whose son would walk off the tennis court giving up when he fell behind in championship matches. His son appeared to be limited by psychological blocking at the moment when momentum changed in the match. When his son believed that he was going to lose within this window of time, that is when he gave up. Strength would transition to helplessness at the point of a momentum shift during the match. As I talked with his father about the types of things that would be helpful, I recognized something in the dad that was being held back from his son. There appeared to be a need for his son to connect with his father outside of the usual conversation topics. The father was a physician who worked long hours. His time with his kid was limited to performance experiences – at tennis matches or school plays. It was rare, however, for shared fun time. In fact, family dinners, father-son down time, unstructured activities, and silly time was "almost never." Further, his son's blocking was embarrassing for the dad and occurred repeatedly. Dad had a hard time disguising his facial expression. Limited intimacy, short conversations, and "disgust" during and after tennis matches appeared to be barriers in authentic connection.

The breakthrough in this relationship and in taking some of the pressure off the boy was improved intimacy and longer conversations with Dad. Essentially, the antidotes were family dinners, father-son down time, unstructured activities, and shared silly time (i.e. laughter). Dad wanted something concrete in terms of conversations – what to talk about. I inquired from the dad if he'd ever had experiences growing up when he gave up or got close to giving up. It turns out he didn't try out for his basketball team in the 6th grade due to fear and didn't finish his 8th grade baseball tryouts when it appeared he wasn't going to be good enough. Each of these vignettes had several fascinating details. As he went into some of the emotionally moving components of his 6th grade story, I found myself thinking, "this is the story his son needs." As he proceeded, I couldn't contain my enthusiasm. Impatiently, I blurted out, "Your son needs this story!"

I was talking to a gymnastics mom whose daughter was now experiencing anxiety associated to stuck points and blocking. She could do front handspring and front handspring vaults a few months ago. Now, the young gymnast was pausing, hesitating, and showing reluctance on skills she previously did well on. Her mother wondered if increased competition between girls two months ago was the origin of the anxiety. We also discussed the key issues of self-imposed pressure and parental pressure. I asked the mother, "Why get frustrated when she doesn't perform a skill?" It seemed that Mom's frustration only adds to the pressure for her daughter. In our conversation, we agreed that (1) letting go, (2) unconditional acceptance without pressure, (3) loving the sport again, and (4) having fun were the key things to return to as a family. During my conversations with the parents, I learned about Mom's exciting volleyball background with multiple ankle sprains and her father's triumphant (and painful) journey with his violin through childhood and adolescence. I was surprised that lessons learned embedded in expressive stories were never brought up. "What does Lynn know about her Dad's triumphs and pains in his young music career?" "Oh, she knows he has a violin but that's it."

## WORDS OF WISDOM & STEPS FOR TAKING ACTION

- Reflective parents can identify (1) most embarrassing moments, (2) favorite achievements, (3) most distressing experiences, (4) moments of breakthrough, (5) conflicts with friends, (6) relationships hardships, (7) great and not-so-great moments with teachers, (8) and the ups and downs of each year chronologically or in their particular grade levels through childhood and adolescence.

- Some people have an easy time remembering key events and the details surrounding them. In that case, you are ready to tell your most important stories to your children. For others of us, while we may remember the fact that there was a significant event, we can't actually recall the details surrounding it. If you are in this category, you are free to fill in the details. The truth is in the larger event and how it impacted you. By filling in the smaller details with your imagination, you are just making the story-telling more engaging and fun for your children.

- How? And Why? The answer to "How" is not formulaic. It simply takes time and reflectiveness. The goal is to share your life with your kid. Reading and storytelling are 100% more substantially meaningful than TV before bed.

- As tweens transition into teenagers, they don't need to be told what to do. Rather, they need Mom and Dad's wisdom, defined by knowledge that is gained by having many experiences in life.

- Teenagers don't need parents to be PREACHY! Instead, they need parents to be VULNERABLE!

- Authentic connection involves vulnerability, not guarded lessons that reflect "I told you so" types of expressions.

- Story telling is about timing.

# WORDS OF WISDOM & STEPS FOR TAKING ACTION
## - CONTINUED -

- Apply the following golden keys to storytelling:
    - The goal of storytelling is not to draw attention away from the child.
    - The earlier you start, the better!
    - Repeating the same story with no reflectiveness triggers the "I know Dad" response.
    - Connection requires reflection.
    - Recognize the time and your type of story:
        1. Overcoming – classic David & Goliath experience
        2. Renewal or Rebirth – Miniature "It's A Wonderful Life" examples
        3. Quest – a mission, a move, transition, a journey; your Jordan moment- leaving basketball to play baseball
        4. Tragedy – minor to major; depressing tales
        5. Comedy – embarrassment, humility, laughter
        6. Dreams – Rags to Riches stories, painful lessons

# THE POWER OF STORYTELLING

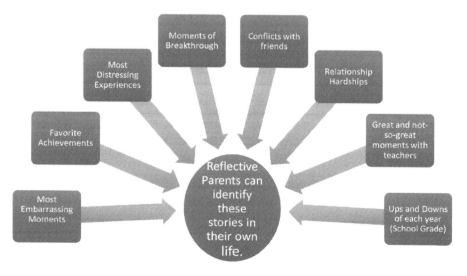

# DECISION MOMENTS THAT INCLUDE REGRET

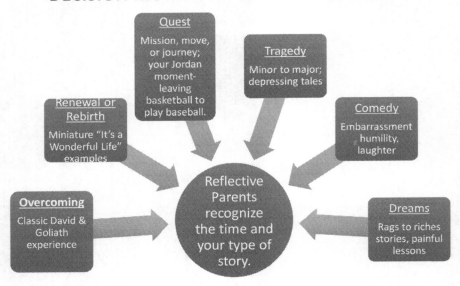

It seems to be popular to maintain the belief to "live without regret." There tends to be two schools of thought on regret. On one side, you have the idea of valuing regret. People have thoughts such as: I regret a lot (or some) of my actions. I wish I could live parts of my life over. I think "if only" a lot (or sometimes). And, then there are those thoughts for people who are determined to not have regret. They might think thoughts such as: I prefer to focus on the future than the past. I rarely think what "might have been." I like to approach life with "no regrets." The reality is that regretting brings on anxiety.[6] It makes sense why people don't want to regret. Guilt and shame often keep us from valuing regrets. The answers to guilt are forgiveness, understanding, and compassion. For those with a propensity to be hard on ourselves, having compassion and gentleness on ourselves is a way we can help our children and prepare them to be compassionate in the future.

Shame is a sticky and complicated emotion and much different from guilt. Shame is related to who you are. Characterological defects and beliefs of inadequacy tend to keep people from embracing regret. Overcoming shame-based thinking is a complicated process but embracing one's authentic self and embracing a sense of self as lovable and loving toward others brings healing. On the positive side of life, embracing regret builds wisdom and other psychological benefits[7]. When a person is not held back by guilt and/or shame, the psychological benefits of learning, wisdom, perspective, depth of thinking, relationship outlook, an expanded range of reactions, and humility can result from embracing regrets.

Regret is often expressed as a desire to go back and change a past experience. I've talked with husbands who abused their wives, registered sex offenders, and 90 plus year olds and centenarians who reflected on their many decades of life. Regret is a consistent aspect of life experience that falls along a spectrum of being owned with honesty to being ignored and suppressed. Those who own it come across as authentic.

People with different types of anxiety reveal different types of regret. It is common for individuals with PTSD to have survivor guilt, and it is usually related to some form of regret. I'll never forget talking to a man in his early 20s whose fiancé died in his lap after they were hit by a semi-truck. He had regret about his driving that he was convinced could have resulted in a different outcome. Or, a Vietnam Veteran tells his story of how his peer was shot by a sniper when he left his guard post to smoke a cigarette. Individuals struggling with social anxiety regret "not being the friendly one when I was in high school, reaching out to those who could be friends with me. My avoidance started a pattern." Individuals with generalized anxiety disorder regret "not finding a way to manage my worries earlier." These types of regret are real, rich, authentic, and meaningful life experience. And, talking about these experiences are immensely moving for youth trying to figure out the world and their place in it.

For most of us parents, even those of us not struggling with anxiety, regrets may be one of the more valuable assets in our life experience. These regrets build wisdom and stories for our children. They offer enriching life experience and help our children to move them toward what is good, true, and beautiful.

---

## TIPS FOR REFLECTION

- It is a myth that successful and happy people live without regrets.

- Embracing regrets in life increases wisdom and other psychological benefits.

- Upon readiness, reflective parents can profoundly influence their children by sharing regrets and the lessons learned. At age appropriate disclosures, when children hear adults reflect on their regrets, lessons learned provide valuable wisdom.

- Parents sharing regrets is the deepest level of vulnerability. While wisdom and caution should be taken when interpreting the appropriate age to reveal regrets, this level of vulnerability invites honesty and authenticity into the relationship.

---

Growth Mindset Interventions

As we discussed, one of the barriers in front of parents in today's world are those things that reinforce "a fixed mindset" and prevent the belief about a "growth mindset." It seems that the path of least resistance for youth, and therefore parents, is the fixed mindset rather than the path of struggle, growth and development. As an example, more and more young adults are taking the position that they are introverts and this introversion defines who they are. Society is moving towards the idea that its job is to get comfortable with individuals who have introverted personalities. In society, this fixed mindset has teenagers gradually establishing themselves as being comfortable with who they are as opposed to actually making changes in who they are – leaving their comfort zone, meeting new people, taking risks with friendliness, and learning to speak in front of groups. First, these are more reflective of social anxiety than they are of introverted personality traits. This notion of "being comfortable with who they are" leads teens to stay rather than grow. Unfortunately, we have compassionate teachers making accommodation for public speaking (e.g. speech before class only in front of teacher) which actually reinforces the fear. In the last few years, in a review of Amazon, lots of books have been published espousing the "specialness" of introverted personalities. I suspect that social anxieties and introversion are not clearly separated. But, this is just one example. Parents and youth are more and more inclined to define themselves in "fixed" terms: this is who I am, rather than in "growth" terms.

Consider the problem of being overweight[8]. One of five children in the U.S. is overweight or obese. Only in rare cases is being overweight caused by a hormonal problem or some other medical condition. The most common causes are lack of physical activity and unhealthy eating patterns. Consider some of the following beliefs of those teenagers who are contemplating a weight management plan to get healthier. "It's hard for me to lose weight." "I'm a procrastinator when it comes to exercise." "I'm not a natural athlete." "I am genetically predisposed to be bigger." "I'm not good with following through on exercise plans." All these beliefs are examples that represent a fixed mindset.

Are there things parents can do to develop a growth mindset? Are there interventions that can be implemented? Some of the key growth mindset interventions include what we talked about in Chapter 2 on praise, specifically process praise – praising the process rather than the outcome. The following are types of praise that reinforce a growth mindset: (1) Strategy praise, (2) Specific praise, and (3) Effort praise. Strategy praise involves praising your child for their strategy in math, for example; "You found a really good way of solving that problem." Specific praise involves praising your child for specific tasks (e.g., "You did a great job implementing those written questions after you read each chapter). Effort praise involves praising effort rather than the outcome (e.g., "Your persistence on your beam concentration has really paid off.")

Children who learn to take on tasks that are hard without immediate results have a stronger tendency toward developing a growth mindset.[9] Youth with a growth mindset embrace challenges and understand that tenacity and effort can change their learning outcomes. The first step for parents is to see that mindsets are malleable. In other words, a healthy approach is perceiving mindsets as "able to shift." And, each type of praise needs to come out of that mental framework of a growth mindset.

The next step is emphasizing effort over ability. Praising effort ("I really like how you struggled with that problem") versus praising a talent ("You're so clever!") is one way to reinforce a growth mindset with your child. Naturally, this mindset can be difficult because the child's genes can be viewed as an extension of the parent's intelligence. Regardless, don't praise kids for "being smart" or for their intelligence because it has a reverse effect. Research suggests that kids are less likely to view themselves as intelligent[10]. Instead, acknowledging effort moves kids away from fixed traits. Process praise acknowledges the effort; talent-praise reinforces the notion that a child only succeeds (or doesn't) based on a fixed trait. The spelling bee champ had the right genes, Gabby Douglas had the perfect DNA, Nick is naturally so very quick, Tommy is innately good at reading, memorizing history lessons appears to come easy for Lorraine, Tomeko appears to be a born natural at softball. A title of a favorite American sports movie—"The Natural"—deemphasizes the hard work of Roy Hobbs to return to baseball.

There is an acknowledgement of genetics and talents; for example, if I was 7 feet tall, St. Thomas would have probably developed me and given me a spot on the basketball team. But, talent-praise comments emphasize fixed traits and are problematic for kids long-term. The most compatible element of a reflective person with an optimistic approach to adversity is a growth mindset. Parents can foster growth mindsets in their children.

---

## WORDS OF WISDOM & STEPS FOR TAKING ACTION

- Recognize that there are specific things parents can do to develop a growth mindset.

- Praise children for their strategies, problem-solving, and effort in specific ways.

- Change praise from "You are so smart" to "Great job persisting and overcoming that challenge."

- It is appropriate to tell your children how smart and intelligent they are because it builds up their self-efficacy. The key is that following an achievement, you praise their effort, not their intelligence.

# Chapter Five

## Vision & Purpose Starts with an Internal Locus of Control

*There are many things both in and out of your control as a parent. The waves of the sea are out of your control. Your son and daughter's dance performance of life is out of your control. Your children will do things that you didn't influence. In contrast, there are also many things in your control – and it starts with our positivity. We can purchase things for our children without complaining about the cost or how expensive everything is, even if we are on a tight budget; I've worked with parents who seemed to set a goal of making kids feel bad about having little money. We can approach youth decisions without cynicism that the world is falling apart—how many of us say "not again." We can lose the negativity and jaded sarcasm; instead, we can express positive things to our children. Rather than being negative, cold and distant, we can be positive, warm, tender, and compassionate. We can express appreciation to our children for all that they do in their job as students. Rather than nagging, we can express gratitude. Our positivity can lay the groundwork for helping our children establish purpose and vision for their lives.*

The goal written out in this book is that our parenting will accomplish three goals. As a result of our parenting: (1) Our children will become solid, productive, and contributing members of society, (2) our children will help our culture be more healthy, and (3) our world will be a much better place to live because of our children. How does this happen in practical ways? This results from our children having a clear vision and purpose for their lives. What is the psychology that bridges the gap between vague ideals and actually making a difference in our real-life settings? The psychology of an internal locus of control bridges this gap and provides clarity for the vision and purpose of our youth.

<u>Poise under Pressure</u>

Let's begin this conversation with how the details of family life and four recommendations for maintaining balance can begin to establish an internal locus of control in our children. When we think of family life, there is a lot happening for parents these days. There is a great deal to be concerned about. Waking up kids, preparing and serving breakfast, preparing lunch or arranging payment for school lunches, checking backpacks, signing permission slips or other forms, driving kids to school or getting them to a bus stop. There are chores, dishes, keeping the home clean, doing the laundry, car maintenance, and of course work and paying bills.

There is plenty to manage: Driving kids to sports practices, music practice, and if you have kids or teenagers of different ages, you have multiple things to balance. And, for many parents, you have working parents juggling work, finances, and family life. Back to school shopping, meal planning including squeezing in the weeknight dinners, haircuts, schedules and routines and the list continues. Of course, family objectives and configurations change according to numbers of kids and type of education. I've talked with home-school teachers and while things may look different, responsibilities remain hectic and even more so with some things.

So, the question is, in all this busyness, how can parents avoid the risk of coming across as task-masters, or managers, or administrators? What is the key to slowing things down while keeping up with everything? The first step in establishing vision for young people is establishing vision for the family. There are four recommendations for maintaining poise on the balance beam of family life. And, the first is the primary recommendation therapists give to families.

(1) Balanced families have family dinners. The best prediction of successful children in nearly every way one would define success is strongly influenced by the regularity of family dinners. You might say, "My parents had family dinners and it didn't do much for us." Nowadays, many families don't have family dinners. Parents who do have family dinners also focus on the quality of the family dinner.[1] Parents can set a timer, with a consistent amount of time for each child to sit, particularly when they are young. There is no magic number but a minimum of four dinners per week is a great place to start. It helps if parents can plan ahead on conversations. Here are some conversation tips:

**Ages 2-7**
- Tell stories and ask questions about the stories.
- What are three things that make you happy?
- What do you love most about spring time?
- What do you love most about our pets?
- If aliens came to our earth, what would we want them to know most?
- What are you most grateful for today?

**Ages 8 – 12**
- What was your favorite movie last year?
- What was your favorite book from last year?
- What was the best vacation you ever had?
- What are the best ways to stop other children from bullying?
- How could we reach a classmate who is bullied?

**Ages 13 +**
- What is the best way to respond in an emergency situation?
- What are three things you could give to or do for a close friend that would improve his/her outlook?
- What are the qualities that you admire in a good friend?
- What are your hopes / goals / plans for the upcoming school year?
- In the midst of all our busyness, do you have any recommendations for family activities this fall?

**All Ages**

How many of us ask "How was your day?" and hear "Fine," or "OK." Instead of asking how was your day, how about asking some of the following questions:

- Can you share an example of kindness you showed to another?
- Were you inspired today? If you weren't, what small thing could have happened that would have inspired you today?
- What is something that you saw that made you think?
- How were you brave today?
- Did you learn any new words today? What's our family's word of the week?
- Did anyone in your class get in trouble today? What advice would you give that child?
- If your teacher got sick and you were the substitute, what would you teach the class tomorrow?
- Did you help anyone today?
- What did you do today that was creative?
- What did you do today that showed grit?
- Did you read anything today that captured your attention?
- Did anything make you laugh really hard today?

(2) Secondly, healthy families practice family intentional connectedness. This includes slowing things down and engaging in at least two moments of warmth each day. One of the ways love is expressed is warmth. These are moments of eye contact, engaged listening, and expressions of love. Similar to the number of family dinners per week, there isn't a magic number. But, many go with zero moments of warmth as a daily average. Then, moments of warmth happen on birthdays, holidays, and after achievements. This results in limited feelings of connection between family members. Instead, two daily moments of warmth, even for three minutes each, is critical to achieve the golden balance for a healthy family.

(3) Third, parents who maintain consistency in behavioral principles are more likely going to be balanced. Praise, reinforcement of chores, and consequences – both positive following desired behavior and penalties following undesired behavior all require consistency. Rewards and the withholding of privileges are essential but consistency is the primary principle for balanced success. When children grow up with a sense of solidity and reliability, their interior lives develop a sense of security and esteem. When children can depend on consistency, their ability to adapt and be resilient in the face of adversity increases.

(4) Finally, rituals and traditions are the bedrock of family generations going back centuries. Accelerated learning, advanced communications, enhanced technology (i.e. people watching videos on watches), and improvements in so many areas of life don't change the fact that reliable families of strength have routines and traditions. As children transition to college or independent living, they still rely on Mom's pumpkin pie at Thanksgiving or Dad reminding Mom that pulling the bag up in the garbage is "standard procedure." While the latter may be scoffed at, the deeply held traditions of the family provide a foundation for families and are never sneered at. Holidays, birthday traditions, extended family get togethers, fami-

ly vacations, Thanksgiving hats, grandma's unique recipe for lemon meringue pie, unique toasts, Sunday brunch traditions, and the list is endless.

## WORDS OF WISDOM & STEPS FOR TAKING ACTION

- Establish a nightly routine of family dinners with engaged communication and without television. It is expected that dinners are in the screen free zone.

- Parents express two moments of warmth with each child per day. Planned or spontaneous.

- Establish consistency in all parenting principles.

- Maintain and build upon family rituals and traditions. Healthy families don't leave this by chance; a dedicated effort is made to carefully think through traditions, holidays, food, vacations, games, and conversations.

Locus of Control

Balance in family life is critical in a child's development toward seeing how they can control how events influence their lives. Locus of control refers to the extent to which individuals believe that they can control events that influence their lives.[2] A person's "locus of control" is either internal or external. An internal locus of control means that one believes that one's life is controlled by themselves, regardless of environmental factors. The outcomes from their own actions is a result of their skills and abilities. An external locus of control means that they believe that their life is controlled by environmental factors, which they cannot influence. Essentially, an individual controls their life or their life is out of control and dictated by external forces. So, luck or effort!

Consider the following examples of internal locus of control. College students work hard in their classes believing that their grades depend on their effort rather than the attitude of the professor. Job applicants perceive that effort, communication, and an explanation of their skills influence their future employment more than luck. Finding the "right relationship" depends on dating skills, ability to articulate, manners, charm, character, interest, and motivation rather be at theright place at the right time, like the probability of a coin flip.

**TIPS FOR REFLECTION**

- The following items are based on the locus of control scale. Look at these two alternatives. Which do you agree with more?

- (a) In my case, getting what I want has little or nothing to do with luck.  OR (b) Many times we might just as well decide what to do by flipping a coin.

- (a) When I make plans, I am almost certain that I can make them work.  OR (b) It is not always wise to plan too far ahead because many things turn out to be a matter of luck anyway.

- (a) Trusting to fate has never turned out as well for me as making a decision to take a definite course of action.  OR (b) I have often found that what is going to happen will happen.

One of the things parents are most concerned about is the health of their children.  An internal locus of control is strongly related to improved health: smoking cessation[3], diabetes[4] hypertension[5] arthritis[6], cancer[7] and heart and lung disease[8].  There are long-term health advantages to an internal locus of control.  It is worth the effort and the attributional lifestyle to foster these types of views.

An External Locus of Control Leads to Learned Helplessness

Many years ago, Seligman[9] researched the idea that if a dog is forced to endure something unpleasant, it will stop trying to escape. Learned helplessness theory suggested that clinical depression, chronic anxiety, and other psychiatric conditions result from a perceived lack of control over the outcome of situations. If your son (Sam) studies but repeatedly fails tests, then he may come to believe that no matter how much he studies, he won't pass.  "What's the point, I'm going to screw up again?"

> *Decision is a sharp knife that cuts clean and straight; indecision, a dull one that hacks and tears and leaves ragged edges behind it.*
> – Gordon Graham

One of the most important goals of parents is to impart within children an internal locus of control.  Besides the four recommendations for maintaining poise on the balance beam of family life, what are the other ways that parents develop an internal locus of control in their children?  One of the best ways to accomplish this task is to amend helplessness beliefs in the heat of the moment, within the circumstances. Sam believes that failing the test is inevitable. Belief change usually involves incrementalism – a gradual set of steps that advocates for looking at things differently.

One of the first steps is reviewing any past success that involved overcoming setbacks. We know that one of the best ways to take on today's challenges like the "possibility of failing the test" is drawing upon our memory bank of internal resources. Second, setting small achievable goals that are easily manageable and obtainable helps Sam learn to control what happens. This can initially be something like work on a task for five minutes. Third, identifying those larger things that are in Sam's control: seeking help from a tutor, recognizing effective and ineffective study strategies, identifying strategies to compensate for learning disabilities, and finding tools to cope with test anxiety.

The fourth step is cleaning up all language that reinforces helpless beliefs. My wife, Dr. van Ingen, is a math education professor and researcher on training future math teachers. She has seen first-hand that any child can learn math and research supports this view, apart from more severe forms of intellectual disabilities. Dr. van Ingen points out how detrimental some statements are for young people. Long-term educational goals are undermined when parents say something like, "That's O.K., our family isn't very good at math." Other misguided statements made by parents include, "That's too hard for you" or "We all have strengths and weaknesses, math is just not your thing."

If Sam is struggling at math, more effective statements can help him exert control over his circumstances. "Let's identify some strategies that you have found to be helpful." "Let's figure out some ways that will help you do this yourself." "You can be good at this." "It will just take some work and the right amount of practice." "Let's figure out how we can make it fun."

Math is a great example of how an internal locus of control can result in a positive attitude. An internal locus of control reverses helplessness, exerts control over circumstances, and positively reframes self-talk for young people. And there is no doubt that a subject like math (or any school subject or interest) requires a positive attitude. Research has shown that math is the least favorite subject among elementary education teachers, who usually teach most subjects. How does this affect the kids? Young people end up with unfavorable attitudes towards math. And, what do negative attitudes toward math result in? Correlational research has shown that teachers miss the same problems as their students. Students don't learn because of their teachers' attitudes toward math. But worse than math skills is the kids' unfavorable attitudes. If young people learn to love math, their ability in the subject will drastically improve.

## REFLECTION EXERCISES

APPLY THE FIVE STEPS TO RAISE YOUR CHILD'S INTERNAL LOCUS OF CONTROL

1. When facing a present obstacle or challenge, review a past success that involved overcoming setbacks.

2. Set small goals to help the child to see the benefit of their efforts and how they can impact their circumstances.

3. Identify specific things that are in your child's control.

4. Practice eliminating language in self-talk that leads to helpless beliefs, such as "bad luck," "life is a game of chance," "mostly a matter of fate," "twists of fate determine a person's life course," "luck played a large role."

5. Inspire your child by incorporating language in self-talk that leads to empowered beliefs, such as "my effort determines my results," "reap what you sow," "grades are determined by my effort and hard work," "getting people to like me results from being friendly and my interpersonal skills," "you decide what will happen to you," "I persist well."

### Change Talk Versus Stuck Talk

Since we are social beings, our interior life is very much influenced by what we say and how we talk. When I was a young man, one of my mentors named Bill used to consistently remind me to value what I say. It was his small way of nudging me towards talking about what I believe and believing what I am talking about. Sometimes how we talk can be influenced by how we think, specifically whether we believe things will change or stay the same.

When it comes to change versus stuck talk, there are multiple ways to communicate about a topic that either moves us forward or keeps us in the same place. Consider the examples below referencing change talk, change and internal locus of control talk, stuck talk, and stuck and external locus of control talk.

Switching schools might make things better in the long run [change talk]. I can adjust and be a good friend wherever I go to school. [Change and Internal locus of control talk]. Compare these ideas to the following: I'm not sure I'm ready to change schools [stuck talk]. It doesn't seem like that other school is a good fit and it doesn't seem like there's a good chance of making friends with kids who have already been there a long time [stuck and external locus of control talk].

I'm ready to make some changes in how I approach my math study schedule [change talk]. I've realized that my effort in developing my writing and spelling skills is entirely on me [change and internal locus of control talk]. I told my tutor that I couldn't make it because I had chores to do at home [stuck talk]. Since my SAT practice exam failure, I've realized there is nothing I can do so I'm not going to study at all [stuck and external locus of control talk].

> *Knowing is not enough, we must apply. Willing is not enough, we must do.* – Johann von Goethe

What is the take home message here? Parents want to teach their kids change talk and internal locus of control talk in the "midst of those moments of adversity" or during family dinners during reflection time as the adversity. Engaging in conversations about what the child can do in those uncontrollable circumstances – substitute teacher changes the lesson, a new basketball coach emerges this season, a best friend moves away, or the theatre director chooses someone else for the preferred part. From failures to rejections, adversity can strengthen us even further with change talk and internal locus of control talk.

Longitudinal Research on Locus of Control

CHANGE TALK VERSUS STUCK TALK

**Change Talk**

*"Switching schools might make things better in the long run."*

**Stuck Talk**

*"I'm not sure I'm ready to change schools."*

Parents influence with change and internal locus of control talk.

**Change & Internal Locus of Control Talk**

*"I am able to adjust and be a good friend wherever I go to school."*

**Stuck & External Locus of Control Talk**

*"It doesn't seem like that other school is a good fit and it doesn't seem like there's a good chance of making friends with kids who have already been there a long time."*

Research has shown that today's teenagers are more entitled[10], narcissistic[11], selfish[12], and believe their destinies are based on luck and randomness. Over the past 50 years, locus of control has been one of the most widely studied psychological constructs in psychology[13]. Longitudinal studies show significant changes in locus of control scores at all age ranges. The average college student in 2002 had a more external locus of control than 80% of college students in the early 1960s[14]. The increase in externality also appeared in studies on children. Children have gradually had an increased external locus of control as each year has passed over the last 40 years. This is true for both elementary-age students and middle-school-age students based on 41 samples with data from 6,554 children aged 9 to 14 years. Here is a disheartening and frightening quote taken from the research, "Children, even those as young as age 9, increasingly feel that their lives are controlled by outside forces rather than their own efforts." These trends of increases in external locus of control are related to increased depression and anxiety, drug abuse, and diminished academic achievement.

There is something very surprising and worrisome about the research over time. Research trends suggest that millennials, those born between 1982-1999, exhibit a set of personality characteristics that is a gradual result of change over the last 50 years. Rather than sudden generational shifts, the changes we have seen from generation to generation appear to be steady, linear changes. In addition to the shift in locus of control, both self-esteem and narcissism have also gradually increased and are much higher among college students than in years past[15]. And, as we know, something that gradually changes is more resistant to reversing back than traits that change and shift. What is the problem with the combination of increased self-esteem and narcissism that is becoming more resistant to change? Contrary to popular belief, individuals with high self-esteem are sensitive and more likely going to react defensively to criticism. Following criticism, these individuals are less friendly. Narcissists have interpersonal difficulties; they have problems with conflict, problems getting along with others, lack empathy and compassion, and have problems taking someone else's perspective[16].

<u>Teenagers Need Purpose</u>

As I mentioned, I often suggest the movie Good Will Hunting (1997) to extremely talented college students struggling with purpose. The lead character Will Hunting (Matt Damon) had an incredible talent and was able to solve difficult problems in algebraic graph theory. He was unable to fully appreciate his talent and was unwilling to be vulnerable and get close to people because of emotional pain from neglect and abuse. Clarifying purpose was a key issue in the movie. During a therapy session, when Will refuses to give an honest reply about what he wants to do with his life, his therapist (Robin Williams) shows him the door. [Spoiler alert!] The movie ends with Will leaving the town he never wanted to leave to find his girlfriend and begin to find his purpose.

*We are shaped and fashioned by what we love.*
- Johann von Goethe

Will began to find purpose at the age of 20 after some good psychotherapy work. Ideally, teens need to find purpose sooner. In a movie targeting teenagers, *Chasing Mavericks* (2012), the character Jay Moriarity (Jonny Weston) is saved from drowning by his next-door neighbor, surfer Frosty Hesson (Gerard Butler). This ignited his zeal and passion for surfing. One morning, Jay sees his friend ride a "gigantic swell" wave. He immediately set this as his purpose. The funny thing about purpose is when we have clear purpose, we learn valuable lessons that are even unrelated to the actual purpose. In the movie, Jay was singularly focused on his purpose of riding this "gigantic swell" wave. But, he grew in discipline as he trained, such as being able to tread water for 40 minutes. He set small goals such as being able to hold his breath for four minutes. He learned the value of learning from a mentor and receiving guidance. He learned the ability to be reflective as he wrote essays about what he was learning and observing about the water, the currents, temperature, and other knowledge learned in his training. Jay appeared happier and motivated to help others. In the movie, you'll see Jay doing his mother's laundry, encouraging her nutrition, helping out his friends, and helping his mentor build his wife's kitchen cabinets.

*Everybody is a genius. But if you judge a fish by its ability to climb a tree, it will live its whole life believing that it is stupid.*
- Albert Einstein

*You must be the change you wish to see in the world.*
- Gandhi

Let's break down some of the developmental areas identified in the aforementioned character. Discipline, goal-setting, mentoring, reflectiveness, learning life lessons, increased happiness, motivation, and helpfulness were all seen after gold was struck. These character strengths and positive attributes that were absent before became evident after purpose was found.

*Firmness of purpose is one of the most necessary sinews of character, and one of the best instruments of success. Without it, efforts are wasted in a maze of inconsistencies.*
− Lord Chesterfield

Teenagers who have vision are living with purpose. Teenagers living with purpose speak freely about their dreams and hopes, and have ideals about their approach to their education, relationships, sports, faith, and possible career paths.

> *The roads we take are more important than the goals we announce.*
> *Decisions determine destiny.* – Frederick Speakman

For years, I have seen funny pictures posted on Facebook of my friends holding a gun while talking in some way about his teenage daughter approaching the dating scene. Usually, the father is comically causing alarm for anyone who might want to date his daughter. Some of the fathers look serious, making me wonder about how much the daughter is externally controlled. Anyhow, these jokes led me to reflect on what parents would want in a young man. Consider the choice and for the sake of simplicity, both young men are doing well in school and headed to college. Young Man (A): He sleeps in until noon, plays several hours of video games every day, relies on fast food, and never communicates any dreams, hopes, or causes that he believes in. OR Young Man (B): He wakes up early and balances studying, exercising, and friend time. He feeds his body with healthy meals but remains a balanced teenager, enjoying an ice cream from time to time. He loves culture, studies Spanish, has already done two mission service trips to Haiti, and loves to communicate dreams about making a difference.

> *I would rather die a meaningful death than to live a meaningless life.*
> - Corazon Aquino

> *At no time in history has so large a proportion of humanity rated love*
> *so highly.* – Morton M. Hunt

A very good resource for teenagers and college students is the book *Intentional Dating: When You're Ready to Leave Behind the Liars, Losers, and Lemons – 15 Keys to Finding Love for a Lifetime* by John Buri (2014). There may be many variables that differentiate the young men in the aforementioned hypothetical choice. Clearly, one of the differences is living with purpose. Many parents that I've interviewed have reflected on the teenage years and described a moment in time when a light bulb went on and their teenage children began to do things differently. The observed difference was related to finding some purpose in their lives, whether it was a sport, a relationship, or a faith encounter. Other parents have talked about their success through the teenage years, which of course consisted of many ups and downs, related to purpose that extended throughout adolescence and through college. Sometimes purpose can develop early. *Akeelah and the Bee* is a heartwarming inspirational movie based on a true story of an 11-year old girl who unites her school and neighborhood as she wins the Scripps National Spelling Bee. Purpose can develop from anything that derives meaning and helps teenagers be a part of something bigger than themselves. This could be spelling or raising money for a food bank or realizing their passion for medicine. Teenagers can find purpose in seeing injustice in their community and becoming determined that he or she will become a lawyer. Teenagers may realize that they can impact people by the words that they write so they become determined that they will become a writer. It could be teenagers realizing how important mentors were in their life and decide to become a mentor for elementary kids in academics and or sports. Teenagers are changing the world through inventing things and starting businesses. Below is a great model for self-reflection on finding purpose. Purpose is where your passion, mission, profession and vocation interconnect.

> *Patience and tenacity of purpose are worth more than twice their weight of cleverness.* — Thomas Henry Huxley

## Purpose Doesn't Solve the Tough Adolescent Problem, but it Helps

As inspirational as it is to consider how teenagers are changing the world, it is mind-numbing to consider those tough adolescents who need our inspiration in different ways. Who are the difficult teenagers? These are individuals most often diagnosed as having oppositional defiant disorder or conduct disorder[17]. Oppositional defiant disorder often begins in childhood and results in open defiance of rules. Conduct disorder is also oppositional but includes serious behavior problems such as aggression to people or animals, theft, running away, and truancy among others. Other dysfunctional behaviors are associated with mood disorders (i.e. bipolar disorder), complex ADHD, and substance abuse. The increasingly frequent combination of bipolar disorder and ADHD is a difficult set of problems requiring psychiatric treatment and psychotherapy. And, many of these problems comprise various anxiety problems and possible comorbid diagnoses of anxiety disorders. Research supports evidence-based treatments for a variety of these problem behaviors and psychiatric conditions. The challenge in these psychiatric conditions is not an absence of treatments but accepting the reality that changes in the family are required. This usually starts with the parents, who will need to change to bring about modifications in their tough adolescents. Reading this book is a start, or most likely, a continuation of what has been started.

Difficult teenagers engage in running away, truancy from school, fighting, threatening suicide, alcohol and/or drug experimentation. A myth around these behaviors is that the parents are unable to make decisions that influence behavior and maintain parental leadership in these situations. Some problems may be perceived as associated with underactive or unbalanced neurotransmitters, but it is often more productive to identify the solutions as behaviorally changeable. While medications can alleviate difficult symptoms, neurotransmitters can be balanced in several ways naturally. One way is good nutrition such as fish, almonds, and fermented soy like tempeh, which can boost dopamine, a hormone related to motivation and focus. Another way is making lifestyle strategies such as incorporating relaxation training or meditation that elevates GABA, an inhibitory neurotransmitter that puts the breaks on stress and distractibility.

Ultimately, the most significant change agent for boosting optimal neurotransmitters is changes in the family system. Successful parenting requires maintaining the belief that the child is responsible for his or her behavior without surrendering leadership. I have talked with hundreds of parents who surrender the behavioral control to the neurobiology and the lack of medications. Or in many cases, when the emotional condition stays the same or worsens, complaints are focused on the lack of effectiveness of these specific medications. In other words, when behavior remains problematic, parents place their focus on the "ineffective medications." Parents have been duped to accepting medications as the externally controlled answer. But meds are no different from any other outside force, whether we are talking about the adolescent's counselor, a police officer, a juvenile probation officer, psychiatric hospitalizations, a social worker or psychologist and medication therapy. While all these services have their purpose, and can be a huge help, when parents lean too heavily on these external forces, they inadvertently undermine their own leadership and effectiveness.

## Enforcing Rules and Consequences

Many parents experience some disbelief, almost shock, when they realize that "what we're doing isn't working." It is almost like a "bad dream" when parents start having thoughts of helplessness about their teenagers. They realize that their kids are always two steps ahead. Teenagers have the ability to foresee the number of steps required to curtail their parents' rules. Difficult teens won't back down from confrontations. They may even look for those opportunities where they can push the buttons of authority figures to gain some degree of control.

This ability to think two steps ahead has been described as "enhanced social perception[18]." This perceptual reasoning skill is often applied to predicting parental behavior. Teenagers are extremely adept at pushing their parents' buttons and can predict their moods and typical reactions. When teenagers feel controlled, they will push their parents' buttons in a variety of ways so parents will get angry and lose control.

I recently worked with a 16-year-old teenager named Lisa. She has had problems that include truancy, fighting, self-cutting, and defiance. A notable pattern in the family is a mother-daughter routine that involves arguing and screaming at each other. Approximately three times a week, the mother raised her voice and engaged in emotionally exhausting screaming. Each time, the mother and daughter were crying together and hugging at the edge of the bed two hours later. Clearly, the mother's anger and loss of control was triggered by her daughter's button pushing.

The key problem is that parents lose control of their emotions and have difficulty consistently enforcing rules and consequences. It is critical for parents to stay neutral, maintain calm and poise, and not engage emotionally with the teenager. When a parent gets angry, they send the message that he or she has lost control.

## Working on Our Hot Buttons

Parents can quench hot buttons with preparation. Personal hot buttons take on a mild to severe range. Mild jabs usually consist of your general complaints: "You never help me." "You always say no." "You never let me go out." "You are always too busy." "You are always late." Of course, to a type A neurotic parent, these comments strike a deep chord and can trigger a major reaction. Perfectionists hate criticism.

*Self-reflection is the school of wisdom.*
- Baltasar Gracian

The types of hot buttons that elicit reactions are subjective to each person. These interact with a parent's personal weaknesses and insecurities. And, teenagers generally know what our insecurities are. To one mother, who spends a lot of time looking in the mirror and is overly concerned about weight, hearing the comment, "You're looking really fat" can cause a major blow up. Another parent may work hard trying to connect with his teenager's friends. His hot button that leads to hurt feelings is, "All of my friends hate you!"

The most severe type of hot button that interacts with caring parents' personal insecurities relates most strongly to the parent-child relationship. "I hate you." "You are the worst mother in the entire world." "You have no idea how to talk to a teenager." "You don't understand me at all; you're the worst parent. My friends' parents understand them." On aside, the issue truly is whether parents care. Engaging emotionally and "flying off the handle" is usually because parents do care. They just need to work on their parenting skills and emotional intelligence.

These hot buttons trigger parents' own personal weaknesses and insecurities. The way to prepare is through personal reflection on our issues. The goal of personal reflection is to know our own insecurities and to separate our personal hurt from our teenager's inappropriate comments. If feelings of hurt are elicited, (1) staying neutral, (2) maintaining poise, and (3) recognizing that statements made by the adolescents are inappropriate behaviors.

> "*The person with insight enough to admit his or her limitations comes nearest to perfection.* – Johann von Goethe

### Ending Criticism

Criticism is hard to endure, no matter how hardened the environment. I worked with a 14-year-old adolescent male (Justin) who endured constant criticism by his father (Jack). When it happened in my office during a family therapy session, I asked Justin how often this occurs. Initially, he was reluctant to share but eventually expressed that "it happens all of the time" and he felt nothing would be good enough for his father. In the past, I successfully helped a father reduce his swearing by paying his wife $20 every time he cursed. I suggested this idea as an intervention that Jack could implement following each criticism but he decided to modify his behavior on his own "without an intervention." Nevertheless, I didn't let them off the hook until we could agree on a strategy to end criticism. We came up with and agreed to a 3-step strategy:

- Jack would agree to learn to initially observe without communicating his judgments.
- Jack would then take deep breaths counting to five as he inhales and counting down from five as he exhales.
- Jack would agree to journal something or tell his wife something that could be construed as criticism.

Jack acknowledged that the new strategy helped him to reflect on his level of criticism. After a week, there was a dramatic change in family interactions. Justin felt that the home was more positive. Jack reported that he gained insight into his quick reactions and began to find ways to be more positive. He eventually set out a goal to end criticism in his family.

### Finding Purpose

There is no doubt that parents find themselves "overwhelmed" by life and feel like they are just "hoping things turn out for the best" for their children. And, some parents view raising teenagers as a badge of honor. Some parents approach their teenagers with an external locus of control. You've heard the bumper sticker "hire teenagers while they still know everything."

There are conversations that parents can have with their children to foster reflectiveness on finding purpose. Finding purpose is an experiential adventure, rather than a linear process. There are key questions that every adolescent and young adult faces. As they think about their Identity, they will wonder –who am I? As they reflect on their Importance, they inevitably wrestle with the question -- do I matter? As they think about their roles in life and their impact, this leads them to inquire – what is my place in life? Reflecting on these issues starts with family discussions.

*If one does not know to which port one is sailing,*
*no wind is a strong one.* - Seneca

Who am I? How can I influence? How can I leave my mark? What will my legacy be? The latter two questions tend to be long-term reflections that aren't important to most 18-year olds. However, questions such as 'what is my mission in life?' And, 'what is my life message?' These types of questions begin to be answered by choices teenagers make now.

## REFLECTION EXERCISES

APPLY THE ONGOING "ENGAGING" REFLECTION QUESTIONS FOR DISCUSSION TO ESTABLISH LIVING WITH PURPOSE

- Engage in personal reflection on hot button issues. The goal of personal reflection is for parents to know their own insecurities and to separate their feelings from their teenagers' feelings. Reflect purposefulness by not matching anger with anger, anxiety with anxiety, or despair with feelings of dread.

- Engage in empowering teenagers, regardless of mood or behavior issues, by naming positive qualities and building up their strengths rather than engage in criticism. (a) observe, (b) count, (3) and journal is one 3-step solution to ending criticism tendencies.

- Engage in sustained discussion regarding three major areas of reflection on building purpose:

1. - Identity:     Who am I?

2. - Importance:  Do I matter?

3. - Impact:      What do I want to do with my life?

# Chapter Six

## Sustaining Cognitive Flexibility in the Face of Adversity

*Relationships on the cargo ship of life consist of approach and withdrawal, engagement and disengagement, or moving toward and moving away. Underlying much of these behaviors that involve disconnection – withdrawal and disengagement – is anxiety. The very thing that can undermine a dance performance is anticipating the worst of a situation, such as a tsunami wave. When the tsunami wave hits the cargo ship, boom! It's over. Anticipating bad outcomes is referred to as anticipatory anxiety. Most of the time, the wave is not a tsunami, but it feels like it. There are thought patterns and perceptions that young people can develop in their self-talk. Positive, calming, and encouraging self-talk brings down anticipatory anxiety. This is a great place to start for us as parents. Be positive with our kids. Be accepting. Be optimistic. Build upon your capacity for fondness. Express to your children their value. Communicate how you treasure their inherent goodness. Positive, pleasant, and good-natured parents produce the best soil for healthy self-talk to grow and thrive.*

Let's take some time now to discuss the overwhelming adversity that faces the youth of today. First, let's expound on the epidemic our children face. Isn't this something we all want to know about?

There are several reasons why anxiety has become an epidemic in the United States of America [and worldwide]. Some of the reasons include improvements in mental health which leads to more self-reported anxiety. This is a good thing! This also leads to increased vocabulary to explain problems—the more words we have, the better insight we can have to the stressors. On the other side, there is an increased medicalization of problems and diagnoses[1].

Society is more fearful as we live in a different society than we did just a few decades ago. It was normal for my sister Jane and I to ride our bikes around Bolingbrook, Illinois without a concern of being abducted during the 1980s. Nowadays, parents have elevated fears, which often transfers to fears and anxiety in their children. Still, there is a range of societal factors that elevate anxiety. We are in a post 9-11 world and facing a war on terrorism. Youth experience a media and information overload[2]. Fluctuations in the economy such as the 2008 recession brought changes in many families. Bullying via social media, an unpredictable future, standardized testing and other school pressures, and overinvolved parenting are just a sampling of the stressors. Due to a wide range of stressors, anxiety has elevated to the prevalence of 25.7% of 8-year old children and 21.4% of 17-year old teenagers. Anxiety Disorders affect an estimated 40 million adults in the United Sates age 18 and older, or 18% of the population[3].

There are three ingredients relevant in the cause of childhood anxiety: (1) biological sensitivity, (2) personality traits, and (3) stress overload. The combination of these factors influence the level of anxiety. First, some kids are born with a biological sensitivity. 20% of individuals are born with a heightened sensitivity to anxiety and fearfulness. These kids are more likely to react to a fire alarm. Second, there are particular personality traits that make children predisposed to over-sensitivity and fretfulness. Certain personality traits such as perfectionism, people pleasing, a tendency to avoid conflict, preferences for structure, and minimal assertiveness are personality traits that increase susceptibility to anxiety. In addition to anxiety sensitivity and personality traits, the overload of stressors such as family, school, and self-induced social media (i.e. "how many likes on a post") combine to elevate strain.

What are the stressors for young people nowadays? This was a question I asked recently to hundreds of mental health professionals in Milwaukee, Wisconsin, Springfield, Massachusetts, Pittsburgh, Pennsylvania, and Kansas City, Missouri; to name a few cities across the country—social workers, psychologists, nurse practitioners, school psychologists, and professional counselors—the following is a sampling of comments made concerning all the stressors young people face:

- "Social media! Kids are under constant pressure to be on it. There is more stress if you didn't get 100 likes. Stress multiplies if 'my selfie isn't good enough.'" Some kids delete posts that have less than 100 likes. Other kids are buying likes with parents reporting their credit cards used for "like" purchases.

- "With the constant obsession over social media, kids are constantly comparing their lives to others'. Wherever you are, a kid's life is never good enough and their current location is never good enough compared to their friends."

- "The stressors all add together—parental relationships, friendships, academic testing."

- "Testing—'you have to do well to get into college, get the right job' and be perfect. Kids are being programmed too young –3$^{rd}$ graders are being asked what they want to do with the rest of their life."

- "Conflict never ends. Some kids are up all night with Snapchat engaged in interpersonal difficulties. There is no turning it off."

- "There is an unnecessary added degree of intensity. Teens are watching their friends and making sure they are aware of their friend's suicidal thoughts, or making sure they are aware of a relationship break up. They say it is their job to be hypervigilant and keep track of their friends."

- "Kids are not activating and stimulating their imaginations. What causes this? Too much structure and too many video games. There is a lack of play because of being overscheduled and overly structured."

- "Caffeine consumption is a major stressor and kids are taking in caffeine younger and younger. At our school, 2$^{nd}$ and 3$^{rd}$ graders are drinking coffee."

- "A parent passes away and the oldest child has to take on Mommy's roles like laundry or cooking. Middle schoolers are babysitting the younger kids. This results in unresolved conflicts. These responsibilities take over the schedule and hamper play time and imagination."

- "Standardized testing! Parents put unnecessary pressure on kids. In one situation, a parent told her child, 'If you don't pass this, you will fail second grade.' The kid was so nervous that he was going to throw up. The teacher had to tell the 2nd grader, 'No, that's not true.'"

- "Parents' stress affects their kids. A particular kind of stress is parental peer pressure. Parents feel pressure from other parents to make sure their kids have the latest gadget. Parents are driven to keep up with the Joneses."

- "There is constant pressure to be the best athlete, get the best grades, everything is about being the best and there is no relaxation time. There is pressure to be the best."

- "Sports can be a great thing. Kids learn how to be selfless, a part of a team, and be a part of something bigger than yourself. Kids also learn how to follow directions from someone besides your parents. The disadvantages – Kids are not playing anymore unless sports are scheduled. Instead of playing freely, everything is governed by parents. They aren't learning how to negotiate rules and engage in conflict resolution because parents govern."

- "Kids compare themselves to other people. This is their standard of how they measure up. Do other people approve of me? Do I measure up? Kids find themselves seeking that external acknowledgement."

- "Over involved parents! There is less respect for teachers because families are getting into the job. There isn't an alignment between parents and teachers."

## WORDS OF WISDOM & STEPS FOR TAKING ACTION

- Social media [1. Instagram, 2. Snapchat, 3. Facebook] has quickly become a useful resource for connecting in relationships. It has also become a major stressor for youth. The following are keys for managing media exposure for youth and maintaining healthy families:

- Acknowledge that research shows that more screen time leads to less happiness. And, specifically, more time spent on social media is associated with more unhappiness. For happiness, agree on limits. Parents themselves should be phone free between 3:30-9:00 (awake time after school).

- Encourage teens to uphold communication standards with their friends: "Please don't look at the phone when we talk."

- Make it a priority to have technology free dinners as a family. Establish Screen Free Zones in the house. No phones in the bedroom or at the dinner table. Identify another location to be phone free such as the library or the TV room – when the family watches a movie together, we don't multitask with other screens, as an example.

- Make the car phone free. Come up with red light questions to ask kids that lead to meaningful connection, rather than looking around for a police officer so Mom and Dad can send out a work email.

- Establish a park zone on the counter for phones during sleep time. All family members place their phones in the park zones one hour before bedtime.

- Have regular family discussions on what it means to have FREEDOM from phones. What does it mean to be peaceful without phone access? When teens reach for their phones before their towels after a shower, they have a real need for connection. What are authentic ways to connect besides phones? On the topic of FOMO (Fear of Missing Out), does my child have a fear of being left out and why? How can we approach family vacations without phones?

- Establish a principle of not getting drawn into social media schemes established for the purpose of keeping users on social media for longer periods of time, like snapstreaks on Snapchat. In addition, in the context of discussion on freedom, help teens and tweens develop marketing savvy and think critically about their digital footprint in social media apps, shareable GIFs, product reviews, hashtag campaigns (i.e. selfie #wearthesejeans), and geofilters (creative overlays for Snapchat) which all have the same mission – use kids to do their marketing.

This is just a sampling of the stressors that are facing our youth with phones and social media leading the way. The average teenager of iGen (those born after 1994) are more depressed, more lonely, more isolated, spending less time with friends, getting less sleep, putting off job opportunities, and putting off getting their driving license. This is largely due to being hooked on their phone and stuck in their bedroom. Since 2012, typical youth stress has increasingly become phone stress.

This chapter emphasizes the pivotal points of cognitive flexibility that make a difference in the face of stress and adversity. In psychology, these points are referred to as cognitive behavioral interventions; these solutions make a difference in alleviating the anxiety and providing solutions to stressors. Parents who apply these interventions make a difference in their children's ability to cope with stressors. The following interventions are the best mental health tools when faced with depression, anxiety, and other life stressors like being left out or not getting enough likes on a post. More importantly, integrating these points of cognitive flexibility sustain us when overwhelmed with real adversity. One thing we all know about life is that adversity is around the corner. Consider the following windows of adversity:

- John's teenage boy secretly dabbles in pornography, and the resulting addiction leaves him spending more time alone, withdrawing from friends, and skipping baseball tryouts.

- Jenny's spouse passes away after a tumultuous battle with cancer over the last 6 months. She noticed that her daughter Kim had become less expressive during Dad's battle. To her surprise, she learned that her daughter began using recreational marijuana with a couple of friends a few months ago as a way to grieve.

- After Jeanne noticed her daughter's nausea, fatigue, and swelling around her ankles, their family's pediatrician determined from the urinalysis, blood tests, an ultrasound, and a biopsy that her daughter had chronic kidney disease.

- Tamika is a three-sport athlete who loses her left leg in a horrific moped accident.

Every single one of these windows of adversity requires compassion at the highest level. What do you say to a parent who is experiencing some of these kinds of adversity? First and foremost, compassion is needed. Kindheartedness and concern expressed facilitate connection. Only the coldest of hearts doesn't feel a deep consideration when hearing these types of stories. When we hear a parent whose child is going through something tough, our inner selves tend to clench our teeth and hold our own kids close. While we might not say it, some of us are thinking gratefully that "my child is not going through this." In my thousands of interviews with children up to centenarians, I have learned that there are two major human things that are not for wimps: (1) getting old, and (2) parenting. Of the latter, if our children aren't going through adversity now, it's around the corner.

Several years ago, the American Psychological Association had a mantra of taking psychology to the streets. This chapter sort of captures the spirit of that motivation. I want to emphasize that by utilizing these interventions, it should NOT be a substitute in place of a parent bringing their son or daughter to a professional counselor, which is needed in a variety of situations. These very difficult periods of adversity often need more support—in which a clinical psychologist or a professional counselor may be the best source of support. That being said, these tools build an inner strength, a resilience, an ability to persevere, and a mental and emotional outlook that will be more positive and connecting with others during tough times. And, with the growing level of potential starting younger and younger, there are more reasons to make these techniques accessible to parents. These points of cognitive flexibility act as a buffer when confronted with adversity.

> *There is little difference in people, but that little difference makes a big difference. That little difference is attitude. The big difference is whether it is positive or negative.* - W. Clement Stone

## We All Need the Big 3

First and foremost, the best way to manage stress in our lives is with the Big 3 – healthy nutrition, regular exercise, and good sleep practices. It's never too early to start our children on healthy nutrition – fruits, vegetables, superfoods, and lean proteins. Nutrition education is potentially one major advantage children have compared to previous generations. My sisters and I find it humorous when we reflect on our lunches and food options growing up. But the fact is, as a culture, we know so much more about nutrition than we did in the past. Many kids relied on fast foods, processed foods (i.e. oatmeal cream pies), soda and candy in previous generations. Daily intake of candy and soda was a norm in middle class families. Kids were sugar addicts but we didn't even know it. Have things changed? Unfortunately, it is a misnomer to believe that kids are eating healthier. A gym teacher recently shared that one of his students was walking in the hallways at 11:00 am having not eaten breakfast while eating from a large bag of cotton candy and drinking a large mountain dew. A quick Google price search shows that a typical price for 32 oz of cotton candy is $4.50 and a typical large mountain dew runs a couple of bucks. With some education, there are lots of healthy nutritious breakfast options for $6-$7. The problem is that reversing this sugar craze trend is difficult. It starts with teaching our children to have a healthy relationship with sugar. Recent research shows that 39.8% of adults and 18.5% of youth are obese, with a 33% increase in youth obesity since 1999. Parents can reverse this trend and make a difference in helping this relationship with sugar by leading by example (i.e. checking your sweet tooth, snacking on produce). Parents can teach kids to notice their body's reaction and describe the difference they feel in response to a healthy sugar like a plum versus a processed sugar like a Twix bar. Parents can gradually facilitate a processed sugar free home while emphasizing fruit, dates, nuts, and honey as alternative snacks.

Second, it's never too early to get our kids going with exercise, fitness, and fun. On the one hand, one of the stressors young people face is the over-scheduling of sports in their lives. On the other hand, schools are cutting gym and recess while screen time has amplified in quantity and quality. When I was growing up in Bolingbrook, Illinois, many of us kids would meet out front on Churchill Drive and pick teams for our basketball, football, baseball, soccer, and wiffle ball games. I'll never forget the fun I had with Jermaine, Danny, Charles, David, Jason, Chad, brothers John and Brian and so many others. When teams were picked, Todd was always chosen last in every game because he was the least skilled. In the current generation, while the better athletes are primarily participating on traveling teams, the Todds in neighborhoods across the country are playing video games.

Engaged families need their fathers teaching their children everything from kickball to badminton to ping pong to soccer and football. Kids need to learn the fundamentals of a jump shot, catching the ball with the hands (and not the chest), a Maradona futbol dribble, and the proper holding of a bat. Most importantly, kids need to have fun. The joy of sports and exercise far exceeds the fun that comes from sedentary activities. Yes, I love the old board game Risk as much as anybody, but games like Star Wars, Trivial Pursuit and Monopoly don't reinforce fun with exercise. Those family games are so much better than screen time, but supplementing those with sports outside is so much fun for kids and teens.

## TIPS FOR REFLECTION

- Give children healthy food from the very beginning so they can live a healthier life. At a basic level, serve mostly foods that are high in nutrition, such as fruits, vegetables, whole grains, lean meat, poultry and fish, and low-fat dairy products and limit those foods with no to little nutritional value.

- Children and teens should consume less than six teaspoons of added sugars per day and no more than eight ounces of sugar-sweetened drinks per week according to the American Heart Association.

- Family dinners are critical and the best predictor of success! Take time to integrate the use of super foods as you enjoy a range of foods and have conversations about things that matter. Visit the Family Dinner Project.ORG for a great resource on conversation starters, fun with food prep like "guess the ingredient" and recipes that adjust for food allergies, dietary restrictions and picky eaters.

- Spend as much unstructured fun time playing sports as possible. Attending your kids' sporting events does not count.

- Parents [DADS], delay golf until the kids go to college.

Third, it's never too early to start with good sleep practices – getting the TV out of the bedroom and parking smartphones outside of the bedroom are a couple of immediate strategies. First and foremost, let's clarify the recommendations for each of the age groups by the American Academy of Pediatrics (AAP). The following sleep hours are recommended to promote optimal health:

- Infants 4 months to 12 months should sleep 12 to 16 hours (per 24 hours).
- Children 1 to 2 years of age should sleep 11 to 14 hours.
- Children 3 to 5 years of age should sleep 10 to 13 hours.

- Children 6 to 12 years of age should sleep 9 to 12 hours.
- Teenagers 13 to 18 years of age should sleep 8 to 10 hours.

The AAP also suggests that screens be turned off 30 minutes before bedtime. At parenting talks, I recommend that parents create a park zone for their teenagers so all phones including parents' phones are parked on the counter one hour before bed to clear the mind. Research shows that blue light from the screens delay the production of sleep promoting hormone melatonin significantly affecting sleep—making it more difficult to fall asleep. TVs, video games, smartphones, fill in the blank, all need to be turned off well before kids go to bed.[4]

For teenagers, there are several factors to consider on this issue of sleep. Routinely, I run into parents all the time who struggle with this issue and are resigned that teenagers will learn to make their own decision. First and foremost, training teens that sleep is essential to their success is critical. Most teens get 6 ½ to 7 hours of sleep but need 9 hours of sleep per night. An important factor is the change in the body during puberty. Before puberty, a kid's body makes them sleepy around 8:00 or 9:00 pm. When puberty starts, this rhythm shifts a couple hours later. For teens, their body is now telling them to go to sleep around 10:00 or 11:00 pm. This natural shift in the circadian rhythm, which is called sleep phase delay, can be an adjustment. That being said, there are consequences for teens who routinely go to bed after midnight such as a weakened immune system and increases in BMI and obesity.

The big three helps us with cognitive flexibility. So, what are these points of cognitive flexibility when confronted with adversity? Mental strategies are those things we can do that help us navigate our journey in a healthy way – Perspective taking, adjusting, clarifying problems, gentleness on self, courage, acceptance, self-regulation, and perspective taking are some of the key ingredients to mastering anxiety and growing in cognitive flexibility. The following are cognitive techniques that help us with perspective broadening, adjustment with changes, clarifying solutions, staying gentle when we are our own worst critic, maintaining courage under stress, acceptance, self-regulation, and perspective taking. Each of these emotional and intellectual elements are trainable over time for the youth of today.

PRACTICING Cognitive Reappraisals

A critical element of anxiety-mastery involves helping children recognize that multiple perceptions of the same situation exist. At the heart of cognitive flexibility is the idea of having multiple perceptions of the same situation. The first step with children starting at ages 4 or 5 is to help them see there are multiple perspectives. With children's books, we might ask, "What is another way Fancy Nancy can view this problem?" Legendary cognitive psychologist, Jean Piaget, identified the preoperational stage occurring roughly between the ages of two and seven. It is during this stage that it was suggested that young children are unable to take the point of view of other people[5]. Things have changed over the last 50 years and it appears that taking on multiple views can start much earlier than previously thought, depending on the child.

Retrospective processing usually leads to insightful interpretations. It is normal to look back and see things better than one did initially. The relationship break up feels better than it did last month. With so many hormonal and emotional experiences, a "break-up" is felt deeply by adolescents. The playoff loss feels a little better a month later. After getting cut from the baseball team, Billy is a little more used to performing in the band instead. It is typical for teenagers to look back and appraise things differently. Getting rejected from the Ivy League school "kept me in state at Illinois and I was able to help Grandma in her last year of life."

Besides looking back, what about flexibility during the initial appraisals? At the time of the failure, disappointment, setback, or hardship, isn't It normal to feel disappointed? I sat down and talked with Cindy who was having trouble making sense of her recent setback. "I wanted more than anything to make the varsity team." I found myself moved with compassion for her. I was also surprised with how she questioned "feeling bad." "I don't understand why I'm feeling this way." Cindy appeared to fight back her feelings as she tried to diminish the importance of making the team. "It's not a big deal. It's not that important anyway." I tried to reason with her but her sadness and disappointment was mixed with anger. She didn't begin to settle down until I reminded her that her feelings showed how much she cared. I gave her some good old fashioned advice. "Cindy, it is much better to go after something and experience a setback, than to stay on the sidelines of life. And, when you experience a setback, when you come up short, you should feel disappointment. It is normal to feel sadness. It shows how much you care!"

There is certainly a place for the setbacks of life. But, what about those times that aren't significant moments like tryouts, exam scores, or acceptance letters. There are lots of other times when we can make more problems than actually appear. These are primarily related to worries about the future, not significant moments in the present. Cognitive bias towards negatives can influence kids to remember information selectively, or may lead them toward bias about future worries. Initial perceptions of challenges or perceived challenges can fall along a spectrum from possible to impossible, tolerable to unbearable, and manageable to extremely overwhelming. It is common for teenagers to get stuck in a mode of making cognitive appraisals that lead them to see situations as impossible, unbearable, and overwhelming.

### "It's Impossible, Unbearable, and Overwhelming!"

When I work with individuals with good insight, they are able to identify those moments when anxiety starts to go up or worsen. With zero as completely relaxed and 10 as the most anxiety that they can possibly imagine, there is what I call a therapeutic window when the physiological reaction intensifies. For some, this is the beginning onset of panic when anxiety goes up from a 2 or 3 to a 7+, for example. It is during this therapeutic window when problems seem "impossible, unbearable, and overwhelming."

Even if teenagers don't struggle with anxiety, every parent can attest that irrationality in spurts is normal. I was talking to Melissa about her application process for colleges. She had her school preferences ranked and by all accounts— she seemed to be an excellent candidate with great potential. Her academic credentials were in the top percentile. She was a balanced student athlete. She had high test scores. She had volunteer service. She had plentiful leadership experience. Getting into a state school appeared to be a formality. Yet, before Melissa received her acceptance letters from Florida State University, University of South Florida, University of Florida, and University of Central Florida, as well as some other out of state colleges such as Georgetown, she insisted that her chances were low. Is this normal? The nervous wait certainly is common. For Melissa, the wait and the pending result was "impossible, unbearable, and overwhelming."

The truth in Melissa's case is that it's possible, tolerable and manageable. In fact, it is helpful to find evidence of how this challenge is completely possible to solve, very tolerable, and absolutely manageable. It is a delight for teachers when they occasionally come across a student who views all challenges as completely possible to solve, very tolerable, and absolutely manageable. Yes, usually the complaining is minimal in these individuals.

> *The emotions are not always subject to reason...but they are always subject to action. When thoughts do not neutralize an undesirable emotion, actions will.* - William James

### First Outside, Then Inside

Practicing cognitive reappraisals of external events prepares young people to practice cognitive reappraisals for internal events. Internal event? Yes. An internal event is not something out there your kid is anxious about. An internal event is something inside of them that makes them anxious.

First, let's consider an external event. Consider the classic speech anxiety, termed glossophobia. To show how things have changed, I took an outstanding public speaking class in college. More than 20 years later, public speaking is now being taught in the 2nd grade in many schools. Despite earlier training, speech anxiety remains a chronic problem with an estimated 75% prevalence rate[6]. Consider a teenager named Bob with stage fright. When I see him after his big speech, Bob reports that he gave a lousy speech. "It flat out sucked. Of course, it was lousy." First, I ask him if anybody threw tomatoes at him. He smiles saying, "Of course not." "Did you vomit in front of the class and run out screaming?" "No." After a series of questions, it became clear that he got through the speech, gave an introduction and closing with points in between. He accomplished his goal by speaking the message he wanted to communicate. What he thought was a D or a F with his initial cognitive bias ended up turning out to be a B+. So, of course, a week later the speech felt better than it did right after he gave it in class. Prior to receiving his evaluation, I had seen Bob a day after his speech and after my series of questions, he felt better because his initial cognitive appraisal was changing. His reappraisal of his speech was that "it may not have been perfect, but he accomplished his goals."

" *If you don't like something, change it.  If you can't change it, change the way you think about it.*  - Mary Engelbreit

Reappraising a speech, a spelling bee performance, a dance recital, or performance on the basketball court is one of the essential goals of parents on an as needed basis.  What about reappraising internal events?  The spirit of this book is that parents foster reflection through conversation.  Families promote an atmosphere of reflection through questions.

Starting with external events is easier for young people to embrace as the first step in practicing reappraisals.  The second step is reappraising internal events, the self-talk that views situations as impossible, unbearable, and over-whelming."  These internal sensations, quiet whisperings, and reactions to stress are all important.

Nipping Panic in the Bud

A common example of a second step is reappraising panic feelings during the therapeutic window.  Panic is a cluster of physiological sensations often appraised as impossible, unbearable, and extremely overwhelming.  Sufferers of panic attacks often report a fear of dying or of having a heart attack.  In 2014, a woman reported that she was told not to return to Bayfront Hospital in St. Petersburg, Florida because her four visits to the emergency room in one month were due to panic attacks, not heart problems.  Common panic symptoms include trembling, shortness of breath heart palpitations, chest pain, hot flashes, sweating, nausea, dizziness (slight vertigo), light-headedness, hyperventilation, sensations of choking or smothering, paresthesia (tingling sensations), and derealization.

Panic feelings often spiral into a panic attack due to the initial cognitive appraisals.  Panic elevates due to catastrophizing, a type of thinking that views panic feelings as catastrophic and dangerous.  Thus, the feelings feel impossible to cope with, become unbearable, and are extremely overwhelming.  The process of reappraising involves seeing these feelings as possible to cope with, tolerable, and manageable.  Decatastrophizing involves viewing panic as inconvenient and mildly uncomfortable.  Have you ever noticed that high school graduates will not miss graduation parties no matter how dehydrated or how painful their headaches are?  Most of us can tolerate headaches without missing work and performing the activities of daily living.  In the same way, equating panic sensations to headaches is a helpful solution.  The headache overlook intervention is an example of a cognitive reappraisal.  The intervention consists of three steps: (1) identifying panic symptoms, (2) equating panic with a headache, (3) and beginning to overlook the panic sensations much in the same way that one would overlook a headache.

Jenny, a 16-year-old sophomore, started having panic attacks after she switched schools and began helping her siblings while her mother received treatment for cancer.  She began to withdraw from friends and her effort and subsequent grades in school suffered.  When she came to therapy, she commented, "I dread feeling panicky. It is often that I feel like I'm going to die. It has gotten so bad that I haven't wanted to leave the house. I quit volleyball and told the coach I had to take care of my mother because of her cancer. I really quit because of my panic attacks." In therapy, Jenny used the headache overlook intervention and learned to follow the three steps as she practiced reappraisals. Over time, her symptoms were viewed as possible to solve, very tolerable, and absolutely manageable. Of course, Jenny needed professional therapy. If your child suffers from symptoms like Jenny, they may need a professional to build coping within the therapeutic window. Nonetheless, an appraisal in the therapeutic window was instrumental in beginning to see the possibilities, strengthen her tolerance threshold, and manage the stress. After Jenny applied herself in therapy and practiced the headache overlook intervention, she returned to socialization and even started practicing with the volleyball team again.

---

## WORDS OF WISDOM & STEPS FOR TAKING ACTION

- The goal of practicing cognitive reappraisals is to increase flexibility and reduce catastrophic misinterpretations.

- The first step in practicing cognitive reappraisals is (1) reappraising external events: sports tryouts, choir performance, the recital, a speech, a spelling test...

- The second step is reappraising anxiety. The three steps of the headache overlook are (1) identifying a feeling, (2) equating it to a headache, and (3) overlooking the feeling the way one overlooks a headache.

- Reappraising involves seeing problems as possible to solve, experiencing feelings as tolerable, and viewing coping as manageable.

---

### ADJUSTING with Must Checks

Must checks are reminders to loosen up on how life must go. Let me say this as direct as I can—many of us get "jacked up" or "weird" about life because of how rigid we are. This rigidity leads us to control others in relationships or stifle others' feelings. The ability to not be rigid but able to adjust is key to our well-being.

The ability to adjust to adversity and life changes is a critical emotional skill. Albert Ellis, one of the original leaders in cognitive therapy, used to encourage clients to get the "shoulds" out of their thinking. Sometimes, as the therapist, Ellis would yell at his patients in order to get them to stop "shoulding" in their thinking. If you only look at Ellis' approach with people, clinicians are uninterested in trying to adopt or incorporate his therapeutic style. When I speak at conferences, clinicians still laugh at some of his methods but nobody takes them seriously. And, I wouldn't recommend his communication style to parents either. As we've pointed out, anger doesn't work in parenting. And, yelling, which usually accompanies anger or making crude comments, don't usually work either. That being said, sometimes our words need to be vegetables and not just Twinkies.

Professional therapists prefer to replicate the therapeutic styles of Carl Rogers and Aaron Beck. It was Rogers who said that the therapeutic relationship is both necessary and sufficient. Beck believed that the therapeutic relationship is necessary but not sufficient. Ellis directly stated that the therapeutic relationship is neither sufficient nor necessary. He flat out told people that good therapy didn't depend on a "strong therapeutic alliance." He even suggested that a good relationship can get in the way of flexible thinking to counter the "should" and "must" thinking. In retrospect, his view about the relationship as unimportant is no longer taken seriously.

While Ellis was wrong about the value of the relationship, his take home A-B-C message is worth the value of gold. His A-B-C message need not be confined to psychologists' offices. His A-B-C message is critical for teachers, mentors, and coaches. Most importantly, this message is essential for parents. The essential ingredients of Ellis' Rational Emotive Therapy was rooted in the fact that it was not the Activating Event (A) that causes the Consequence (C) – the distress, but it is a person's belief (B) about the activating event that elevates the distress (C). Relationship turmoil, test results, and application letters are primarily influenced by rigid beliefs about the outcomes. When a person's belief is how things "must happen" or "should occur," then the distress is much greater. It is the rigid belief about what must happen that elevates the distress.

> *It is not only the most difficult thing to know oneself, but the most inconvenient too.* - Josh Billings

When I was a 22-year-old college student, my girlfriend came to see me at my dorm (right after she saw her old boyfriend) and decided to break things off. A few days later, I made up my mind to do everything I could to win her back. I borrowed my step-brother's car and drove four hours to her father's house in Wisconsin. I bought long stem sunflowers that she scoffed at when she answered her father's door. A few hours later, I was on my knees vomiting in her toilet as she knocked on the bathroom door wondering if I was O.K. This was one of the lowest moments in my young life. When I tell this story, I often hear laughs when I wonder if roses would have done the trick. Probably not. In this scenario, the Activating event (A) was the relationship break-up. But, the break up didn't cause my intense distress to the point of nausea and vomiting. It was my belief (B) that we "must stay together" that caused me such intense emotional problems. The other significant problem is that I was interpreting my experiences through my emotions.[7]

Virtually every client that comes through my office has emotional problems that require must checks. They require checkups on their reflectiveness and meta-cognition – thinking about what they think about. At the root of their thought processes are musts in their thinking. The solutions to many problems are must checks. This involves checking their musts at the door of life.

I was recently working with Jeanne and her daughter, a gymnast who was experiencing some psychological blocking and having difficulty with some skills that she previously had accomplished. Jeanne was showing considerable disappointment following her daughter's tumbling on her floor events as well as her other routines. It became immediately clear to me that Jeanne was putting tremendous pressure on her daughter. I listened intently as Jeanne talked. "Every event is critical in her development. She is not going to master the skills unless she can get through this blocking." As we sat down and we began to talk, I was struck by the sorts of things Jeanne had mentioned. Her daughter didn't seem to be having fun. But, her mother was more concerned about her performance than any enjoyment her daughter was experiencing. "Jeanne, does your daughter see your facial expressions. What I mean is, does she notice you react after a routine?" Jeanne looked at me with a surprised gaze. "Probably, she knows how much I care." By this time, Jeanne had shifted her body and appeared curious. She leaned forward, intently waiting for what I was going to say next. "I have a question for you. Why react?" She didn't have an answer but nodded in agreement. "My thought on the matter is that by reacting, you add undue pressure on the outcome. Too much emphasis on the outcome takes away the enjoyment of the journey." I had another question for her. She appeared to listen thoughtfully. "Do you expect her to make the Olympic team?" Her 30 seconds (literally) of silence was a jolt to my nervous system. We went on to discuss ways her daughter could experience enjoyment once again by reducing pressure. My perspective was by regaining love for her sport, her daughter would begin to have less anxiety around the outcomes. "It's time to get back to having fun!" I left that meeting with Jeanne concerned for her daughter's long-term enjoyment of gymnastics. Kids often "burn out" when they experience undue pressure to achieve particular outcomes. At the heart of the gymnast's pressures were "musts." And, the musts were coming directly from her mother. As parents, we need must checks!

Establishing a precedent of eliminating musts can make a difference for the future of family members. A family principle of flexibility with external circumstances sets kids up with improved well-being. Flexibility with external circumstances out of direct control is the antidote to must thinking. It is recommended that parents discuss must checks during reflective exercises. Is that too "psychological" for the dinner table? It doesn't have to be. It's a great discussion topic for families.

At the heart of coping well is eliminating musts. Let's be honest, when it comes to our kids, it's natural for them to say things like, "I must have this. Must have that." Let's take a step back and clarify that we are talking about problems outside of daily living. From the kid's perspective, they may be referring to, "I must have ice cream." From the parent's perspective, we aren't talking about eliminating the musts like household expectations such as taking out the trash or regular chores. Readers might be visualizing their son exclaiming, "Aren't we trying to eliminate musts around everything which includes trash and chores."

No—we are also talking about those things outside of our control and usually the bigger things in life beyond ice cream and chores. For young people, this usually consists of performance related evaluations, sporting events, relationships, and steps in a trajectory (i.e. getting into college, choosing a major). The solution to musts is preferences. I prefer to win the election for FBLA (Future Business Leaders of America) president in my High School, but I can cope with losing the election. I prefer that I advance to the state cross-country meet, but I can handle coming up short with grace. I prefer getting into Honors English class but I will find another solution if it doesn't work out. I really hope that Angela attends the prom with me, but I am fine attending with a group of friends as well. In each of the aforementioned examples, musts that raise the level of distress are modified to preferences that incorporate flexibility and improve well-being.

---

## REFLECTION EXERCISE

**Cognitive Reappraisals and Must Checks Are More Manageable When We Teach Kids & Teens Mindfulness Skills**

**<u>Mindfulness Skills for Kids</u>**

- **3 Ss: Keep it Short (5 minutes), Simple, and Specific**

- **Have Fun by using Humor**

- **Use a 5-step progression of mindfulness skills**

  1. **Teach outer awareness (i.e. nature)**

  2. **Teach awareness of breath with deep breathing practices (i.e. listen to the sound of your breathing)**

  3. **Teach awareness of sensory experience**

  4. **Teach awareness of bodily signals**

  5. **Teach self-reflection and awareness of thoughts (i.e. what thought went through your mind?)**

---

<u>Valuing Failure Talk</u>

A positive way to incorporate flexibility and buffer against musts is failure talk. During parenting talks, I recommend to families that they engage in family conversations at dinner time about failures. "Did anyone here fail today?" "Has anyone failed at something this past week?" When a kid responds, we praise the effort to leave one's comfort zone. Inevitably, parents raise their hands ques-

<u>**Mindfulness Skills for Teenagers**</u>

- **3 Rs: Keep it Relevant, Relaxing, Responsive**

- **Keep it Relevant by practicing mindful eating, mindful texting, mindful focusing on schoolwork, mindful attentiveness when with friends.**

- **Keep it Relaxing by using music in mindfulness listening skills; facilitate a quiet environment using screen free zones for 15 minutes.**

- **Keep it Responsive by applying mindfulness to daily life activities for a few minutes each hour: walking, brushing teeth, texting, and driving.**

- **Engage in activities to keep mindfulness fun and engaging, not boring.**

  1. **Teach mindful neurobiology by having kids draw a picture of a brain. This helps letting go of musts.**

  2. **Increase mindfulness of nature by writing a poem about flowers, images, visual beauty, sunsets, fish, butterflies, nature, etc. This makes eliminating musts easier.**

  3. **Practice mindful smelling by baking chocolate chip cookies or melting dark chocolate (superfood).**

tioning this discussion topic. In one talk, Susan raised her hand and waved it noticeably. As she began, I immediately noticed the argumentative and passionate tone of her voice. "For those of us who can squeeze dinner into our hectic lives, it's hard enough to get our kids focused on the positive." Susan's dilemma is not unusual. Yes, we do want to focus on the positives, the solutions, and build up their optimism to see problems as temporary and not permanent. It usually takes some convincing but positive conversation about failures is done with a long-term vision. The effect of regular family conversations about failure produces the following fruit: (1) fearlessness about risks, (2) resilience when kids experience setbacks, (3) improved ability to reflect and appraise.

Ultimately – we want to desensitize our children to failures. By discussing failures freely, we encourage our children to take risks which is the essence of boldness. We also help our children not react so strongly to let downs and setbacks. The more things kids try (listen to the song, "Try Everything), the less things they avoid. Check out these lyrics by Shakira that should inspire every kid:

*I messed up tonight*
*I lost another fight*
*I still mess up but I'll just start again*
*I keep falling down*
*I keep on hitting the ground*
*I always get up now to see what's next*
*Birds don't just fly*
*They fall down and get up*
*Nobody learns without getting it wrong*

*I won't give up, no I won't give in*
*Till I reach the end*
*And then I'll start again*
*Though I'm on the lead*
*I wanna try everything*
*I wanna try even though I could fail*
*I won't give up, no I won't give in*
*Till I reach the end*
*And then I'll start again*
*No I won't leave*
*I wanna try everything*
*I wanna try even though I could fail*

## CLARIFYING PROBLEMS with Worry Mastery

Most worry is self-defeating worry. The opposite of worrying is problem solving. The solutions to self-defeating worry are clarifying and normalizing the worry and problem solving. According to international research[8], the top teenage worries are coping with overwhelming stress, school or study problems, body image, family conflict, and coping with depression.

One of the factors behind worry is viewing failure as negative. This is why failure discussion helps them to see failure as positive. Viewing failure as negative starts with the parents. Another key factor is seeing worry as unsolvable. Again, the opposite of worry is problem solving. Engaged parents don't solve all their kids' problems. Things are done at age appropriate levels – but we help teens gradually brainstorm solutions as the remedy to these problems.

Let's identify some fears and worries that parents help their children navigate through in life. What are the normal fears of children and adolescents? The fears for children 0-2 years of age are loud noises, strangers, separation from parents, and large objects. The fears for children ages 3-6 are imaginary things such as ghosts, monsters, the dark, sleeping alone, and strange noises. From ages 7-16, fears are more realistic such as injury, illness, and school performance. What are typical worries among children in this latter age group? Yes, school performance. Other worries include friends, appearance, social acceptance, and death of a parent. Is "concern about what others think" still a major issue among youth? Of course.

What if the thing we worry about actually happens? First of all, let's take a step back and reflect on our parenting worries. Every parent worries about their kids. Let me correct myself---every engaged parent worries. When I first became a parent, older parents advised me that the challenges in life, which were my biggest concern in the past, will pale in comparison to concerns about what could happen to my kids. The new loves of my life were now my priority, my responsibility. These treasures were the new burden I carried about in life. Yet, enjoying our kids in the moment is more important than worrying about what could happen to them. Like most things in life, the key is moderation versus excess. Excessive worry leads to over-protectiveness and anxiety in our kids. And, very often, our worries about our kids have a carry-over effect.

Let's go back to the question for our kids—What if the thing we worry about actually happens? Taking time to discuss this question has shown to be essential for children and their ability to cope. Secondly, if this happened, could you cope with it? Studies have shown that the notion, "don't worry about that", often spoken by family members and friends is not supported by evidence.[9] Instead, mastering the worry is the goal. If parents can apply worry mastery in their own lives, it becomes easier to teach to the lives of their children. What is worry mastery?

Identifying the worries is the first step. Not so easy. But, awareness of consciousness is power. Anything we focus on expands in our consciousness. What has been expanding in our conscious? What do you worry about the most? Problem solving is the second step. The opposite of worry is problem solving. Ranking worries from least distressing to most distressing can be a helpful strategy. The main goal is to identify worries and brainstorm solutions to those worries. Parents can make a difference brainstorming three to five possible solutions. Sometimes, empowerment occurs when the worries are categorized into those things in your child's control and those things outside of control.

> *There is a time when we must firmly choose the course we will follow, or the relentless drift of events will make the decision for us.*
> – Herbert V. Prochnow

## Being Gentle with Ourselves

Consider the negative belief: "I am ugly; I can't make friends." This self-defeating belief can be addressed directly with Socratic questioning—a series of questions to get at the truth of things and open up about issues. Attempts to reframe can be difficult if the teenager has repeatedly heard that she is ugly and has lots of evidence of potential friends rejecting her over time. The solution is gentleness. Defusion techniques can help.

Occasionally, we see a relationship in a movie that has an impact on the audience. I enjoy a father character interacting nicely with his overweight son who is constantly bullied at school. Audiences are moved when movies show the development of relationship and a dad's gentleness with his son emerge as they tackle bullying problems. If these can happen in movies, these relationships can happen in real life.

Defusion techniques help young people distance themselves from self-defeating beliefs and see them for what they are – changeable thought processes or streams of words that can dissipate. In the context of gentleness, there are some techniques that can be used to help in this process. The leaf on a stream technique involves taking time to close eyes and place a negative self-statement on a leaf and watch it float away on a stream. Phylicia visually sees the belief, 'I am ugly' on the leaf as it floats down the stream. The ocean wave technique involves placing a negative self-statement and placing it on a wave. The wave dissipates on the beach as a metaphor for a negative belief dissipating in our minds. Miguel sees the belief, "I am incompetent" dissipate on the wave as it crashes on the sand. Another technique that can help create distance from negative is the sound it out technique. This involves saying difficult thoughts very, very slowly and saying positive replacements aloud, "I am beautiful, and I am a good friend." The loud voice drowns out the negative belief (i.e. "I'm not good enough.") minimizing its impact. For those with a sense of humor, the silly voice technique entails using a Donald Duck voice to say "I am ugly; I can't make friends." Then, the voice says, "No, I am attractive, beautiful, and accept myself completely." Having worth, being treasured, believing one is loveable are essential to well-being. All these are small techniques that can help in those key growth windows.

Each of these techniques are examples of the type of thing that we can do for our children in those growth windows. Essentially, these defusion techniques capture a small part of the larger need our kids have from us as parents – encouragement. If you have taken the time to have family dinners, engaged in two moments of warmth per day since birth, reinforced privileges and restrictions consistently, and regularly implemented family rituals and traditions as the family foundation, then you have established an influence in your child's life like no other. And when adversity hits, the thing you have to offer more than anything else is encouragement. That may be in the form of wisdom, revelation, a solution. Essentially, it is encouragement that they need more than a technique [but these can help]. If you have taken the time to invest in your child's life, the following comments can have a profound impact at the right time, in the right moment, and in the right circumstances:

- "I believe in you."
- "There is something inside of you that will know what to say to your friend in that moment."
- "I have a lot of compassion for you. And, I know that you can get through this."
- "You have tremendous integrity."
- "You are a wonderful girl. You are a wonderful boy. I am so proud of who you are."
- "I am 100% confident that you will make the right choice at the right moment."

### Being Courageous Despite Fear

One of the best treasures that we can draw out of our children is courage. Being courageous is a great gift and one of the virtues that we can elevate in the lives of our children. Consider the example given in *Chasing Mavericks*. Frosty tells the teenager that fear is normal on a gigantic swell wave but panic is "what gets you dead." He explained this during a scene when Jay (lead character) panicked as he saw a shark while they were diving. Panic prevents rational decision-making. Fear is what you are supposed to have. Panic "gets you dead." Now, the language used to establish distinctions here was not made using medical language or psychiatric nomenclature. Regardless, it highlights a distinction that is helpful for kids. Normalizing fear is good for children. Normalizing fear at the appropriate times is not reinforcing it, but providing encouragement at key growth windows for kids. "Being afraid is normal."

The distinction serves some teenagers by learning how to have normal fear without panicking in situations that may involve training: surfing, scuba diving, skiing, parasailing, rock climbing, cliff jumping, sky diving (after turning 18), or even social situations. Generally speaking, we want to encourage our children to overcome their fears. Identifying fears, normalizing them ("what you are experiencing is normal."), and helping them to overcome them is the best course with all tough things.

ACCEPTANCE by Accepting Counterfactual Thinking

Let's review. We've discussed must checks with failure talk as a buffer, worry mastery with problem solving, defusion techniques with words of encouragement, and overcoming fears. What about the setbacks of life? Failure talk captures some of this. Some setbacks just sting. Let's look at how we can help our children accept counterfactual thinking with the setbacks of life that seem to leave a lasting sting.

When I was a senior in high school, I was the starting point guard on a very bad high school basketball team. I was named team MVP at the end of the season despite only averaging 6 points per game while leading the team in assists, steals, and inspired teamwork. Our team finished the season 2-18, but we did have our very brief moment in the limelight during the playoffs. We played our last and only playoff game with vigor and tenacity and held a five-point lead with two minutes to go against one of the top ranked teams in the state. The start of our opponents' comeback began with a 10-second back-court call due to my dribbling in the backcourt. Naturally, I watched the video and the referee appeared to speed up the 10-second count and miscount. The crowd appeared to influence what was a true 8-count on video. Even an objective eye watching the video would suggest that the ref appeared to be influenced by the deafening noise in our opposing team's gym. Regardless of the call, I took responsibility for the backcourt call. The other team outscored us by 10 after that in the last two very sad minutes. I have engaged in counterfactual thinking for 25 years, particularly from the starting point of that backcourt dribbling that led to my violation.

Counterfactual thinking is the human tendency to create possible alternatives to life events that have already occurred. It consists of how things could have turned out differently. The details in the basketball example are important to absolutely nobody else. I have created my own reality in my mind of how things could have turned out. Yet, this is not uncommon.

Excessive counterfactuals can lead people to excessive worry about their problems[10]. Problem solving these scenarios help young people worry less and critically think more. The benefits of counterfactuals are preparation, to avoid making the same mistake, and the process of acceptance, accepting reality and our shortcomings. An advantage of parent-child bonding is the process of mutually sharing counterfactuals with each other. Naturally, this process requires vulnerability, understanding, and accepting each other. Children need their parents' vulnerability and their counterfactuals. How do we go about sharing our counterfactuals?

It starts with storytelling. Every parent can become a good story teller. The following are some questions to trigger conversations with your kids. Have you ever shared your (age-appropriate) regrets with your children? Have you ever discussed mistakes that replayed in your mind over the years? Do you remember your last game in high school or college in your particular sport? What parts about that game do you wish could have gone differently? Is there anything that you wish you had done differently in that game? Elaborating on details, honesty, and vulnerability are the keys to capturing the experience for your children.

### SELF REGULATION with the Reaction Clarification Method

In the midst of telling stories and living life, there's something that happens in our experiences of life that is helpful to understand. A piece of psychological insight that can help is the distinction between the two origins of our emotional states. Emotional reactions are the result of either: (1) A classically conditioned response or (2) An interpretation of an experience. Every reaction is either from a trigger we have learned to respond to based on our classical conditioning history or a result of our thinking—an interpretation. Every experience of anxiety is a result of a triggered stimulus or a thread of thoughts.

> *I do not think much of a person who is not wiser today than he or she was yesterday.* — Abraham Lincoln

Classically conditioned responses are reactions elicited by an external trigger. When Jenny with test anxiety sits down to take a test, her anxiety is often a classically conditioned response. Likewise, Fred has endured lots of abuse from his alcoholic father and is often triggered into fear responses by loud noise, somebody yelling, a crashing sound, or visual images of helpless individuals in fights. Sam, who has repeatedly been bullied, experiences triggered anxiety in reaction to the sound of a slammed locker. Somebody yelling may remind Jacklyn of her bipolar mother. A crowd cheer may scare Johnny who saw his dad get injured at the 2013 Boston Marathon. Realizing the birthday party involves swimming brings a feeling of terror for Maggie who lost her twin sister to a drowning accident. Each of these responses are triggered – a test [that elicits test anxiety], a loud noise, a locker slamming, someone yelling, a crowd cheer, and swimming.

Most emotions are not triggered. The above triggers are based on classical conditioning experiences. A personal experience is tied to fear, anxiety or panic feelings and stimuli associated to this experience become associated triggers that elicit reactions. Most emotional experiences are not a result of previous anxious experience. Most emotions are the result of the thought life that influences interpretations of experiences. Previous experience can influence interpretations, but that is based on the thought processes. To put it simply, emotions result from (1) triggers or (2) thoughts.

Many young people are confused by their emotions. Some may believe that "everything makes them" feel the way they do. Learning that one can consciously control their emotions is empowering. This happens when they realize that their thought life (self-talk) is evoking their emotions. When Louis checks the wall list to see if he made the baseball team, his emotions are influenced by his self-talk. Tom cheers for his team in the playoffs after getting injured and missing the rest of the season. Rather than self-pity, his inspiring encouragement is a result of selfless focus on his team (selfless thinking). Sadness from a break up is often a normal reaction in response to thinking about the loss. Happiness from good news such as an acceptance letter from one's preferred college is based on an if-then thinking set up. "If I get into this college for reason A, B, and C, then I will be thrilled!" Feeling loved by her parents reinforces the belief that Vicky is loveable. All these examples are based on inner thinking and the interior thought life (one's self-talk). While anxiety is often triggered, most reactions are based on the thought life. Self-regulation is based on self-talk. In the spirit of this book as your child's best psychologist -- this is a strategy on how you can empower your teenagers. Help them separate triggers from thoughts. This by itself is an empowering piece of insight that can last a lifetime.

## PERSPECTIVE TAKING with the Trigger Downsizing Technique

Again, emotions result from (1) Triggers and (2) the Thought life. When the emotion is triggered by something external, the trigger downsizing technique is a worthwhile strategy. Triggers that do elicit distress result in a range of anxiety. An easy scale is 0-10. In the emergency room, nurses often ask patients to scale pain from 0 – 10. "On a scale of 0-10, what is your level of back pain?" In the same way, scaling anxiety from 0 (completely relaxed) to 10 (maximum anxiety) provides clarity on distress. Obviously, scaling your children on a daily basis is overkill. Scaling on a weekly basis may also be too much. But, occasionally, helping us identify a set point on our level of anxiety helps all of us parents and youth alike. Consider the following examples and their level of anxiety based on the level of scaling and the subsequent valuable insight.

Jenny with test anxiety used to be a 10, but accommodations (i.e. extra time), cognitive reappraisal practice, relaxation training, and reflective exercises with must checks (i.e. changed her musts to preferences) have lowered her scaled anxiety to a 3. Now, when she approaches her tests, her confidence has increased.

Chad endured lots of abuse from his alcoholic father. When he came in for therapy, he was encouraged to reflect on his life and his experiences and begin to separate triggers from thoughts. This is not an easy task but with some reflection, insight can develop. Over time, Chad could recognize that he was often triggered into fear responses by loud noise, somebody yelling, a crashing sound, or visual images of helpless individuals in fights. This latter trigger caused him to overreact in the hallway at school when two boys were horsing around and he inadvertently approached the situation too strong, believing one of the kids was in a helpless position. As Chad gained awareness on his triggers, he was able to use scaling as a way to describe his experience. He realized that when his triggers elicit a 9 on his distress scale, he started to smoke marijuana, which began at the age of 16. By the age of 17, he now smoked as soon as he could following a triggered reaction. He realized that his scaled anxiety of a 9 was locked in. Instead of feeling his anxiety and developing coping strategies to bring his anxiety down, he relied on avoiding his feelings. This insight was instrumental for Fred as he began to make changes. Instead of suppressing and avoiding, he began to feel and cope.

Sam has been repeatedly bullied and used to experience triggered anxiety in reaction to the sound of a slammed locker. Sam found support talking to his parents about the bullying. He sought help from the school counselor. With Sam's permission, the counselor spoke with the principal and some teachers to arrange a safe place for Sam and other students. Additionally, Sam observed that the school worked harder to enforce an environment of respect. Sam found relief from the support and felt safer in his learning environment. As an amusing exposure, he was open to a strategy of overcoming the locker slamming trigger. Sam practiced an exposure intervention with his friend Kevin repeatedly slamming the locker. The locker slam that used to trigger a 9 was now a zero. The reaction was extinguished as a result of this comical intervention.

In each of these examples -- somebody yelling may remind Jacklyn of her bipolar mother, a crowd cheer may scare Johnny who saw his dad get injured at the 2013 Boston Marathon, realizing that the birthday party involves swimming brings a feeling of terror for Maggie who lost her twin sister to a drowning accident; the trigger may increase or decrease depending on cognitive reappraisal practice, relaxation training, and reflective exercises.

As a parent, your child's experience may be completely different from the above. The use of the trigger downsizing technique helps kids reflect on their feelings. Identifying our emotions can be empowering and identifying the "downsizing" of the feelings can be enlightening. Key questions that can help in the downsizing process—the process of lowering the level of stress: How anxiety producing was it six months ago? How anxiety producing was it one month ago? How anxiety producing is it now? The best way to downsize a trigger is exposure. Being around crowds will help Johnny bring down his anxiety. The more Maggie swims, the less swimming will have a hold on her. So, Yes! Age old wisdom known by parents of several generations past—get back on the horse remains true today. Initially, anxiety goes up but through exposure – the trigger is downsized.

## REFLECTION TIPS

- Techniques are helpful to a small degree. The most important and essential parenting ingredient is our unconditional love for our children. Techniques are like icing on a birthday cake.

- These techniques help preserve the essential goals of optimal reinforcement, encouragement of boldness, healthy and secure attachments, meta-cognitive optimism, and finding purpose with an internal locus of control.

- Professional counseling is a reliable resource and may be an additional supplement for good father/mother - child discussions. Professional therapy ought not to diminish or squelch parent-child talks. Conversations ought to be strengthened, not replaced.

- The goal for children is "continuous freedom," defined as nothing outside of your child having a hold on them.

# Chapter Seven

## Happiness is Balancing Flourishing and Contentment

*Is it the enjoyment of the choreographed dance at the historic Detroit Opera House moved to the middle of the ocean or is it the result of the performance that makes us happy? Those who derive more happiness from the result are more likely going to worry about the shakiness of the cargo ship or the appearance or synchronicity of the dance performers. When we put too much emphasis on the destination, we miss out on the process. Joy is in the journey, and not the destination. How do we live that out? It certainly makes sense when we hear it. How do we carry that out within our parenting? That seems to be the question as we enter this last key of why you are your child's best psychologist.*

### Happiness Attitudes

This chapter is loaded with ideas and information and can be best summarized by the 3 As of Happiness boosters—attitudes, actions, and patterns of attention. As you read this chapter, be mindful of how this relates to an attitude, an action to take, or how we can channel our own or our child's attention. First, we'll start with the attitudes of a happy parent based on extensive interviewing. Then, we'll explore happiness and unhappiness in parenting, happiness boosters, and how attention relates to the health of the family (i.e. TV is very often an unhealthy focus of attention for families). Finally, we transition into evidence based techniques that improve the health and happiness of family life.

Let's start with the big question—what makes a happy parent? One of my research studies that served as a foundation for this book involved completing 45 comprehensive interviews with licensed professionals who work full time with parents and families. On aside, all these professionals were parents themselves. My interviewees consisted of licensed clinical psychologists, licensed professional counselors, social workers, and registered nurses. The interviewed professionals averaged 16 years of experience working with parents. These interviews were completed in Minnesota so there are geographical limitations to the qualitative data. Data that emerged from my semi-structured interviews provided insight into the attitudes of a happy parent. Each of the following gems recorded the highest percentage of responses.

### Appreciation and Learning

*Happy parents have an appreciation for professionals and display a willingness to learn from them.* This is important because parents who take on a life long journey of learning incorporate professional viewpoints into their communication with their children. This book title suggests that parents have the primary role and support professionals such as coaches, teachers, academic support staff, mentors, pastors, mental health professionals, licensed clinical psychologists, guidance counselors, neighbors, grandparents, aunts and uncles and friends all have a secondary role. You are your child's best psychologist, even without the professional working title. Interviews with licensed clinical psychologists said that appreciation and openness to learning were key for parents.

I worked with Louise recently who called me up to request help for getting her teenager out of her bedroom. She had a teenager who was refusing to leave her bedroom and listen to her mother and the experience had lasted more than 36 hours. On the phone, Louise spoke in a staggered state: "Isn't there anything you can do? I've been at this for hours! She won't talk to us and refuses to leave her bedroom!" Astounded myself, I tried to be of service, "Let me see if I can walk you through some steps that might help." As I brainstormed immediate and long-term solutions for her daughter, Louise was surprised that I couldn't immediately come to her house and solve the dilemma or provide some "magical" difference-making solution over the phone. While Louise expressed appreciation, she appeared to overly depend on others without trying to learn. She had difficulty differentiating short-term from long-term solutions and was flooded by the immediate turmoil. Subsequently, she came across as meek and helpless in the stressful moment. I personally had a lot of compassion for Louise. But, I also picked up the notion that her meekness appeared to be a problem for her opinionated daughter. And, overly dependent on secondary help appears to be a long-term problem for Louise. Depending on others is a problem with passive-aggressive and meek parents. Children and teenagers like Louise's daughter absolutely need parents who are direct communicators.

Balanced & Independent Life

Happy parents have a balanced life and report a high level of satisfaction in their life and in other relationships. This is critical for readers – a balanced life makes a great parent. We live in a time when anxiety and stress is an epidemic for young people. Overscheduling, academic pressures that start early, and subtle achievement demands are just some of the stress inducing challenges youth face. Some are losing the joys of childhood and forced into independence too quickly while others delay their independence—not learning how to do their laundry until well into college. In contrast, it is common for kids who lose a parent to death or divorce to take on some roles too early (i.e. cooking, laundry) and end up attempting to bring organization and leadership to their younger siblings before he or she is ready.

The antidote to many of the common stressors young people face is a balanced parent. A balanced person is a relaxed person in the face of high stress. A common question: "How do I stay balanced with house repairs, car repairs, diapers to change or purchase, taking the dog to the vet, soccer games, etc.?" The answer to obtaining balance is certainly not easy and new parents figure out a way through scheduling, communication, and seeking help. Consider Dr. Johnson, an orthopedic spine surgeon who was driven to see more and more patients until his own back and neck problems forced him out of work. His drive led him to succeed but also caused him to miss much of the last 10 years of his 16-year-old son's life. Unfortunately, Dr. Johnson worked 80 hours a week and missed out on a lot. No words from my psychology tool bag can alleviate guilt and regret. Dr. Johnson is realizing that he has learned a tough lesson about balance after being forced out of his unbalanced life.

*Happy parents have an emotional life that is independent of their child or teenager.* This is best captured by one social worker's comments, "They (healthy parents) are confident people. They are confident in their love for their child. They are confident in the child's lovability. They see the child as a separate individual from themselves."

## Consistency & Flexibility

*Happy parents are consistent and can demonstrate flexibility.* This balance is critical as many parents err on the side of being flexible. Consistency is interwoven throughout this book. It is a critical element in healthy parenting and reinforced in this research. Consider one mom who brought candy home all the time, but then would get mad because her son (non-athletic) would gain weight. Or, one social worker noted, "A parent didn't want her daughter to have caffeine but then would get angry when her father stopped her from buying orange jolt." The mother took the position, 'don't say 'no' to our daughter.' These examples of inconsistency reveal confusion, not flexibility. In stark contrast, flexibility entails wisdom marked by an ability to adjust on the journey of the child's development. As an obvious example, approaching high school, John doesn't need a star chart that helped him 15 years ago. Flexible parents adjust and grow in their parenting.

## Fostering Freedom and Independent Decision-Making

87% of the parents that were interviewed noted that over-involved parents on their case load tend to be involved in every decision. This may be helpful for young children. But, for college students to call Mom for advice on the type of notebook to use for note taking is beyond real. Yes, sometimes this is just a reason to connect. But, less self-efficacy on small decisions (i.e. what should I study tonight?) definitely is problematic. In response to a child asking basic 'what should I do' questions, many balanced parents hear this and respond, 'Are you kidding?'

Mom, let me say these aren't kids with special needs. These are accomplished high school graduates and fully functioning adults at Big 10 universities. But what happens in parent-child relationships for this insecurity over small things to become the norm? Something like this is a sign that young adults have not had enough freedom in their own decisions.

What were the other themes that emerged in the data about unhealthy parenting? Unhealthy parents are demanding, have low frustration tolerance, and are rarely satisfied.

Reflective Parents Process Grief

*Happy parents have successfully dealt with their own grief or guilt.* After Trent was married and began exploring some family of origin issues with his wife, he wanted to talk to his father about some difficult things in the past. Unfortunately, Trent walked into a locked door with steel locks. His father refused to engage in the discussion. He offered no details, dismissed Trent's interest in the past, and repeatedly exclaimed, "It's in the past, there's nothing we can do about the past." Research in the use of the Adult Attachment Interview suggests that unreflective parents provide scripted responses like, "It's in the past, there's nothing we can do about it." Reflective individuals are willing to work through tough issues and develop a coherent memory pattern about their past – both the good and the bad. Reflective parents can rationally discuss mistakes and parenting errors. They can say, "Yup, I wish I could have done it this way" and coherently articulate those other courses of action. What Trent needed was his father (and step-mother) to not only acknowledge errors but approach the past with coherence, while elaborating and explaining issues. Regrets are not the problem. Unprocessed grief or guilt with incoherent and scripted responses are the problem.

Unwillingness to discuss the past with humility robs individuals like Trent from a chance to experience further understanding and clarification about his upbringing. This is a normal desire, especially adult children who grew up experiencing a parent's divorce. Have you ever come across a person who takes something like the following stance, "Yeah, I wish we would have approached that situation differently. If I could do it again, I would do it this way." This is often a refreshing experience! This takes immense reflection on life. Most people have difficulty with this degree of introspection.

Many times, it's less about right and wrong and more about acknowledging the messy situations and the subsequent feelings. In situations of divorce when the mother gets custody of the children, it is not uncommon for the father to be spoken of in negative ways by the mother. Sometimes, shedding light (without assigning blame or criticizing) on what went on during those difficult years provides clarity. And let me say, as a caveat, life is short and letting sleeping dogs lie may be most helpful. Sometimes, it is better to just leave this stuff behind and let it stay dormant. That being said, in Trent's situation, discussing these matters and taking responsibility for things the father would have done differently is a springboard for wisdom. These types of conversations go best when love and wisdom are the goals. If this can be agreed upon as the goals with hearts in the right place, healing and bonding can result. If individuals can't cope, can't process, and only anger and resentment shows its ugly heads, then focusing on the here and now is the best course of action.

What is the real reason Trent's father was unable to discuss the past? His father is locked into unprocessed issues. He has never taken a personal inventory and reflected on both the helpful and positive ways he parented and the unhelp-

ful and negative ways he parented. Very often, the keys to these unprocessed issues or locked feelings is Trent's father unlocking how he himself was parented by
his own parents. This, of course, requires extensive reflectiveness. Only through
reflection are parents able to reveal a level of humility and humor about their
journey.

These discussions with parents can often be a bridge to reflections on
different ways to parent in particular situations. They also have the potential to
increase insight into how any of Trent's father's (or mother's) HURTS were passed
on to Trent. All of us are susceptible to HURTS that end up lingering in our relationships and having an impact on our parenting. HURTS are Human Unresolved
Responses to Trauma, those response patterns that develop in response to those
small T traumas. Rather than Large T Traumas (e.g. assaults, life threatening car
accidents, combat), it is those small Ts such as criticism (e.g. "You are so fat."
"You'll never amount to anything." "Melinda has such big feet.") that are most
common and do emotional damage to our minds and souls.

Some of the ways that this emotional damage manifests as HURTS include
self-centeredness, insecurity, inconsistency, cynicism, or disagreeableness. Consider Lee's father who's discussing a matter with his wife and daughter and turns
to Lee remarking, "Your opinion doesn't matter right now." Lee personalizes this
and generalizes it to everything. As a way to compensate, he forces his opinion on
others and becomes disagreeable in relationships. Lee had trouble maintaining
his work because this HURT stuck to him like glue. He lost his first two jobs out of
college because he was unnecessarily disagreeable. In therapy, Lee experienced
a breakthrough when he began to separate himself from his father's opinion and
learned to value his own opinion. He also learned to value coworkers without
fully agreeing or feeling that he needed to be disagreeable. In this example, disagreeableness was a result of emotional damage to the soul that affected how
Lee approached relationships.

While it is ideal that parents like Trent's and Lee's are willing to discuss
past events, it is important to not hide our feelings of powerlessness, helplessness and vulnerability when they don't. It is common for parents to not want to
discuss messy scenarios of the family past or small Ts that might be hard to face.
"Leaving it in the past" is usually a strategy in moving family life forward. When
this is a common choice, it is important to not stuff our feelings. Instead, expressing our feelings and losing the anger that builds a wall between us and others
keeps us mentally healthy. Very often, this is best accomplished by forgiveness.
Wisdom is balancing two key ideas—the past doesn't have to determine your
future but nothing should be swept under the rug.

Despite any disappointment from past walls, it is critical that these types
of walls don't form between us and our kids. Stuffing past HURTS can build a
wall between our parenting and our kids. A sure fire golden sign that we have
processed and expressed our own feelings is that feelings are fully welcome in
the family. Finding different ways to let go of unreleased resentments and grudges toward our own parents can help us NOT make the same mistakes with our

own children. Even if our parents are unwilling to discuss the messiness from the past, our healing from small Ts and unresolved issues results from processing past HURTS with willing others (i.e. including professionals), acceptance and forgiveness, letting go, and intentional effort to do things differently with our children—being affectionate, expressing our feelings, saying 'I am sorry,' allowing disagreement, explaining the rationale behind parental decisions, changing our minds, and allowing children to negotiate are examples of a renewed and recovered life.

## Lots to Learn from Parents with the Greatest Challenges

Happiness can be simply defined as raising normally developed healthy children. When it comes right down to it—a healthy child makes all the difference in the world. What about raising unhealthy children or children with significant disabilities? Raising these kinds of children is often a special calling and requires extraordinary love.

How do parents with the greatest challenges find happiness on the long roads of difficulty? Another study that was foundational for this book were interviews with 20 experienced parents of adult children with significant multiple disabilities. These parents have children who are grown up, so these parents have experienced the full gamut of life, but not the typical "get them through school and onto college" type of experience. Instead, they raised their children with immense challenges including intellectual disabilities (formerly mental retardation), psychosis, autism, intermittent explosive behaviors, uncontrollable seizures, genetic disorders such as microcephaly or Smith-Magenis, Tourette syndrome, and aggressive behavior were some of the difficulties these parents faced over the years.

As you can imagine, these parents were not on their first rodeo. Their degree of challenges out-distance most of us parents. Yes, every one of us has our own set of problems on our unique child raising journey. Those of us with a newborn struggling to get some sleep might find our situation more appetizing than the neighbor with three including a newborn. Synchronized napping is no doubt a tougher task with toddlers needing care. A parent struggling with one teenager may find her task significantly less daunting than her sister with three teenagers. Regardless, every journey is unique. We all know not to compare. But, can we help it when a friend is balancing a household of 12 children when we struggle to make lunches for two kids? And if we were to consider comparing our situation – most would agree that raising children with serious medical problems and disabilities like the above list is indeed the most challenging.

I worked with one mother whose son with severe sensory issues would race into his parent's bedroom at night beginning at the age of seven and attack them by hitting and biting and this went on for years. It became considerably more difficult into his pre-teen and teen years as he grew in strength. This ranks at the top of the list as the toughest nights of sleep that I've ever heard of. And, consider if child-raising involves relying on group homes for care and support and loving a child who is nonverbal but can never say "I love you" in return. This challenges any of our thoughts about what unconditional love truly is. Many parents are blessed to receive love and affection in return; but what if this never occurred? Could you love anyway?

I talk with these parents who loved anyway and sought nothing in return. There is wisdom to tap into when talking to experienced parents who have endured the pain of loss and the torment of children suffering with a variety of problems. Parents dream of having a child but when they do, they end up in the impossible situation of moving him to a group home because they are not capable of meeting the child's needs. Imagine visiting a group home on a regular basis worrying excessively and deeply desiring to connect with their child. One parent commented on her struggle from years past, "I learned from other parents in a support group that a strong effort is needed in transitioning my son. He left our home and went to Cambridge (Minnesota treatment facility) when he was 14. We drove up there twice each of the first six weeks and explained everything we could from his bedtime routine to his aversion to the color yellow. I knew that I would explain stuff enthusiastically that wouldn't be captured in their questionnaires."

There is so much richness in talking with these parents. Consider Sandy, a mother of a 25-year-old man with autism, bipolar disorder, and severe attacking and biting problems. The medicine that helped stabilize his mood the most caused him seizures. Without it, he bit staff recklessly. How about that scenario? A mother had to choose between seizures or biting the only people who could help her son. Yes, other medications were tried and staff implemented reinforcement plans and behavioral interventions, but that was a choice during a critical window of time. This was a medical and mental health ethical dilemma. The treatment team ended his doxepin (a tricyclic anti-depressant that caused him to have seizures) and his attacks became so vicious he was once again hospitalized for psychiatric reasons.

My interviews with parents like Sandy provided rich perspectives. One important theme that emerged in the interviews—Parents maintain healthy involvement by investing dedicated energy to balance doing whatever it takes to help their children. 70% of parents endorsed "passion" as essential in their advocacy efforts. As you can imagine, it can be an exhausting process if you place your child in a group home without assurance of the group home being a possibility long-term. Parents learned to stay involved in the ways that would help most. One dad said, "We learned the importance of staying involved. If there are any threats to funding, we felt free to write to our representatives making our voice heard. And, we did respectfully but passionately. We now do that on many levels besides our son."

Parents also acknowledged that some situations required more than passion, but letting go and trusting professionals. One parent stated, "We thought he couldn't get along with female staff. When my sisters, his aunts, would come over, he reacted strongly and resisted spending time with them. While we knew nothing bad had happened, we were aware that this problem had gone on for years. When he began living in a group home, we were convinced that female staff members were not going to work. We argued that our son's preference for male staff needed to be a requirement for the home. It took us some time to begin to realize that he could change. The coordinator convinced us that he could learn the skills needed to get along with different people. He was learning to trust and we were as well."

Another emerging theme from the data—Parents maintain healthy involvement by accepting help. One parent talked about the challenge of coming to this realization, "I heard from everybody that I couldn't be a parent and a therapist and a teacher. But, it wasn't until I realized it for myself. I actually was watching a sunset one evening and was reflecting on what was best for Fred. That is when I finally touched base with reality." Another mother was reflecting on how she came to the place of accepting help and improving her self talk, "It took me a while to realize that I didn't have to call every day to demonstrate my love. I am finally able to admit to people that it took years for me to realize that having a week go by without a visit or call didn't mean I was a bad mother." She stated that she was able to finally admit to herself that she 'was a good mother.'

These final comments stated by a mother of her son with disabilities may strike a chord for those of us parenting college students. I recently worked with seven colleagues across the country and we completed a groundbreaking study on the popular phenomenon known as "Helicopter Parenting." The term was popularized several years ago but had gone unstudied and lacked the scientific credibility until recently. 190 college students participated in a study that revealed some specific psychological problems experienced by college students who have helicopter parents. Even 10 years ago, helicopter parents were averaging up to 10.4 forms of communication (i.e. email, cell phone, text message) per week which doesn't serve the college student's independence or autonomy[1]. So, what are the problems with all this communication that people call reduced autonomy? Our research showing significant empirical evidence suggested that helicopter parenting is associated with low self-efficacy, alienation from peers, and lack of trust among peers. When individuals give me feedback about this research, it usually makes sense that helicoptered kids have less belief in their own abilities. But, it's usually followed up by the comment, "What about this peer alienation or peer mistrust?" Yes, peer connection as a buffer to peer alienation becomes a college goal. Kids experience feeling more alienated and are trusted less by peers. Yes – our kids' relationships start with parents letting go.

---

# WORDS OF WISDOM & STEPS FOR TAKING ACTION

- Happy parents are life-long learners, live a balanced life, are emotionally independent, and remain consistent.

- If you experienced a HURT from your family of origin, don't stuff your feelings of powerlessness, helplessness and vulnerability. Work through these issues. Draw a line in the sand and assure your children that their feelings are welcome in the family.

- Evidence of a resolved past includes: (1) Accepting and forgiving, (2) Letting go, and (3) Intentional effort to do things differently with our children—being affectionate, expressing our feelings, saying 'I am sorry,' allowing disagreement, explaining the rationale behind parental decisions, changing our minds, and allowing children to negotiate are examples of a renewed and recovered life.

- If you are a helicopter parent of a young adult, consider reducing the frequency of communication.

- Welcome your adult son or daughter's attempts to establish boundaries without reacting.

- What is the wisdom derived from parents with the greatest hardships in raising kids with immense difficulties? Happy parents love fully, even with nothing in return, are dedicated and passionate, and accept help.

---

## Is Parenting a Happy Endeavor?

Now that we've presented the research on the attitudes of "a happy parent," and the rich life lessons of those parents whose children have significant disabilities, let's get into the actions of happy families. Family happiness rituals are at the center of happy and content families. First, a question: Is parenting a happy endeavor? OF COURSE! Parenting is the best mission in life. But, why do we see unhappiness in the parenting process? Let's take a moment to discuss some of the unhappiness that you see in parents. Ample research shows that parenting reduces happiness from the perspective of hedonic pleasures but boosts meaning[2]. In other words, parents are constantly inconvenienced which results in more unhappiness. Parents experience discomfort frequently—from the baby's crying at 2 am to the toddler's temper tantrum in the middle of the library to your 13-year-old daughter's withdrawn behavior to your teenager's new driver's license. Parenting is also accompanied by less pleasure—from your last $20 bill handed to the teenager for dinner with the team after her basketball game to cleaning up your kid's vomit, instead of finishing your Marguarita and guacamole.

So, yes, the inconveniences, discomforts, and decreased pleasures get in the way of happiness. In contrast, meaningful moments and richer experiences increase. Sure, laying by the side of the pool is more pleasurable than cleaning up vomit. But every 90-year-old and centenarian will say the same thing, "enjoy every moment of it. It all goes by so fast."

Every parent can relate to Lori's recent hair pulling experiences. She comes into my therapy office pulling her hair because she "doesn't get any relaxation time." She described some scenarios that had us laughing. The laughter, life's best medicine, brought tears to her eyes and some much-needed emotional relief. When she had a minute to go to the bathroom on the previous day, her 7-year old son was using the dish sponge to clean his dirty shirt while helping his two-year old brother use the potty, as he is currently being toilet trained. As Lori comes out of her bathroom, she finds the dish sponge that was taken from the sink and now being dipped in the toilet water and drizzled throughout the tile floors of the house. As she is cleaning the house, she finds the guinea pig eating paint and marker that were thrown in the cage.

Are adults who choose parenting happier than those who choose not to parent? Philosophers may debate the definition of happiness here. Certainly, those who didn't go the way of parenting most likely had significantly less moments of being inconvenienced. I've talked with hundreds of 95 to 105 year olds and I've never met someone who regretted having children, even those in prison or estranged adult children for 20 years. While that might not be surprising, I've also met some centenarians without children and they all held regret for not having children. Even if they knew that it was medically impossible at the time, they still wish life would have been different for them. Let me just add that Sarah and I have some good friends who aren't parents and they are living happy lives making a difference for others. But, generally speaking, this book is not written for them. My bold and confident answer is YES! Parents have lived a much happier life!

I think the key to happy parenting is engaged parenting. Engaged parents are certainly happier than disengaged parents. In other words, engaged parents are those parents who take the time to instruct on how paint is not good for guinea pigs. Disengaged parents are intellectually and emotionally removed: they miss out on huge chunks of Sundays (or Saturdays) by golfing; they observe and comment on those observations more than intentionally discuss situations that just happened with their children. Metaphorically, disengaged parents are on the sideline rather than in the game. But, let's shift this discussion to our children and their happiness.

### "I Want My Child to Be Happy!"

When I give parenting talks and ask parents what they want most for their children's future, the majority will often say that they want their children to "be happy when they grow up." The question one inevitably asks is what kind of happiness will the child eventually want, or put from the perspective of the parent, what kind of happiness will a parent want for their child?

Some parents point to a happy marriage as the key criterion in determining happiness. If this is the case, a quick glance at one aspect of marriage research shows an interesting viewpoint. John Gottman, the foremost marriage expert, identified a 5:1 ratio of positive to negative exchanges during conflict as a winning formula for a happy marriage[3]. In other words, if your married son or daughter has five positive interactions to every one negative interaction during disagreements, then the probability is nearly 95% [very high] that he or she will keep the love alive and vibrant in their relationship. So, the question is how do we prepare young people to engage in winning marriage formulas now as a way to prepare them down the road?

When it comes to conflict resolution, one of the key factors in the use of this skill is perspective taking[4]. Some people develop their skill in perspective taking and get quite good at seeing things from another person's point of view. With practice, some become very good at viewing things from another angle. This is particularly difficult in stressful situations, but with practice, some people can become proficient at resolving conflicts when they arise. And, as you can guess, parents can play a significant role in the development of this skill. Families can develop these skills by engaging in debate practice and can start as early as 5 or 6 depending on maturity and other factors. Many of us driving parents know that back seat conflict surfaces repeatedly. This is an excellent chance to teach perspective taking, one person talking at a time, and other conflict resolution strategies. Both debate practice and conflict resolution prepare our children long-term.

Then there is the idea of a "happy career" or a vocational calling. "I want my child to enter a career that will make them happy." An alternative idea is assessing how happiness affects the "calling" as opposed to happiness resulting from the type of work. One study showed that cheerfulness data obtained from college freshmen in 1976 was correlated with increased income around 20 years later. When salaries of this group were examined, the least cheerful people were earning $50,000 a year and the most cheerful individuals were earning $65,000 a year, a 30 percent higher salary[5]. Even when other complicated variables were reviewed such as parental jobs/income and chosen occupations, results still suggested that cheerful 18-year olds made more money as they approached 40. Why is this the case? Results suggest that attitudinal factors influence performance and therefore positively affects promotions and raises. And, as you can guess, parents can play a significant role in the development of attitudinal skills – of having a good attitude. But, attitude is best modeled; when the laundry is undone, rooms are a mess, the in-laws are on their way, and the kids are yelling, can you handle the situation gracefully, patiently, and positively?

150

Parents can approach these tasks one step at a time, intentionally appreciating the moment, and mindfully engaging. Despite the stress with seven things on a parent's mind, the process of mindfully engaging includes noticing our breathing and taking in the moment. "Inhaling, 'I breathe in this moment,' exhaling "I accept this moment." One mindfulness grounding technique that can be used while performing tasks is noticing five things you see, four things you hear, three things you touch, two things you smell, and one thing you can taste. Being in the moment with our kids helps us to convey kindness and appreciation. Our kids need us to generate fondness for each other during stressful times. Being positive, kind, warm, and expressing appreciation for our children builds up the positive attitude in our children.

So, it sounds like communication skills and cheerfulness lead to more happiness (and additional benefits like job promotions and income) for our children. What else? What specifically about money? A 30% higher salary is shown in the cheerfulness study. Lots of parents hope that our children will have the money that they need to accomplish their goals and vision for their lives. Most importantly, raise our grandchildren without our help.

Most people link money with happiness to some degree. Let's briefly review some of the research on money. We have all heard the stories of tragic life scenarios following lottery winnings. People win huge fortunes but then flounder a short time later – they lose their fortunes and relationships. Of course, these isolated examples are usually the ones we read in the newspapers, magazines, and websites. Despite hearing about the unfortunate stories, this doesn't lead us to reject inheritances or lottery fortunes. Are there any of us that would? The broader question is --- Does money equal happiness? There are several studies by economists that demonstrate that increases in sums of money (e.g. lotteries or inheritances) correlate with significant increases in happiness on average, despite those isolated bad examples of windfalls ruining lives[6]. Other results show that these individuals also experience less unhappiness than they had before the windfall. Usually, the level of happiness returns to the pre-inheritance happiness level a few months after the initial happiness increase. However, money can be deceiving. There are several reasons behind those who report increases in happiness. In another study, 49 rich people (a study of the Forbes list of millionaires) were studied and the specific contributing factors to their life satisfaction and happiness were not the things usually associated with more money: vacation homes, expensive cars, yachts, and all that comes with extravagant lifestyles. The types of things mentioned were similar to the things us regular folk would identify: family relationships, helping people and making a difference, and meaningful work and accomplishments.

More money doesn't explain why some poor people are happy and some wealthy people are not. Contentment is best explained when our income is sufficient for our desires. When our income exceeds our desires, then an individual is more likely going to be content. Rich people whose spending exceeds their means "feel poor," and people with a low-income who spend within their budget are content.  Research shows that attitude toward money is more critical for a happy lifestyle than net worth.  A winning attitude towards money includes spending within a budget and having happiness that is independent of income.  An unproductive attitude entails spending that exceeds a budget and an overemphasis on materialism and stuff money buys.  The factors most linked with happiness measured in many different ways include a person's attitude.  Positive attitudes influence contentment and clarity that we are spending within our budget.  A second significant factor is generosity, traditionally a classic happiness action.  And, as you can guess, parents can play a significant role in the development of generosity.  Finding ways to give to others and teaching children to give reinforces generosity.

## WORDS OF WISDOM & STEPS FOR TAKING ACTION

- For the sake of long-term relationship health, practice perspective taking during sibling conflict and family meetings.  As a matter of practice, could you please explain the other's point of view?

- For the sake of developing long-term positive work attitudes, parents encourage cheerful work habits and model positive attitudes about going to work regardless of job or day of the week [Eliminate TGIF language that suggests more love for work on one day of the week]

- Start "giving" at an early age.  Teach children that money consists of saving, spending, and giving.  Reinforce and model generosity as a regular part of family life.

- Teach children that true wealth is in relationships, not money.

*To get the full value of joy you must have somebody to divide it with.*
*- Mark Twain*

<u>Building Buffering Strengths</u>

Perspective taking and a healthy attitude towards finances are just two of the effects of something deeper in who your child is becoming.  Your child's happiness flows out of a depth of who they are in their character.  This book definitely teaches a mental tool box that can significantly change a teenager's interpretations of their experiences and happiness.  But leveraging character occurs

152

at a deeper level and starts early. Lessons taught early on such as "catching lies," or "this family never steals," establish a character road map. Family mantras like "a Jones never cheats, lies, and steals" is critical. Honesty as the best policy, both in how we teach, but also in how we model, sets up our teenagers to have secure identities perceived by others to be rock solid and completely reliable in all that they are and do. Secure boys and girls have "rock solid" character.

In the field of psychology, leaders of a positive psychology movement have researched those deeper things that we call character. One of those leaders is Martin Seligman, Ph.D., former president of APA and professor of University of Pennsylvania. In his last column as APA president in 1998, he wrote about building strengths as one of the key factors in helping people. In other words, great progress in changing others' lives is made when we can instill hope, draw out courage, and encourage others by pulling out inner strengths such as perseverance and grit.

How does this relate to parenting? Our goal is to spend a lifetime instilling hope, drawing out courage, and reinforcing persevering character strengths. Shaping character is central to parenting. Rather than being disengaged observers, parents need to impart, instruct, develop, invest, and shape. Youth who experience engaged parents end up with secure attachments, a healthy reinforcement history, openness to taking healthy risks with boldness, approach life with optimism, and maintain vision and purpose for their lives. Engaged parents address issues of stealing, lying, dishonesty, deception, and corruption at the smallest levels. Engaged parents shape character at the core of who they are and blanket them with unconditional love. Most importantly, engaged parents teach children to live reflective lives and facilitate a relationship with God as central to who they are.

When I directed a day training and habilitation (DT&H) program for adults with intellectual disabilities and challenging behavior from 2001-2006 in Minneapolis, Minnesota, I provided leadership for 25 staff including two coordinators, seven supervisors, and several program trainers. A few years later, I coordinated a PTSD program and provided leadership for social workers and therapists serving veterans at the VA Medical Center in Detroit, Michigan. These two work environments couldn't be more different — from clients unable to live independently to emotionally wounded warriors who fought for our ability to live independently. However, in both situations, it was easy to emphasize symptoms and behavior problems at the expense of drawing out the treasure in each individual. In both these environments, we changed the culture by incorporating character strength programs. Staff were encouraged to identify and document strengths in clients based on a list of character strengths. Change didn't happen quickly but positivity increases over time. Whether the environment is a school, a hospital, a rehabilitation program, a YMCA, or foster homes, character strength programs that draw out strengths and positive personality characteristics is a critical necessity for youth. But shaping character goes beyond perceived personality characteristics like outgoingness. Shaping character involves taking personal responsibility, learning to make choices that garner respect, enduring difficulty and hardship with patience and courage, and the list goes on. But, programs that involve shaping character and identifying and reinforcing character strengths are most effective when positive people engage in positivity with intentionality.

A key point is that when we look for the treasure in others, it influences them to look for the treasure in themselves. The truth reveals itself time and time again; in the end, we reap what we sow, and those who sow seeds of positivity and strength end up reaping positive attitudes and strengths. Think about it, one of the benefits of positivity, pleasantness, and encouragement is an encouraged, positive, and pleasant son or daughter. You might say, "Not my teenager." If we sow negativity, we reap negativity. The best replacement behavior for nagging is gratitude. Gratitude is the most efficient strategy for strength finding. As parents' gratitude increases, and verbal expressions of gratitude, so too does an individual's compassion, congeniality, helpfulness, kindness, and positive teamwork. Research shows that grateful teenagers transitioning into adulthood are more likely to lead happier, healthier, friendlier, better adjusted, more loving and successful lives.

From a parenting perspective, parents lose sight of positives when overwhelmed by negatives. Every parent is susceptible to becoming overwhelmed by their child's symptoms and behavior problems. It is common for parents of children of all ages to become overwhelmed by behavior – hyperactivity, irrational decisions, back talking, or sleep problems. Rather than draw out the treasure in each son or daughter, and sow goodness, loving kindness, and pleasantness, this overwhelm leads parents to overemphasize symptoms and behavior problems and place less emphasis on the strengths of their kids. The principle of reap what you sow is significant in the minds of parents. Whatever you focus on expands in your consciousness. If you sow negative thinking repeatedly into your perspective, it is only natural that the filter of your mind will see what's not going well in your son's homework habits, athletic discipline, or efforts in relationships. Such thinking only leads to greater negativity and greater ingratitude to our children. Just like a clinic, a hospital, or a school, identifying strengths is a positive and refreshing change our culture needs. And, most importantly, it will be a refreshing change that your family needs.

Being a Pearl Finder

At my bachelor's party in 2002, I will never forget the encouragement I received from a friend who encouraged me to be a pearl finder in all the areas of my life. These words of wisdom are perfect for parents raising teenagers. Finding pearls is critical for parents often inundated and overwhelmed by typical teenager behavior. Finding pearls in the face of lying, manipulation, teenage tempers, and various other complex behaviors can be difficult[7]. Establishing a culture of honor prior to teenage years makes a difference. Remember – rather than becoming embittered, hardened, and distant, sowing into our children the capacity to express fondness and gratitude will pay huge dividends. And, it is never too late to start pearl finding.

Since the late 1990s, a classification of character strengths and virtues has been researched and developed. The Classification of Character Strengths and Virtues is the result and it provides a foundation for parents to become pearl finders[8]. As pearl finders, parents can help children find true happiness, which is found in a virtuous life. The following is a list of virtues and their categorized strengths.

- Wisdom: Creativity, Curiosity, Good Judgment & Critical Thinking, Love of Learning, Perspective & Sharing Wisdom.
- Courage: Bravery & Valor, Perseverance & Persistence, Honesty / Authenticity & Integrity, Zeal / Enthusiasm & Vigor.
- Interpersonal Skills: Love & Valuing Close Relationships, Sharing & Caring, Kindness / Generosity / Nurturance & Niceness – doing favors and good deeds; & Social and Emotional Intelligence
- Justice: Teamwork & Loyalty, Fairness, and Leadership.
- Temperance: Forgiveness, Humility, Prudence, & Self-Regulation / Self-Control
- Transcendence: Appreciation of Beauty and Excellence [Awe, Wonder] and Noticing Excellence in Others, Gratitude, Hope, Optimism, Humor, and Playfulness; Spirituality [Faith & Purpose].

<u>Strategies Toward Pearl Finding Include Going Against Your Own Reinforcement History</u>

Parents will ask, "How do I find pearls when my daughter tells me I'm the worst mother in the world?" "I hear 'you're a bitch' on a regular basis!" Another overwhelmed and desperate mother exclaimed, "She screams and swears. This is not the Godly daughter we raised. She is better than this. My women's group prays for her. But something happened when we sent her to that public school." Another mother described her attempted intervention with her daughter diagnosed with bipolar disorder and ADHD; she would engage in 2-3 hour arguments twice a week with her daughter in an attempt to change her mind and this went on for years. For our children with whom we love with all of our hearts, it is easy to become enmeshed with their behaviors (i.e. disordered eating, paranoia, cutting, defiance) and find it arduous to name positives. These may trigger our own issues and lead us to withdraw.

The answer to emotionality, hostility, and erratic fluctuations isn't disengagement and parental withdrawal. An understandable but unfortunate coping strategy for parents is to withdraw. In fact, I've seen faithful parents withdraw and pray saying, "I will trust in God. There is nothing more I can do." Maintaining a neutral position while remaining engaged is the best stance. Neutrality means not reacting and staying calm. Remaining engaged is the best stance and is critical to helping your son or daughter get through this critical window of development. It is during these moments when parents are tested. In my own life, I grew up around a lot of anger with my step-father. My anger issues stem from childhood, and this anger carried over into my own family. Although I've worked hard to reduce the anger and have made good progress, my battle isn't finished and remains a life-long challenge. For parents who struggle with this vice like myself, neutrality may be the most important objective for a healthy and happy family. In the face of emotionality, a focus on pearl finding can help ease the emotional tension.

I also grew up with a lot of fear because of the anger. I never knew when I was going to be hit or come face to face with anger. Naturally, this results in feelings of rejection. It can be disheartening for kids to be afraid to leave their bedrooms until their mom comes home from work. These emotions such as fear or anger will definitely be activated or triggered when we are faced with the "hard stuff" that goes with our own parenting or the "hard stuff of life" that we mistakenly bring home to the family. Whatever is happening, in the face of these emotions, parents can focus on pearl finding with their own children to ease these feelings.

Pearl finding can ease some of the difficulties if it is done with integrity and honesty. While teenagers lack fully developed neurobiology resulting in deficient maturity to discern and self-regulate, their ability to read authenticity is usually a strength. The last thing they want is "fake compliments" or pseudo-positives. Neutrality as a parent involves staying engaged but not "sucked in." Taking a neutral stance involves not yelling back while communicating expectations calmly. Evidence of a parent maintaining perspective despite the current problems is being able to pearl find – identify strengths and positives and speak these into the lives of their children. Selfish parents are unable to move past their hurts and speak good things about their children. Thus, if our own parents came from a very difficult background that was emotionally abusive, angry, shaming or critical, it is common for these parents to struggle in moving past these hurts. It was a tough task for these parents to focus on what is good about their own children. Very often in life, we can get stuck and kids inherit the pain. Selfless parents, or those parents making a concerted effort to focus on their kids, are able to move past these hurts and parent based on what is good about their children. Unfortunately, some parents never do this until the children have grown into adulthood; by this time, it's too late. I will be the first to say that God can do anything and relationship healing is always possible, but no restoration with an adult child can restore what was lost in childhood.

Sometimes, overwhelmed parents are limited in their ability to articulate character strengths toward their sons and daughters. Developing selflessness is not easy. Based on personal experience, I will be the first to admit how much of a challenge it is. While it's hard, purpose in parenting helps us get outside of ourselves and speak strengths to our children.

Are you a forgiving person? Do you hold grudges toward your children? Are you slow to let things go? Is it difficult for you to ignore an offense or problem solve and let go? Do you have long-standing bitterness and resentment toward your children that has built up over years of reinforcement? Are there layers of bitterness and hardness that has established a wall in your thinking that prevents an ongoing experience of gratitude and affection? If your answer is "yes" to any of these questions, forgiveness may be your answer to help you engage in pearl finding.

Have you worked through your own issues so you don't make the same mistakes that your parents made? If you struggle with anger and fear or other emotions that are rooted in childhood, have you worked through these issues to find healing? Have you taken the time to draw a line in the sand and officially end the generational dysfunctions in your family line? Have you taken the time to experience the healing you need so that you can find pearls? If you have experienced abuse and rejection, have you taken the time to process this experience? Have you taken the time to fully forgive your parents or a particular parent? Have you experienced freedom so you can take ownership of your own stuff without resentments or bitterness? If your answer is "no" to any of these questions, take action now with a therapist or a counselor. You will want to experience healing so you can engage in pearl finding with your own children.

Establishing New Family Traditions & Rituals

In addition to strength finding, family traditions and new rituals also reinforce happiness. It is not uncommon for parents in their pursuit of a breakthrough and desire for changes in their family systems to establish new rituals. Creating new rituals is a time honored American tradition, particularly as New Year's resolutions. In contrast to three-week diet plans, establishing new family rituals can make a difference in improving the quality of relationships when strength finding is a focus.

Honoring is a ritual that can make a huge difference for families. When I was a director of an agency from 2001-2006, one of the positive changes we made in our culture was incorporating a tradition of honoring a supervisor on the anniversary of their employment. Other supervisors were invited to speak positives about their colleague on their important day. When the day arrived, we honored the supervisor in my office at our 7:30 am Friday morning meeting. Some supervisors squirmed, particularly if they didn't feel like they had a close relationship with that colleague. Others spoke about some positive aspect of their work performance that they appreciated. And, occasionally, our group struck gold when a colleague spoke from his or her heart about the treasures in the other person. Yes, sometimes this process of "honoring" was fake, sometimes it was forced, and once in a while, it was sincere. As the director, I didn't wait for the "right time" or the "right office feeling" or the "right feeling of camaraderie" to make this activity happen. Instead, it was a consistent part of the program that supervisors came to expect as a part of our positive culture. Of course, this led to some planning with some individuals. As time went by, individuals began to plan and prepare to speak positivity. Naturally, this encouraged us to learn to perceive positives in others more. More attention was given to positive qualities in others.

In 2006, upon my departure, I was honored to receive a BBQ lunch with my favorite ribs [Rudolphs, Minneapolis] in the midst of 14 colleagues: seven supervisors and key leaders, coordinators, other directors from two other agencies, the HR coordinator, the business administrator, and the executive director and owner. During the lunch, each person took time to honor me with positive words. The experience was quite moving. I share this experience not to draw attention to anything that I did well during my time; I certainly had my strengths as well as my weaknesses. And, I humbly appreciated the way each person was able and willing to overlook my weaknesses and articulate my strengths in a positive manner. The ability of my colleagues to articulate positively shared experiences spoke loudly about the strong and positive characters of each of my colleagues. Certainly, my life is better having worked in a social service non-profit agency with wonderful colleagues concerned about relationships. But, the lunch was an event of magnitude for me and indeed provided me an unforgettable life lesson. In addition to hearing positive things about things I accomplished or differences I made that was a great source of encouragement for me, the lunch provided evidence of how building a culture of honor can bring about significant changes and positive outcomes in relationships among colleagues. I never could have planned to be honored by 14 professional colleagues in such a moving way. Again, I remain deeply grateful for that moment in my life; but, the honoring had less to do with me, and more to do with the culture of honor that was facilitated over the years. If you build a culture of honor, people are shaped and respond to that culture. This example demonstrates the power of a culture of honor and is exactly the kind of thing families should implement. Similar to honoring a supervisor on the anniversary of their employment, families should honor children at set times.

*The deepest principle in human nature is the craving to be appreciated.* – William James

A culture of honor can be developed even more effectively within families with the obvious personal benefits compared to a work environment. Here are some ways to establish a permanent set of routines for all family members to become pearl finders and establish a culture of honor within the family:

1) On birthdays—beyond birthday cake and ice cream and presents and other traditions, family members take time to honor their child or sibling. Parents lead by example by taking time to specifically "Honor" the family member by speaking positively about their character strengths. Many times, attention is placed on accomplishments. Experts recommend drawing attention to their response to changes from the past year, overcoming adversity, and other interior qualities. In other words, it is easy to draw attention to achievements such as the excellent report card or the two goals scored in one game last fall. An even better area to place attention on is shared experiences (i.e. "we had so much fun

talking on the Ferris wheel last month.") And the best form of honoring is taking time to draw out personal strengths and speaking to the treasures in the son's or daughter's life.

In a culture of honor, brothers and sisters are trained to honor their siblings. As they do, practice will accelerate their pearl finding skills. As they mature, positives will become more meaningful and deeper beyond "you have nice hair." Sometimes squirming, and superficial or memorized comments are all part of the process, but the family culture of honor deepens with love, respect, and expressing goodness over time.

> *How we talk to each other reflects the quality of our relationships*
> *as well as the depth of our character.*
> - Dan Allender & Tremper Longman

2) Another time to express honor is on Mother's Day and Father's Day—similar efforts are made to express love and how much the particular parent means to the other family members. Going one step further, time is taken to speak to the internal qualities of the parent. In married households, the father takes the lead on Mother's Day and vice versa. With effort, single parent homes can facilitate this process as well. An emphasis is placed on gratitude for the relationships. Reflecting on favorite memories and experiences from the past year increases positive emotion and bonding. These reflections give life meaning, purpose, and passion.

3) On a regular basis, parents inform children that they are proud of who they are. While accomplishments are important, attention is placed on unconditional support and care. The comment, "I'm so proud of you" often follows accomplishments. This is normal and typical parenting. A problem with this approach is when these words are only spoken after achievements. When parents are glued to the "I'm proud of you" statements that are only spoken post-achievement, it reinforces the conditional love phenomena. One of the parenting goals is to emphasize unconditional love and being proud of who your children are, not just what they accomplish. Of course, it is normal to be thrilled for your child's accomplishments. Let me say this here --it is common for parents to react if anyone implies that they should deemphasize accomplishments; they will quickly point out that their own parents gave little attention to their spelling tests and athletic exploits and they plan to reverse the trend. As Bill sadly shared, "We won the Illinois state baseball championship and my dad missed it as he was still more concerned about drinking." So, yes, we absolutely are there for our children at every volleyball match and music recital that we can be and remain their biggest cheerleaders. But, expressing how proud of our kids we are must go beyond the

post-achievement moment and extend into ordinary life. To elevate our children, building up who they are is much more important than what they know or what they do.

4) Children are regularly told how loveable they are. Intermittent statements: "You are worth it!" "You are so precious!" "You are loveable!" "I am so proud of who you are." In addition to hearing how proud of them we are, they need to hear that they are lovable and good enough. Positive comments are regularly shared with their children. "You are a wonderful boy." "You are a wonderful girl." "I love you so much!" "I value who you are." Acceptance is a significant characteristic of a family that builds a culture of honor. When children feel accepted for who they are, this has a significant influence on their internal working model—how they see themselves and how they fit in with others. I've trained therapists throughout the country and I will often ask the seminar group the following question – "How many of you are currently working with someone on your current caseload whose father told them that they aren't good enough?" At every single talk, the majority of the hands go up when I ask this question. The children of America need to hear from their parents that they are "enough" and they are "good enough."

## WORDS OF WISDOM & STEPS FOR TAKING ACTION

1. Be a pearl finder for your children. Find specific treasures about your children and draw them out on a regular basis.

2. Identify and reinforce character strengths. Reinforce honesty, kindness, generosity, teamwork, fairness, humility and self-control.

3. Establish a culture of honor within the family and create new rituals in the family system. Teach children to be pearl finders with each other. Establish a routine and train family members to honor each other on birthdays, key holidays, celebrations of accomplishments, and other momentous occasions.

Happiness Theory

Character strength finding, establishing new family rituals, and building a culture of honor can strengthen the family happiness levels. Now – let's look at some of the other happiness strategies and habits that can bolster families.

According to Sonja Lyubomirsky's work, research suggests that 50% of the differences among people's happiness levels are a result of genetically determined set points[9]. These set points are compared to set points for physical set points such as weight disposition. Some people have a skinny disposition and their food consumption doesn't change their set point, which appears to be genetically related. Many of us have met people who have a "dream" type of metabolism. Others, like me, have to work at portion control, superfood consumption, eliminating processed foods, and minimize added sugar and useless carbohydrate intake.

Happiness set points work in a similar way. The implications of this happiness research is like genes for intelligence or cholesterol, the degree of our innate set points governs our level of happiness. In Lyubomirsky's research findings, 10% of happiness is determined by life circumstances. And, many know that significant lifestyle changes can bring cholesterol ranges into ideal ranges. These types of behavior changes account for the other 40% of what determines happiness, according to this theory. Our intentional activity, our thinking and behavior patterns, control our level of happiness. Research in education has recently shown that in the right environment, an IQ score can increase by one standard deviation. I have seen kids in the inner city perform in the borderline IQ range with an IQ of a 75. After assessing these kids, it is common for psychologists to come away thinking that if this child was raised in a healthy family – books read regularly, family dinners, TVs out of the bedroom, and regular family meetings – then this child's IQ of approximately 100 would be in the normal range. If this can happen for IQ, why not for happiness? Families that produce a positive environment of frequent laughter, resilient attitudes, positive strength finding, and a culture of honor can raise happiness for children by more than one standard deviation.

Thus, 50% of happiness is our genetic set points, 10% is the right circumstances, and 40% entails intentional activities that are in our control. Do you believe this idea? So, whether you agree and believe that 40% is in your control or it is easier for you to believe that 100% of your happiness is in your control, it helps to identify what those choices are that increase happiness. The following is a sample of thinking and behavior choices that studies show happy people do on a regular basis.

- Extensive time is devoted to family and friends; they believe that the quality of their lives is dependent on the quality of their relationships.

- Gratitude is expressed on a regular basis.

- They help their coworkers and are service-oriented. They deliberately find ways to help people with specific service-oriented actions.

- They are able to live in the present moment and savor life's pleasures.

- Optimism is applied to their visions for their future.

- They hold deep commitments to lifelong goals and values.

- They smile and are pleasant with others, are sociable, and are affectionate[10].

- They spend time in prayer, worship, and personal reflection.

> "When one door of happiness closes, another opens, but often we look so long at the closed door that we do not see the one that has been opened for us.  - Helen Keller

Breakthroughs Bring About Profound Change

These determinants of happiness are within the realm of choice and can certainly be taught to young people.  In the last 20 years, each of these happiness ideas—gratitude, present-centered living, savoring, optimism, service—have been researched and supported in comprehensive studies on strategies that help people become happier.  It is common for personal breakthroughs in high school or college when doors close and windows open.  Some examples include changes in majors based on an epiphany about one's future, relationship breakups or startups, graduate school acceptance letters, or some other bend in the road of life.

Let me dive into two quick personal stories.  The first has to do with my personal breakthrough when I had to adjust to the end of a dream at the age of 20.  For many years, I dreamed of playing college basketball and tried for two years but was unable to make it. During my second year, my determined focus led to dehydration, weight loss, and a hospitalization due to pneumonia.  I had a touching moment with my dad at the hospital after the second week of tryouts when he delivered the heartbreaking news that I was cut from the team.  I made the best out of a personal heartbreak as I engaged as a practice player, volunteered as a manager, and engaged as a videographer and broadcaster all while I worked on my game.  But, I eventually had to accept the inevitable.  During my third year, I was forced to accept a different plan.  I could acknowledge that I wasn't good enough and say it with confidence.  Of course, it was very hard at first but accepting and letting go was a huge breakthrough.  What made it most difficult was that my personal identity revolved around basketball.  Broadening my perspective felt like taking a step into the unknown.

A second breakthrough involved a change in my major.  I went into college with dreams of being a broadcast journalist.  I loved basketball but I loved and deeply appreciated broadcasting basketball and all sports.  As a young boy, I walked around my house on Churchill Drive in Bolingbrook, Illinois announcing baseball and basketball games in their entirety.  I developed my unique style and appreciated my favorite broadcasters of my youth: Vin Scully, Harry Caray, Steve Stone, and Johnny "Red" Kerr.  My favorite announcer was long-time NBA and Chicago Bulls announcer, Jim Durham; Michael Jordan texted to ESPNChicago.com's Melissa Isaacson about Durham when he passed away a few years ago, "The voice of champions, I will miss him."

During the summer after my second year in college, I had an epiphany on the back of Raspberry Mountain behind Pikes Peak in Divide, Colorado.  My knowing context was disrupted and I experienced some newness in my consciousness.

I experienced a profound change in what I wanted to do in my studies. As a result, the second step in my journey was my decision to change my major from broadcasting to psychology. I was inspired and later motivated to see if I could learn the path to happiness and make an influence in others' lives. I wanted to understand every strategy under the sun and every nugget of wisdom that leads to happiness. Initially, my steps included investing in the best of everybody who published self-help audio tapes/CDs and books from Zig Ziglar to Anthony Robbins. Naturally, my college studies led me to study psychoanalysis with Freud and Adler, humanism with Maslow and Rogers, behaviorism with Skinner and cognitive behaviorism with Ellis and Beck. I wanted to study the inner-workings of the interior minds of people and understand what makes people do what they do and gives them fulfillment and happiness. As a liberal arts college, I was also positively affected by great thinkers such as Aristotle, Plato, and Thomas Aquinas. My father is an Emmanuel Kant expert and philosopher of moral education. While our interests had different paths, his critical thinking skills definitely had a significant influence on me as I studied the field of psychology and deepened my ideology on the best ways to help people. My search for understanding happiness eventually led me to my faith encounter experience in 1997. The end of my dream, a change in my major, and my faith encounter was my unique path. This is just one of thousands of different paths young adults take. Victories are in the breakthroughs.

Be Ready for Breakthroughs

During adolescence and young adulthood, the experience of breakthroughs has significant potential for bringing about noteworthy personal changes. Some adolescents or young adults experience God in a profound way. A spiritual experience is described as a conversion or a transformation experience in life. In the late 1990s, thousands and thousands of young adults ran to the Brownsville Revival in Pensacola, Florida and experienced profound encounters with God.

Some understand happiness in a different way, transitioning to a desire to help others achieve happiness. It might be a "aha moment" when Michelle realizes that she wants to be a teacher as she realizes education is the path for freedom and happiness. For another college student, the epiphany happens when Geoff can see clearly that his major will be mechanical engineering. Some transition from a focus on self to a focus on others based on a study abroad trip, a major service or international volunteer trip, or a significant tutoring or volunteer experience in college. Like untrained teenagers, young adults are not experts at thinking about others but this can change based on a profound personal experience. I have a friend who calls college an expensive extension of adolescence – a stage that is often criticized (and well validated) for more focus on self than others – narcissism, self-centeredness, and high self-esteem that can increase self-focus. So, yes, it can take young people awhile to come to a point in life where their vision is bigger than themselves. Change takes time but for some, it can be spontaneous or a surprise. I've never seen a college student return unchanged after a missionary trip or a study abroad trip.

<u>A Simple Positive Discovery in Breakthroughs Has Been Attentionality</u>
  In 1998, the field of positive psychology was established to emphasize and strengthen what is already good about people including personal break-throughs that individuals experience, rather than the traditional medical model of reducing what is already "bad" or "unhealthy" about people. The field of positive psychology is not intended to replace treatment, but to add to it. There are several research questions that are guiding the field in a vast array of areas in this entire area of building what is already good in people. How do we teach children resilience? How do we build grit and self-control? How can the Army use resiliency training to become as psychologically fit as it is physically fit? What are the neural mechanisms of human flourishing? Does experiencing hardship and troubles leave us in a better place than we were before? What can we learn about psychological and medical well-being based on language used in social media like Facebook or Twitter?
  In the last two decades, we have also discovered specific strategies that are based on randomized clinical trials that improve the happiness of individuals. One of the thinking strategies involves understanding the role of attention and its influence on our perceptions and interpretations of experience. This idea of attention is key in being open to breakthroughs.

<u>Essential Ingredients of Using Attention</u>
  The third A of happiness is patterns of attention. One of the essential psychological ingredients for young people is attention. Adolescents are inundated with Instagram messages, how many Facebook friends and likes they receive, excessive texting, tweets, and other data points that increase distractibility and reinforce inattention. How attention is valued, cherished, used, and shifted is a critical component of a young person's degree of positive psychology in their interior life.
  Some psychologists suggest that happiness is determined by how one allocates their attention[11]. Unhappiness results from a misallocation of one's attention. As a result, enhancing happiness is as much about attending to positives rather than negatives. A beginning step might involve writing up a spreadsheet with all the positives in life and all the negative things in life and finding ways to place attention on the positives. Talking through a plan or writing out a plan on how to focus on life's positives can help shift the attention. This is a simple but effective strategy used with adolescents in therapy.
  Savoring is a classic happiness booster that helps people pay attention. Savoring is essentially all about attention. The next time something good happens—stopping, taking a few seconds, and appreciating what just happened in the moment helps people savor. Research shows that people who do take time to smell the roses are happier. This is a particularly difficult concept for teenagers nowadays because each moment is captured on the smartphone and posted to Instagram or Facebook. Sometimes, that "great" moment is missed because of the obsession of the moment capture and the social media post. In addition, sa-

voring one's own moment is hard for teens because of "FOMO" – Fear Of Missing Out. While posting, they review where others are at and what they are doing and compare contrast leads them to believe that others "have it better," or "are doing something I'd rather be doing." The booster effect of savoring is strengthened when individuals pay attention to what they are doing rather than what others are doing in other places. Research found that individuals who regularly took notice of something beautiful in their own experiences were 12% more likely to say they were satisfied with their lives[12].

> Research has shown that slowing down in the busyness of life and appre-
> *The art of being wise is the art of knowing what to overlook.*
> *- William James*

ciating good things can boost happiness. Depressed individuals who take a few minutes once a day to savor and take delight in something that they usually hurry through (i.e. eating) showed increases in happiness[13]. To enhance the experience, individuals can write down ways in which they experience the event differently and how it felt compared with their usual "rushing" through activities.

Over 200 undergraduates were screened for levels of happiness, and the upper 10% (the "extremely happy") were compared with the middle and bottom 10%. Extremely happy students experienced no greater number of objectively positive life events, like excellent test scores or positive relationships, than did the other two groups[14]. You might expect that these students had accumulated more positive events, achievements, or relationships but they didn't. They must have had more money? No, that wasn't a factor. The difference was how they placed attention; their thoughts and their attention were centered on the positive events. This research supports the old rational emotive therapy conclusion from the 60s – it is not the activating event, but your thoughts about the event. Yet, rather than changing thoughts, the emphasis is on shifting attention.

Shifting attention is critical because tunnel vision can become a habit. Professors at Harvard University found that tunnel vision, which helps people excel in some areas, can have a drastic effect on other areas[15]. In the teaching of classes, one professor noted, "I discovered the tax auditors who are the most successful sometimes are the ones that for eight to fourteen hours a day were looking at tax forms, looking for mistakes and errors. This makes them very good at their job, but when they started leading their teams or they went home to their spouse at night, they would be seeing all the lists of mistakes and errors that were around them." These professors observed that the auditors were "stuck in a negative Tetris Effect. We're finding the same thing with lawyers. Lawyers have three times the level of depression of most of the other occupational groups in America. We discovered that many of the lawyers were coming home and started deposing their children or thinking about their quality time with their loved ones in terms of quantified billable hours."

Research has shown that by practicing the shifting of attention, we can get unstuck in our patterns, and this is effective even for auditors and lawyers. And, with effort, we can also get stuck in desirable positive patterns. In other words, if we can be fixated on things that bring us down, we can be engrossed in things that are good, healthy, and positive. To develop a pattern of being gripped by good, the ability to balance being absorbed in the present and shifting attention is the golden mean.

Shifting attention takes conscious practice because a significant amount of awake time is spent on something other than what people are doing. A smart-phone app was used to gather 250,000 data points on individuals' thoughts, feelings, and actions as people went about their lives, and results showed that people spend 46.9% of their awake time thinking about things they aren't doing[16]. In short, a wandering mind leads to an unhappy mind.

There are several interventions that can help a person improve their at-

> *A Jedi must have the deepest commitment, the most serious mind. This one a long time have I watched. All his life has he looked away... to the future, to the horizon. Never his mind on where he was. Hmm? What he was doing.*
> - Yoda

tention and become more mindful of the present, which increases happiness and engagement. Most importantly, integrating these activities into family life makes a significant difference—scheduling, modeling for young kids, for discussions at the dinner table, etc.

- Five minutes of meditation every day can improve breathing and present-centered awareness.

- Prayer and worship strengthens one's relationship with God.

- Savoring life's pleasures in the process of trying to live in the present moment.

- The use of mindfulness can help individuals become more present-centered. Mindfulness is a state of active, open attention on the present living in the moment and awakening to experience. This includes observing thoughts and feelings from a distance, without criticizing or judging. Our tendency toward being a self-critic can squash our creativity and our present-centeredness.

- An area this is best applied is with mindful eating, chewing slowly [a bite per minute], absorbing smells, and appreciating tastes over an extended period of time. Cooks are trained on absorbing smells and valuing their sensory experience.

- The following are the Dos and Don'ts of mindfulness that capture the ideas of observing, accepting, and being in the present. These Dos and Don'ts are for a window of time. Establish a clear window of time, like 20 minutes, and go for a walk, sit on the porch, or stroll through a garden. Within this established period of time, engage with these Dos and Don'ts of mindfulness.

P.E.R.M.A. Theory

| DO | DON'T |
|---|---|
| • Observe and notice the feelings and sensations in your body. Notice the location of these feelings. | • Don't try to change the bodily sensations. |
| • Tell yourself to accept your reaction to the situation and to these feelings in your body. Accept these feelings. | • Don't try to push the emotions away. |
| | • Don't wrestle to fight the frustration; let go. |
| • Like an outside observer, notice the thoughts going on in your mind. Observe the thoughts like you're watching a train go by. | • Don't try to push the thoughts out of your mind. Don't try to force the discomfort to go away. |
| | • Don't reject your feelings. |

## WORDS OF WISDOM & STEPS FOR TAKING ACTION

1. One theory suggests that 40% of happiness is in our grasp. Regardless of the degree of control (40-100%), there are specific actions that can increase happiness: relationships, service, gratitude, savoring...

2. Engage the present by being sensitive to one's focus of attention is critical. Develop strategies with teenagers on fully engaging in the present-centered activity. Teach kids to focus on one thing at a time such as turning off the music when reading and taking smartphone "checking" breaks.

3. Shifting attention back to the present solves the problem of inattention, which can occur for nearly half of our awake time.

4. Teaching children the advantages of mindfulness, which includes accepting thoughts and feelings, can improve self-awareness of their placed action.

A broad perspective on happiness theory is stated by the PERMA Theory[17]. In the last 10 years, research findings have suggested that happiness results from building up our well-being and satisfaction with life. According to Seligman and positive psychology, the building blocks of well-being consists of five elements: Positive emotion, Engagement, Relationships, Meaning, and Accomplishment.

## Positive Emotion – Kids Need Laughter

Most adolescents have their understanding of positive emotion evolve as they grow, develop, and mature. The ideal is that we all grow up and mature. For most adolescents, their view of positive emotion is physical pleasure and physical comfort. As attitudes progress and mindsets expand, positive emotion is viewed much more expansively. Feeling good includes hearing laughter and laughing at ourselves and with others. Good feelings can be contagious, especially when I smile or laugh, which can make others want to smile or laugh. Kids need parents to laugh and produce laughter on a regular basis. Recently, I sat down at the dinner table right after getting home from work. Half way through dinner, my son spilled a large cup of water at the table. Sitting in my suit, I immediately and firmly exclaimed, "That's not how you spill water, this is how you spill water!" and I immediately dumped a venti cup of ice water on my head. Our family laughed about this one for an hour.

Feeling good strengthens relationships and leads us to dance, be creative, leave our comfort zone, and take chances and risks. We all bump into those types of people at the grocery store who leave a lasting effect on our lives – they offer encouragement, laughter, or something that stays with us. Sometimes, our hope is that we can be like them or have a similar touch on another's life, to leave a flavor of honey wherever we go. One of the nuggets of wisdom for helping young people is building their tool kit of eliciting positive emotion in numerous capacities.

## Engagement – Kids Need Flow

Strengths like honesty, courage, loving behavior, and hope can be assessed with a valid and reliable measure called the VIA Survey of Character Strengths at www.authentichappiness.org. The results of the survey will show a person's top strengths. When these "Top 5" character strengths are identified, and used during work, job satisfaction, confidence, and productivity increase. This is particularly relevant for teenagers working part-time jobs or summer jobs and finding little value besides the paycheck. One study shows that implementing our top five strengths in our least favorite tasks on the job can improve our job satisfaction. A bright teenager with a creativity strength might find creative ways to reduce doldrums within the realm of the drive-thru protocol as a fast food employee.

At the heart of engagement is flow. True engagement is flow, a research idea that was originated by Mihaly Csikszentmihalyi, defined as a feeling of full engagement that leads a person to experience ecstasy and clarity. When a person is skiing the slopes or rock climbing, this person is not worried about work politics.

An experienced ballroom dancer fully engaged is not preoccupied with bills. A bridge player is not obsessing about his "to do list." Yes, critics of overinvolved parents caution overscheduled kids. On the other hand, uninvolved kids lead to disengaged teenagers. Less interests and hobbies means less engagement. Ultimately, fully investing in activity and one's interests leads to flow, which involves a subjective experience of being completely absorbed and losing a sense of self-consciousness. Parents can develop this flow skill in children by helping children develop their list of top three flow activities. What are your hobbies? What do you love to do? What captures your attention more than anything? What do you love to do that captivates your heart? What energizes you? What are you passionate about? What activity grabs your attention and causes you to lose track of time?

## Relationships – Kids Need High Quality Relationships

In my discussions with older adults, including several centenarians, the word I hear that matters most is family. Family is everything. I recently spoke with a 105-year-old woman and two other female centenarians who all outlived their children. Heartbreak is experienced daily by these mothers. It is common for people who live a long time to outlive friends. But, to outlive your own children is heart wrenching. When a therapy client of mine loses a child (regardless of age), there is no greater pain. Who has words to say to such pain? What can you say to comfort the tears and console the heart? Our compassion is expressed and we join them in sorrow and grief. But, the pain is so deeply felt that mere human words feel useless.

There is a lesson in these reflections. When people get to the end of their life, there is one thing that matters – relationships. The quality of our lives is dependent upon the quality of our relationships. Relationships in all areas are important. Work relationships are important for teamwork, accomplishing goals, service, and productivity. Helping children have childhood friends or allowing and encouraging friends makes a childhood come alive. As I'm writing this, I just sent a "happy birthday" note to a childhood friend. We had great times together playing wiffle ball, baseball, basketball, and trading comic books. An important life lesson for our children and teenagers is learning to appreciate relationships as an end, not a means of feeling better about ourselves, or politicking for a favorable position, or experiencing pleasure selfishly. Relationships are mutual life giving joys of life.

Family shared experiences make a significant difference in childhood, but especially adolescence. However, the best way to secure adolescent involvement is shared experiences during childhood. Regular family laughter, consistent family games, nurturing family talks, steady affection, transparent communication, and recurring family dinners over years establishes a level of emotional family muscle that will provide a secure foundation for years to come.

<u>Meaning – Kids Need Meaning in Virtually Everything</u>

Another important ingredient to well-being is meaning, which is needed in everything that kids put their hands on. A teen reading Fyodor Dostoyevsky's Crime and Punishment or studying the bible experiences clear meaning. Is meaning relevant when a teen is playing the violent video games like Five Nights with Freddy or Grand Theft Auto? From my conversations with school counselors across the country, Five Nights with Freddy is causing significant sleep problems.

Video games in general are causing problems for children, particularly for boys[18]. While the benefits of video games may be developing logic to solve problems, decision making skills and improving fine motor skills, many of these things can be developed in other ways. The negative effects of video games need to be considered – aggressiveness, violence and pornography, attention problems, impatience, and addiction[19]. Kids using video games excessively end up with quick analytical skills and reflexes, but lack communication skills, have few bonds with people, exhibit little empathy, and show minimal self-control[20]

A metaphor for managing video games is considering the effects of high fructose corn syrup (HFCS), which has shown to be more addictive than cocaine. Like the food industry, billions of dollars have been spent on everything from the music in the games to specific types of reinforcement in the games to the design of the video game which is made to suck players in and make them want to spend as much time as they can playing the game. The most important thing is not that our children avoid HFCS or video games. We want them to be free and understand their choices. We want them to understand that the pop tart is made to be addictive. Likewise, the video game is designed to be addictive. We want our children to be equipped to make intentional choices. The answer for our kids is not for parents to forbid these things. The answer is making intentional choices. This is best done by having family meetings. You sit down and talk about your children's responsibilities. You also talk about activities for enjoyment and how much time they want to spend playing video games. There is no question that playing video games is enjoyable for children. What responsibilities are getting put on the back burner? What other entertainment and leisure options are being eliminated if there is excessive gaming?

However your family approaches video games, a key point is that kids need downtime, but they don't need wasted time. Family meetings and reflection time make it more useful time rather than wasted time. Finding meaning also consists of learning that there is something greater than yourself. This is one of the lessons I communicate to the kids when I coach youth sports in soccer and basketball. One of the qualities of good team players is unselfish teamwork. Being a part of something bigger than yourself is fulfilling. Meaning and purpose is the quality that motivates adolescents to get involved in outreach projects, service in shelters, and sports. We also know that adolescents are prone to individualism and selfishness. Outreach, service, and teams can also squeeze out some of the selfishness. As we thoroughly discussed in Chapter 5, being a part of something bigger than yourself establishes a foundation for vision and purpose.

Accomplishments – Kids Need to Feel a Sense of Accomplishment

As indicated earlier, I am a big believer in emphasizing unconditional love and communicating to kids that parents are proud of them for who they are, not just expressing "I'm so proud of you" following accomplishments. Certainly, we want to celebrate with our kids and going out to get ice cream or to a restaurant to discuss the accomplishment is great for positive emotion. It is also great for memory making and placing a memory landmark for increased personal confidence. I have made over 100 highlight videos for baseball, soccer, basketball, and gymnastics for all the sports my kids have been a part of over the years. This isn't overkill nor is it unhealthy. Nowadays, this is done in 10 minutes with apps on smartphones, compared to 48 hours of editing from multiple VCRs, screens, and videos 20 years ago.

When it comes to sports parents, whose kids play youth sports, over-involvement has significant consequences[21]. Unfortunately, one response to the ongoing discussions of over-involved and helicopter parenting is less involvement. Less involvement is not the answer. For many parents (whether they have engaged on the over-involved discussion or not), passive involvement is the status quo. In contrast, huge amounts of energy need to go into our kids' achievements —both to give them confidence and make things fun. I show tremendous enthusiasm on the soccer field with my players. Obviously, not all parents have the temperament to get overly excited when a very quiet kid with little ability scores his first goal. Each parent will approach accomplishments and activities in their own unique way. But, effort, energy, persistent involvement, and enjoyment raises confidence and happiness for our kids.

# REFLECTION TIPS

- Reinforce smiling at every picture. Smile often with your children. Laugh at least once a day. Take time to dump water on your own head and embarrass yourself in various ways for your kids' enjoyment. Help them elicit positive emotion in numerous capacities.

- Find a way to establish an old-fashioned pen pal relationship with a long-distance cousin or friend for each of your children. Remind your child and emphasize this as something that the family merits.

- If video games are already prominent in your household, consider setting limits. If "hours" are being used (and possibly wasted), consider 30 minutes as a daily limit. Consider a more conservative limit of "weekends only." If video games are not yet prominent, consider facilitating a family culture that emphasizes a wide range of entertainment options.

- Remain an engaged parent in school, sports, music, science, or any other extracurricular activity. Expend effort on his or her achievements.

## Evidence Based Techniques

This final section focuses on a collection of happiness building strategies that research evidence suggests builds happiness. At the heart of happiness is gratitude. Have you ever been around teenagers who constantly complain, even on vacation? If you were to ask them to identify events of the day, they would have an easier time naming events that were disappointing, frustrating, or aggravating. Have you noticed that their descriptions of these events tend to make their vocabulary more negative, unpleasant, or upsetting? Vacationing parents hearing these negatives sometimes wonder, "Why are we spending all of this money?" "Couldn't I have experienced this same level of unhappiness, criticism, and pessimism while at home?"

The answer isn't easy, especially with strong willed and independent thinking teens. And the answers may not change things right now if you are actually on vacation and experiencing this negativity. Nonetheless, the solution over time is gratitude. As we begin to focus on events that had been good, pleasant, and encouraging, our minds begin to focus more on positive things. When we as humans begin to express appreciation, we subsequently experience a greater increase in gratitude. The benefits of gratitude and an attitude of gratitude are significant. Gratitude leads to happier connections on vacations (and ordinary life), more love expressed through the ups and downs of family life, better adjustments to life stressors, more productive with family chores and helpfulness with parents to name some of the benefits. The following are four key gratitude elevating techniques.

*We all find time to do what we really want to do.*
*– William Feather*

Three Good Things or The Three Blessings

Some families buy journals for each family member. Near the end of the evening, each family member writes down three good things that happened that day. This exercise reorients each of the family members' attention towards the positive. Each member writes specific good things that happened that day and why. They write out what they appreciated from their day at school, in transportation from school to home, with friends and with family members. During the next family dinner, each family member shares from the previous night's list. Journaling is the best evidence-based method for cultivating gratitude and requires only a few minutes. It may be the best few minutes spent out of all 1,440 minutes in the day.

I have found that incorporating wisdom into the ups and downs of life helps us to remember the good things with more richness and robust gratitude for all that is happening in life. When Regina Brett, columnist for The Plain Dealer in Cleveland, Ohio, turned 50, she offered "50 Life Lessons."[22] Many of these life lessons apply to our parenting, particularly during the challenges our kids and teenagers (and adult children) face on a regular basis.

- Life isn't fair, but it's still good.
- Life is too short to waste time hating anyone.
- Make peace with your past so that it won't screw up the present.
- Don't compare your life to others. You have no idea what their journey is all about.
- If a relationship has to be a secret, you shouldn't be in it.
- No one is in charge of your happiness but you.
- Forgive everyone everything.
- However good or bad a situation is, it will change.
- Don't take yourself so seriously. No one else does.
- Life isn't tied with a bow, but it's still a gift.

> *Love doesn't grow on trees like apples in Eden – it's something you have to make. And you must use your imagination to make it too, just like anything else.*
> – Joyce Cary

Gratitude Technique & Lifestyle

Its best to think of gratitude as a lifestyle. To develop a lifestyle, it usually starts with a technique that can transition into a habit. When somebody thinks that their life has improved after a positive outcome, such as a promotion, then happiness results. But, we get used to our new circumstances and happiness tends to return to our previous level, like the typical return response after a lottery win. Psychologists refer to this "return to our previous level" as a "hedonic treadmill." Often, adolescents are running regularly on this hedonic treadmill when they are constantly focusing on what makes them feel good, as opposed to doing good for somebody, learning something new, or accomplishing a challenging task. One of the ways to curtail this treadmill is expressing gratitude.

Research on gratitude shows that depression and anxiety is reduced due to specific expressed gratitude. One way to implement a gratitude task is applying it at family dinner time. (1) Every dinner, family members identify something that they are grateful for. This can be interwoven with the "three good things" technique and last night's journaling. (2) A more common approach would be to identify five things you are grateful for and why. If family members find this to be a difficult exercise, then starting with the practical basics may help such as food, shelter, education, health, and friends. For young children who are concrete in their thinking, using visual aids such as creating pictorial collages helps them to express what they are thankful for.

Gratitude Letter

Every Sunday, the family identifies one person in their family's life who has made a difference and had a positive impact on one or more family members. A vote for Billy's friend is acknowledged. But, the goal is to identify a person who has had some interaction with the entire family to some degree. The family takes 15 minutes to write a letter to this person. The experience becomes a family ritual. Ways to make it fun include the use of creativity and doing something unique and new each week (e.g. drawing a picture, video of family singing a "thank you" song, etc.). Positive reinforcement can be implemented; winner of an original idea gets to stay up 30 minutes extra, for example. The entire process works best when the activity is driven by the children, rather than the parents. The following is a sample gratitude letter.

*Dear Mr. Sam,*

*We wanted to thank you for being a kind neighbor. You have been nice to us kids. You have helped our dad with your big ladder on several occasions. When we had a broken water pipe, you provided a tool to stop the water from flooding our backyard. Once, you even made cookies or brownies for us, several years ago. We appreciated how you watched our little fireworks show in recent years on 4th of July. You have been a huge help as hurricane Irma came through recently. And, we really appreciate you letting us borrow your saw among other things following the hurricane. Thank you for being a wonderful neighbor.*

*Best regards,*
*van Ingen family*

## Gratitude Vocabulary

Journaling and speaking is influenced by the words that we use[23]. In expressions of gratitude when honoring a family member, writing specific reasons for gratefulness, or writing gratitude letters, increasing consciousness in word choices can increase gratitude. Grateful people tend to use words such as "blessed," "those were blessings," "fortunate," "appreciative," "fortunate," "prosperous," and "lucky." While this tends to naturally come with the gratitude territory, it is worth mentioning that emphasizing the words of gratitude toward children strengthens connections in the brain most related to becoming more grateful.

## Ritual Resolution

We all know about New Year's resolutions. There are several reasons why resolutions don't last. Research has thoroughly studied why these resolutions come to an end rather quickly[24]. The motivation is more extrinsic than intrinsic and rationale has been modified. Then there are those committed individuals like a friend of mine who has exercised every day for six+ years, since a New Year's resolution in 2009. However long the resolution lasts, there is emotional power in making changes in one's life. Resolve toward new rituals brings about changes. Sustaining these changes requires commitment, scheduling, and support.

When family members resolve to create a new ritual, it can create joy and learning that brings the family together. And, it disrupts the routine, which can get bland without creativity in a hurry. One family established a new debate contest every Saturday night. Through their teenage years, they took occasional breaks on vacations or holidays or visits from family relatives. Nearly every Saturday they were given a topic and an hour to prepare their side. At 7:00, the debate began with rules and an enthusiastic atmosphere. The parents took time to find ways to laugh so it remained a positive experience rather than a divisive one. Another family instituted a Saturday night show. Every week, the house turned into a theatre stage. As it evolved, driving by garage sales led to opportunities to shop for performance costumes.

Ritual resolution disrupts the schedule and brings life into the family. Vitality within family life is the goal of changes to make family life more positive and healthy. There are a number of activities that change the quality of the family through ritual resolution: family prayer, turning off the television and playing card games, serving at the homeless shelter, bringing cookies to a different family each week, Sunday football, fall season leaf collecting, weekly letter writing to grandparents, and the list goes on.

Family Exercise

One of the most significant happiness boosters is exercise. As Dr. John Tauer points out, youth sports are great for life lessons, associating positive feelings with physical fitness, having fun, unselfish teamwork, meaning and fulfillment by being a part of something bigger than yourself, and accomplishments. Some disadvantages for youth sports include parental overinvolvement, overscheduling of childhood, and the competition grind. In contrast, competition can cause young people to grow, learn from failure, value setbacks and develop resiliency – all positives. Another negative is that good high school student athletes stop exercising when they get into college because they are so used to the experience of exercising on a team within an organization and within an externally controlled environment.

One way to counter the externally controlled environments is for children to grow up in families that find ways to exercise together, play games together and have a lot of fun together. Family runs, family soccer games, family basketball games, and long Saturday morning bike-rides are great for family togetherness.

I have fond memories growing up with my father facilitating "Pickle games." My father picked us up from my mother's home on a consistent basis. I spent time with my father every other weekend throughout my childhood. On those weekends, my father always found time to facilitate a game of pickle with my sisters and step-brother. We had a great time. "Pickle" is an informal term to describe a rundown in baseball; it is a situation in the game when the base runner is stranded between two bases. In our game, we had two throwers and everybody else was on a base. The simple game involved runners running between bases with the catchers attempting to tag them out. It was incredible fun!

Best Possible Family Exercise

The best possible family exercise is an activity in which family members write about the feelings and events they would experience if their life unfolded as favorably as they could possibly imagine in all areas of their lives: professionally, education, relationships and social life, fitness-exercise and sports goals, and all other areas. Family members are asked to think about the best possible life in each of these areas. Playing college basketball or getting excellent grades as a premed student are examples. This is an annual activity and ideally started comprehensively in the age range of 8-12 depending on readiness and the maturation process. Each family member takes 10-15 minutes to write about their best possible self in any way that they want. As children move into teenage years, individuals are instructed to dedicate some time (i.e. 5-7 minutes) to write about a specific goal that is consistent with the adolescent's best possible self. A key for the success of this activity is that parents put forth 100% effort and articulate transparency with their children.

## Cultivating Gratitude Patterns

There is more to say about gratitude beyond gratitude techniques, gratitude letters, and gratitude vocabulary. Some parents reading this might visualize their teenage daughter eye rolling or their son lacking verbal skills or willingness to express gratitude when this is brought up. Naturally, implementing gratitude strategies will become easier the younger the children started. Expressing gratitude tends to solidify around the ages of 7 to 10, but can begin to develop as early as 3. Even if you have teenagers, it is never too late to begin to cultivate gratitude patterns.

Gratitude exercises were the first types of positive psychology techniques supported in randomized clinical trials. Even before research, smart families have known for a long time the advantage of expressing gratitude in specific ways. There are many ways to express thanks but specific and intentional strategies elevate gratitude and subsequent happiness.

We know that taking five minutes at the end of the day to identify blessings boosts happiness. Taking time at the end of each day to identify things a person is grateful for is a great happiness lifter. Nighttime is a precious time for parents to engage in gratitude expressions with their child. If the child can't write yet, taking a few minutes to identify three things that he or she is grateful for while you snuggle at the end of the night is a great exercise to start. The building blocks for gratitude begin to develop around the ages of 3-5. If a child can write, then having them write out three good things that happened that day is a great exercise. Identify three blessings and why they happened and writing these three good things can elevate gratitude and develop gratitude habits. Establishing this exercise can help it become ingrained within the child and develop a habit of being thankful. This is a habit that leads to happiness. And this is what we all want for our children.

## Reminiscence Therapy

One of the empirically supported treatments for older adults is reminiscence therapy. There are several reasons why this modality is effective, most notably, because it activates feelings associated with an individual's favorite memories. Picture albums do wonders for older adults. There are other reasons as it relates to age. Neuroscience suggests that older individuals have a more positive outlook because the amygdala, the emotional center of the brain, is less active in response to negative information[25].

Reminiscing can highlight family vacations by using iMovie or another app that involves editing family video to the music theme of that experience. Family websites, Facebook posts, family tweets, Pinterest, and Instagram are used to highlight life experience and show the positive uses of social media. While all these applications can assist with memory making and reminiscing, the keys are reflection and bonding. The sun/storm/rainbow technique can assist with daily reflection and bonding and provide deliberate reminiscing and savoring the moments. Each evening, a family member can share their experiences of the day with the sun-storm-rainbow technique. The Sun is something that delighted you that day. The Storm is something that challenged you that day. The Rainbow is something positive you learned about yourself or discovered in the storm. By reflecting with the sun-storm-rainbow, individuals increase their reflectiveness, cultivate reminiscing opportunities, and increase gratitude.

A highlight of family dinners can be BPODs: Best Part of Day. Each family member takes a couple of minutes and discusses their BPOD for that day. On Saturday, each family member discusses their BPOW: Best Part of Week. Naturally, each family member reflects on memorable highlights from this past year on their birthdays.

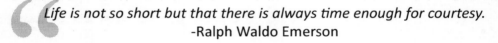

*Life is not so short but that there is always time enough for courtesy.*
-Ralph Waldo Emerson

*As perfume to the flower, so is kindness to speech.*
-Katherine Francke

## Intentional Acts of Kindness

Finally, how can we possibly forget about kindness? Kindness is central to happiness as it brings us to places of pleasantness, compassion, understanding, warmth, and love. Kindness is central to courtesy and politeness with strangers. And kindness is at the heart of our love relationships in the family. Training our children to be kind is something that the world desperately needs. We live in a world where kindness is perceived as weakness; the truth is that active and assertive kindness is the answer to the world's cynicism, despair, criticism, and negativity. Kindness is the answer to combat narcissism. The world needs our families' kindness. Our families need the kindness of our children.

The following are a list of intentional acts of kindness that children can be trained on:

- Visit your favorite social media site and write something kind to three different people.

178

- Write an extensive "Happy Birthday" comment to each of the friends and acquaintances on Facebook.   Snail mail or phone calls are even better.

- Spend Saturday giving an hour at a nursing facility.  Perspective broadening is great for children.

- Send notes of kindness to friends at random times.

- Teach your children that small kind acts matter – smiling, holding a door open for someone, complimenting, and manners, calling Grandma & Grandpa....

- Bring your neighbor baked sweets.

- Encourage your child to send videos to aunts and uncles.

- An act that has been popular more recently is paying for the drive thru order of someone behind you.  Encourage your child to pay for the drink as an act of kindness without immediate reward.

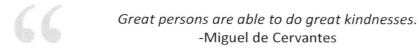

*Great persons are able to do great kindnesses.*
-Miguel de Cervantes


*Kindness is the golden chain by which society is bound together.*
-Goethe


## Summary

Our goal of "optimal parenting" moves us in the direction of raising our children to be contributing members of society, make our culture healthier, and improve our world.  There are seven keys to optimal parenting: (1) Reinforcing a Secure Attachment, (2) Minimizing Reinforcement Errors, (3) Drawing out the Strength of Boldness, (4) Promoting the Reflective and Optimistic Life, (5) Establishing Purpose with an Internal Locus of Control, (6) Sustaining Cognitive Flexibility In the Face of adversity, (7) and Establishing Family Happiness Rituals.

In this last key, family happiness rituals encompass several happiness boosters that essentially falls into three categories.  This chapter is summarized by the three As of Happiness—attitudes, attention, and actions.  Happiness Attitudes, Attentionality, and Actions build up the family unit, strengthen families, and improve the influence parents can have on their children's happiness.

First, viewing happiness attitudes as something to cultivate, as opposed to genetics, captures the essence of an "attitude."  The growth mindset as opposed to a fixed mindset is essential for child-raising here.  And, a general misconception is that kids and pre-teens are happy but teenage life is unhappy.  This is false! Happy parents can influence happy teenagers and vice versa. It all starts with a happy family culture. Life experience shows that parents are happier than non-parents, but in a deeper way than pleasure and comforts. Yes, diapers and 2:00 am vomiting reduces pleasures. But even in the face of routine inconveniences, happy parents rub off on their children's happiness. Parents who are cheerful goes a long way in how their children and teenagers interact with the world – how much they smile, how much they interact, and in their ability to see the bright side of things. This only happens with parents who are fully engaged in conversations on a regular basis while bringing life and joy to their children and teaching them how to approach problems with optimism; it doesn't work for parents who are neutral observers. Of course, happiness is deeper than smiles and rainbows. But, there is no doubt in the research that cheerfulness can have a deep effect. Balance is key, particularly when it comes to having a balanced approach to money. Contentment results from our balanced approach to money. Cheerfulness, generosity, and a balanced approach to money are ways families reflect genuine happiness. Additionally, parents make a significant difference engaging with children by building buffering strengths as pearl finders and building a culture of honor. More than anything, an attitude toward building character and virtue that exudes the fruits of love, joy, peace, kindness, goodness, and gentleness can reinforce the happy life.

Second, there are patterns of focus and attention associated with happiness. Practicing the shifting of attention, being absorbed in the present, and keeping one's mind on exactly what he or she is doing in the moment makes a huge difference. Parents who bring their cell phones to the dinner table or the park distract themselves and model misplaced attention. Attention specifically on what one is doing is critical for mindfulness, and subsequent happiness. Specific methods assist with attentionality --five minutes of meditation daily, in-moment savoring, in-moment observations, mindful eating, and sense absorption. Additionally, prayer is commonly reported as both broadening perspective and capturing in-the-moment experiences.

Third, happiness actions are like habits. These consist of quality time in relationships, regular expressions of gratitude, consistent generosity, service to others, engaging in the present, looking at the future with optimism, and holding a deep commitment to values and living out those values on a daily basis. We finished the chapter with evidence based techniques—those explicit actions that raise the happiness and health of families: counting blessings every night, writing gratitude letters, intentionally incorporating gratitude vocabulary, establishing new rituals, "the best possible family" exercise, reminiscence therapy (i.e. family slide shows), and intentional acts of kindness (i.e. family service projects).

The journey of life is an amazing journey. As interviews of millionaires suggest, the things that matter most to millionaires (or billionaires) are the same things that matter most to the rest of us – family, making a difference, and children. And, the biggest difference any one of us will make in the world will be in our family. There is nothing greater to dedicate our lives to than children.

# Chapter Eight

## Final Thoughts

There are several reasons why families need to look outside for help. I have spent a large portion of my career training providers who work with families who require professional help. So, clearly, "You Are Your Child's Best Psychologist" is not intended to discourage professional help. There are times when licensed psychologists need more from families to make this culture a better place – as do pastors and churches, teachers and schools, social workers and communities, and coaches and teams. I have talked with thousands of providers who are desperate for more from the parents that they work with. Unfortunately, in many child situations, too much falls on teachers, school counselors and psychologists. At the same time, those parents reading this book and the thousands of providers that I have talked with are inspired by the amazing families that they interact with. Personally, I have watched my kids involved with various sports clubs and we have seen some very healthy parental involvement at all levels – academically, athletically, spiritually, and in service. There are healthy parents like these in every county across America. Yet, there are those times when the healthiest among us need professional help for our families.

Many long for the "simple" days of neighborhoods working together to raise kids. However, time and again we have read that we see the 1950s with rose-colored glasses. Even if problems of war and unemployment were just as prominent then, experts will still say it was more of a simple time to raise a family. Today, moral ambiguity, distraction (disguised as technology), and excessive individualism are just a sampling of ways society has deteriorated. This leads us to some key questions. Is this world getting better with so many advancements in health care, technology, and knowledge? Is the world in decline with the breakdown of families, communities, and values? Is it in flux with bad and good people fluctuating in their influence? Regardless of where you fall on this philosophical spectrum and larger conversations, we need our children to grow up to become difference makers, leaders, and problem solvers. While we try and work as a team for each child, many parents and teachers are working hard to raise their children toward being contributing members of society and to be positives for the culture and world. My kids' school consistently reminds our family that parents are the primary educators. This idea applies across the board in every aspect of healthy child development. But, sometimes, on this journey of development, we go through seasons when we need professional help.

<u>When do parents seek professional help?</u>

How do parents know when they need to go about seeking professional help? Although we are the primary educators, many of us certainly rely on the expertise of licensed teachers. When should we rely on the expertise of licensed mental health professionals? The Seven Keys focuses on parenting over the long-term. But, what about those seasons when we don't know what to do. Families go through seasons when life seems bleak. There are countless reasons when a family would need help from a licensed professional. The following are some of those reasons:

(a) Kids are so unruly that no intervention seems to work and your style of communication seems to have no effect;

(b) Your teenager is experiencing a depression that doesn't seem to lift;

(c) The kids are having significant difficulty coping with significant loss (i.e. Dad passing);

(d) Your child is showing signs and symptoms of obsessive-compulsive disorder;

(e) Your child is overly concerned about being humiliated, avoids social situations, and appears to suffer from social anxiety disorder which often starts around the age of 13;

(f) Your family has experienced significant trauma such as a car accident that has led to intrusive memories, flashbacks, and sleep problems;

(g) Fears have overwhelmed your young child leading to acid reflux, headaches, diarrhea, "frequent accidents," and the nurse has been visited on several occasions;

(h) Your child has developed "unstoppable" or "impulsive" habits of skin-picking (exhoriation), pulling hair (trichotilimania), or hoarding behaviors;

(i) Obesity has become an issue with too much TV, video games and processed foods and you need a professional to help change course;

(j) You notice your daughter binging and purging (vomiting up a ton of carbs consumed) and/or a preoccupation with body image;

(k) Your student athlete is experiencing psychological blocking in his/her particular sport and is locking up with previously learned skills (i.e. giving up and quitting tennis matches or avoiding the gymnastics floor routine because of a previous fall);

(l) Your kid is showing learning discrepancies with a bright intellect but underdeveloped reading, writing, or math skills.

These are just a sampling of reasons why professionals should be sought after. In this day and age, obtaining professional therapy is insightful. There remains a mental health stigma but more and more, empowered parents are viewing professional help during difficult seasons as wise. Rather than a sign of weakness, instead, professional help is a sign of strength. During this "winter" season of life, treatment may last four weeks, three months, six months, one year, or in some rare occasions—two or more years.

Dispelling Fears and Myths About Seeking Professional Help

"*Our family problems are too embarrassing to talk about with a thera-pist.*" This is a common yet understandable concern, but licensed professional therapists know how to express compassion, empathy, and supportive counseling. Many families attempt to keep information contained within the unit. Some closed families discourage "talking about our problems" outside of the family. Sometimes this is seen in religious communities or churches where "problems reflect badly" on the parents. If this is you, consider nipping 'embarrassment' in the bud as important for family health. Try to consider your problems as temporary and recognize that bringing them into the light and getting an outside perspective is the best way to develop an effective plan of problem-solving and coping.

"*Families who receive counseling or therapy have parents who are needy, disorganized, and dysfunctional.*" Unfortunately, this is a common belief, but very much false. Most of us go through seasons and may feel that things seem more difficult than other times. It is important to remember that the most organized parents among us go through trials and tribulations. There is no way to organize life in such a way that our family is shielded from life's tough stuff. As we've emphasized, the waves of life are like the waves of an ocean, they never stop. Some seasons or waves are more difficult in family life. Seeking professional help during these times, particularly for one of those aforementioned serious problems, is a sign of function and strength. It is common sense knowledge that no parent has it all together. How many of us have heard from sincere and reflective older parents who are able to acknowledge the many mistakes that they made? None of us have it all together. Parents who seek help show more wisdom than neediness. In addition, a professional offers objectivity and expertise that improves the quality of life.

"*Having someone dealing with my kids' problems undermines my authority as parents.*" While it is true that sometimes your teen may become more interested in someone else's opinion than yours, it is helpful to remember that you are the parent in it for the rest of your (and his/her) life. Another thing to remember is that the goals of therapy should never be to deconstruct your teen's worldview, restructure their ideology, reframe their philosophy in life, impose the therapist's values, minimize the influence of God, or devalue your family's Christianity or religiosity. Generally speaking, contrary to some misconceptions out there, therapists want to simply help with the presenting issues. The goals of a therapist will be to help your child increase their problem-solving strategies and coping skills. Parents ultimately raise their stature by valuing a large network and support team for family success.

Finding a Mental Health Professional

Sometimes the solution is family therapy. This may be poignant when a step-parent is involved and the therapist can help the family improve communication. One problem that sometimes comes up is that a step-parent will withhold relationship effort under the guise of "not wanting to take the Dad's (Mom's) place.  No, what the child needs is effort and expressed love on behalf of the step-parent.  Getting in the game is more important than being a sideline observer.  A family therapist can help a step-parent take this perspective and it sometimes works better when this is communicated by a professional than the spouse.

Sometimes the solution is individual therapy for the child, preteen or teen.  For all the aforementioned reasons and more, a therapist can broaden perspective, increase coping skills, instill strengths, heal shame, and provide evidence based treatment.

There are several ways to find mental health providers.  Here are some of the more common strategies people take:

- Seek a referral or recommendation from your family doctor.

- Ask trusted family or friends.

- Ask your pastor or clergy.

- Ask your health insurance provider for providers who are covered by your insurance company.

- Many people go through www.psychologytoday.com or a similar path to find a therapist.  However, contacting a national mental health organization can provide a particular specialty depending on the issue.  If you as a parent suffer from an anxiety disorder, or if your child suffers from anxiety, the Anxiety Disorders Association of America can be a great resource (www.adaa.org).  Other specialty organizations include the American Board of Professional Psychology, or ABPP (www.abpp.org) and the National Registry of Health Service Psychologists (www.nationalregister.org).  For a Christian counselor, the American Association of Christian Counselors is a great resource (www.aacc.net).

- Another issue to consider is getting marriage therapy.  If you are married, this may be one of the best gifts that you can give your marriage (and children).  I strongly recommend that you find a therapist who has studied John Gottman principles.  Gottman is widely considered the foremost expert on what makes marriages work.  www.gottman.com is a great website that features key information on the The Gottman Institute and a referral source for finding Gottman certified marriage and family therapists.  Other important resources are www.smartmarriages.com and www.johnburi.com.

Conclusion

The bottom line is that there are so many things that we as parents can do to increase the quality of our family life. Yet, there are those seasons in life when we need to stretch our tent pegs of support. There are times when professional help can be an important step towards growth, development, and family solutions. Professionals can add to our efforts to attain successful attachment, reinforcement, boldness, reflectiveness, purpose, cognitive flexibility and family happiness. There are also many self-help resources available as well. These are listed in the Appendix. May we move forward with an attitude of gratitude for our amazing children. Is there anything better than being a parent?

# (Chapter 1 Endnotes)

1        The most important aspect of attachment theory is that a child needs a relationship with a primary caregiver starting at infancy. Bowlby (1969) and Ainsworth (1973) were instrumental in attachment theory. A key concept from Bowlby's contributions includes the internal working model, which involves thoughts, schemas and relationship tendencies formed in early childhood and is carried forward to influence adult relationships. Among Ainsworth's key contributions were her attachment styles that were formed based on a laboratory procedure called the 'Strange Situation.' The procedure consisted of eight sequential episodes in which infants were separated and then reunited with the mother. Based on reunion behavior, infants were categorized into three types of attachments.

2        A fourth attachment style was added by Main & Solomon (1990) resulting in four attachment styles. The disorganized/disoriented attachment was categorized for those infants who displayed fearfulness, contradictory behaviors and did not achieve closeness or some proximity with the caregiver.

3        Research has shown that PTSD growth results from secure attachments. This does not suggest that securely attached individuals are prevented from experiencing PTSD, nor does it suggest that individuals with insecure attachment will automatically experience PTSD, a condition that can result from a traumatic experience. A history of prior exposure to trauma is a potent risk factor for PTSD (Davidson et al., 1991). The type of prior trauma such as a previous assault is a particularly strong risk factor for the development of PTSD upon later trauma (Breslau et al., 1999a). Other risk factors include lower levels of education and income.

4        This is another example of the effect of emotionally absent fathers. Emotionally absent fathers tend to be emotionally absent husbands. One of the best predictors of stable and secure attachments for children is a stable and secure marriage that is thriving and flourishing. For resources on absent fathers and this critical issue in America, see *Man Enough: Fathers, Sons, and the Search for Masculinity* by Frank Pittman, M.D., *Absent Fathers, Lost Sons: The Search for Masculine Identity* by Guy Corneau, and *Fatherless America: Confronting Our Most Urgent Social Problem* by David Blankenhorn.

5        Disorganized insecure attachments have been identified as a primary risk factor for the development of various psychiatric conditions including dissociation (Main, 1996; Ogawa et al., 1997). In longitudinal studies, attachment researchers identified an association between childhood trauma and proneness to dissociation (ogawa et al., 1997). For her healing and trauma resolution, Jenny needed something more than just talk therapy, which touches on things in the mind, but doesn't work through those deeper issues such as implicit traumatic material in how Jenny processes information. Treatment methods such as EMDR or prolonged exposure begin to peel back the deep onion that has caused unresolved

pain. Clinical studies show EMDR to be a leading evidence based treatment in this area. Cognitive processing therapy and prolonged exposure therapy are evidence based treatments that have rolled out in the VA medical system over the last 10+ years.

6          Siegel is a leader in mindfulness and in developing the field of interpersonal neurobiology. His books on parenting and child development include *The Whole-Brain Child: 12 Revolutionary Strategies to Nurture Your Child's Developing Mind*, *Survive Everyday Parenting Struggles*, and *Help Your Family Thrive* (2011), *No-Drama Discipline* (2014), and *Parenting from the Inside Out* (2003).

7          The Adult Attachment Interview is a great resource for clinicians (George, Kaplan, & Main, 1985). In my experience, it is also a great resource for parents who take the time for introspection. Many of my colleagues are quick to point out that parents don't have the time and don't take the time to reflect on their interior lives, particularly due to this new digitalized world we live in. Nonetheless, for those who are willing to take the time, reflection on one's own life can be initiated with key questions found in this resource. http://www.psychology.sunysb.edu/attachment/measures/content/aai_interview.pdf

8          The Parental Authority Questionnaire (1991) consists of 10 items each for the permissive, authoritarian, and authoritative parenting styles.

9          Diana Baumrind (1971) based her parenting styles on some of the following key parenting aspects: (1) parental responsiveness, which refers to the level of responsiveness of the parent to the child's needs. Second, (2) parental demandingness, which refers to the parent expecting more mature and responsible behavior. Baumrind studied the effects of corporal punishment on children, which served as the foundation for the spanking debate over the last 50 years. Baumrind concluded that mild spanking is unlikely to have a significant detrimental effect (Baumrind & Larzelere, 2002). Others counter that even if harm isn't caused, there remains no consistent evidence of its helpfulness (Gershoff, 2002). This debate starts a range of conversations for parents including best ways to engage in behavior modification and help children exhibit obedient behavior. A key study shows that the key factor in spanking is separating anger from the spanking (Trumball & Ravenel, 1996). In other words, the detrimental effects result from parents spanking when they are angry. There is some evidence to suggest that spanking without getting angry is the key if this intervention is implemented. This generalizes to points made in this book. Why get angry? A healthy parent with high EQ can implement a creative or straight-forward consequence without anger.

10        This communication tool is attributed to Lynn Lott. For more information on the positive discipline series completed by Lynn Lott, MA, MMFT and Jane Nelsen, EdD, visit www.positivediscipline.com

11        Research has shown that permissive parenting correlates with a number of family-defeating problems. Children and adolescents from permissive fami-

lies are susceptible to antisocial peer pressure (Condry & Simon 1974; Steinberg 1987). However, such individuals are also more likely to be involved in problem behaviors and perform less well in school, but they have higher self-esteem, better social skills, and lower levels of depression than children raised by authoritarian parents (Strage & Brandt 1999).

# (Chapter 2 Endnotes)

1  1-2-3 Magic is a popular parenting discipline program that teaches parents effective discipline.  Further information on this program can be found at www.123magic.com

2  Screen Free Zones and regular family dinners are two of the key features of healthy families.  Screen Free Zones are recommended by common sense media, a valuable resource on movie reviews, best TV lists, best books, best games, best apps, best websites, and best resources for character development.  www.commonsensemedia.org provides key information on parent concerns in the areas of character strengths, technology addiction, screen time, cyberbullying/haters/trolls, privacy and internet safety, advice on Facebook, Instagram and other social media.

3  John Buri (2015) normalizes the dysfunctions in every family.  Generally speaking, a person is mistaken if they believe that their family is perfect or free of problems.

4  This study was a groundbreaking study (Lepper, Greene, and Nisbett, 1973).  Other studies have demonstrated similar effects.  Children who get rewarded for behavior they enjoy justified their behavior, known as the overjustification effect.  Did the children want to draw or was it because of the reward?  As a youth sports coach, I see this all the time.  Children are affected in complicated ways by rewards.  Moms will give kids donuts to play in the soccer games and some of these same kids enjoy soccer less.  They now connect playing with donuts, not for the fun.  How young are the children who make these associations?  As young as 20-month old infants are less likely to engage in helping behaviors following rewards in a study that shows that extrinsic rewards undermine altruistic tendencies (Warneken & Tomasello, 2008)

5  Praise has been thoroughly researched.  Several researchers, parents, and educators identify praise as enhancing intrinsic motivation (Cameron & Pierce, 1994; Shanab, Peterson, Dargahi, & Deroian, 1981).  The contrasting view

is that praise actually undermines intrinsic motivation by creating excessive pressure to continue performing well, discourage risk taking, and reduce autonomy (Holt, 1982; Kohn, 1993). For a review and synthesis on these ideas, see Henderlong & Lepper (2002). The bottom line is that sincerity is what our kids need. Sincerity cuts through any disadvantages and makes praise substantially meaningful. At the end, it is sincerity that builds a foundation for the parent-child relationship.

6      Several important insights for parents have emerged in the literature on sincere praise. For praise to be interpreted as meaningful, these authors identified perceived sincerity, performance attributions, emphasizing autonomy and standards. (Henderlong & Lepper, 2002).

# (Chapter 3 Endnotes)

1      Parents need to be aware of the psychological consequences of social media, particularly when the kids develop habits of using social media apps as the first activity they do in the morning. While some parents allow and pay for the latest technology for their kids, others are more concerned and trying to figure out healthy limits and boundaries. Regardless, parents need to know the consequences. Research has shown that social media may detract from face-to-face relationships (i.e. texting family member in same room), can lead to internet addiction (Christakis, 2010), which can lead to altered regional cerebral activity and structural brain changes (Yuan, Qin, Liu, & Tian, 2011), as well as reduced self-esteem due to social comparisons (Feinstein et al., 2013). A new rigorous study of 5,208 adults from a national longitudinal panel has assessed well-being changes over time in association with Facebook use. Measures of well-being have included life satisfaction, self-reported mental health, self-reported physical health, and body-mass index (BMI). Facebook use measures included liking others' posts, creating one's own posts, and clicking on links. One of the strengths of the study was that it had three waves of data over a period of two years. Results showed that an increased use of Facebook was associated with diminished well-being (Shakya & Christakis, 2017). The more people use Facebook, the worse they feel.

2      Wood (2004) summarized the evidence of nonverbal communication in this way, "Scholars estimate that nonverbal behaviors account for 65% to 93% of the total meaning of communication (Mehrabian, 1981)" (p. 129). In essence, 35% of the meaning derived in communication is based on what is spoken verbally – the verbal content. Over 65% of the meaning is extracted from the non-verbal components of the communication, for example, gestures, tone of voice, eye contact, inflections, body stance, pauses, physical movements, physical space.

3      The marshmallow study was originally reported in an article by Shoda, Mischel, and Peak (1990). In his work on emotional intelligence (EQ), Goleman

(1995) provided extensive detail around the original marshmallow study. Aspects of EQ has had a huge influence on the culture in education and business over the last 20 years. Educational systems in other countries have incorporated curriculums on "social and emotional learning" based on the work of EQ, and has resulted in programs on character education, violence prevention, and anti-bullying to name a few. There is no doubt that EQ has had a positive influence on concepts such as self-awareness, emotional management, and social deftness. However, from strictly the point of view of the scientific community, emotional intelligence has been criticized. The concept is questioned with researchers pointing to its research methodology leading to an exaggeration of its significance. Questions within the scientific community include: Is EQ a real intelligence? Does it consist of concepts and constructs that are better measured within IQ and the Big Five personality traits (Hunt & Fitzgerald, 2013)? Some critics suggest that there exists a lack of construct overlap and incremental validity when compared to the Big Five or the IQ (Harms & Crede, 2010). Research suggests that the significance of emotional intelligence has been exaggerated due to deficient research methodology (Hunt & Fitzgerald, 2013).

These are good academic discussions. However, the general public uses terms that help people and bridging the gap between the lab and the clinic and academia and real life is what this book focuses on. If kids across the world are finding EQ tools to regulate themselves and have words to understand and explain themselves, a lack of incremental validity is a non-factor in making a difference in this world. EQ is a skill / an art that can be developed but requires (a) undivided attention, (b) practice, (c) concerted effort, and (d) a sincere desire to learn the art. If parents want their children to develop this skill/art, then developing EQ within themselves is the starting line.

4        The field of psychology has been limited in its development of psychological interventions that attempt to foster bravery or courage, according to positive psychologist Martin Seligman (Peterson & Seligman, 2004). He notes that Pearson's (1998) book *The Hero Within* is the rare exception in the area of psychoanalysis, an emphasis on developing a system of archetypes. The topic of courage has been addressed in a variety of ways by philosophers, theologians, and other scholars. Thomas Aquinas, for one, wrote extensively about courage and bravery and noted that teaching bravery depended on fostering a sensitivity to fear and good judgment (Yearly, 1990). I can look at several of my past therapy clients as examples of boldness. Often, one usually considers the charismatic and popular student who runs for class president as the bold one. My favorite examples are those who overcome personal barriers and exhibit boldness. Boldly taking risks consists of perseverance. Expecting positive outcomes can increase motivation to persevere and persist (Peterson, Maier, & Seligman, 1993). Becoming a risk-taking family appears different based on temperament, the big five personality factors, feelings and background of the family members. Leaving comfort zones as a practice sets kids up for success.

5        Research at a human lab at Yale suggests that friendship webs or networks follow certain mathematical and sociological rules regardless of the culture

(Christakis & Fowler, 2013). For more information on friendship and natural selection, see www.nicholaschristakis.net

6        For experiential examples on gender differences in relationships, see Buri (2006). He highlights some of the experiential differences commonly seen in boys and girls growing up.

While differences are notable, see Hyde's 2005 analysis of 46 meta-analyses that were conducted in recent decades that shows that men and women can have similarities in terms of personality, cognitive ability, and leadership. Often, what parents often attribute to gender differences are actually human differences. "He's so boy" may be an accurate descriptor when talking about aggression. "She is such a girl" is not an accurate descriptor when describing shy leadership. While a meta-analysis of psychological gender differences has yielded differences in motor behaviors (e.g., throwing distance), sexuality, and aggression (Hyde, 2005), Buri notes other differences, particularly in communication and ability to connect at emotional and intimate levels. In some ways, marriage involves a process of catching up for many men. Buri (2014) wrote a book that is a great resource for teenagers and young adults (or any single person) to prepare themselves so that they can develop these emotional and intimacy skills in advance. Read *Intentional Dating: When You're Ready to Leave Behind the Liars, Losers, and Lemons – 15 Keys to Finding Love for a Lifetime*. In many ways, our culture is working hard to eliminate the notion of gender differences. Extensive research over decades and centuries of practical experience confirm these gender differences. For example, Tannen (1990) points out that boy's games are much more likely to have "elaborate systems of rules" that are frequently used to regulate play behavior and resolve conflicts.

7        The four-level intervention has been applied in outpatient programs, Hazelden, at a Big 10 University, and has been a key component of clinician training programs in the training of practitioners providing therapy to individuals with social anxiety. Patients who implement the four-level intervention have reported increased confidence, improved social skills, and decreased social anxiety. When it comes to social anxiety, there are three elements: (1) anxiety—which necessitates tension reduction, (2) avoidance—which necessitates exposure, and (3) skill deficit—which necessitates skill development. The four-level intervention targets this third element in developing social skills. For its use in the treatment of anxiety disorders combined with building containment skills, see my book *Anxiety Disorders Made Simple: Treatment Approaches to Overcome Fear and Build Resiliency* (van Ingen, 2014). The four-level intervention is modified from John Buri's (2006; 2014) four levels of communication. Buri designed the levels as a way to describe how communication consists of talking at progressively deeper levels.

# (Chapter 4 Endnotes)

1       The groundbreaking book by Norman Vincent Peale, *The Power of Positive Thinking*, was hugely popular.  Despite the book's success with 186 consecutive weeks on the New York Times best seller list and 5 million copies sold, mental health experts were highly critical of the book.

2       These ideas are supported by research in the area of optimism led by Seligman (1998), widely viewed as a key leader in the positive psychology movement.  His research on optimism has been influential as a counter to the self-esteem movement and the over-emphasis on feelings at the expense of achievements.  Dispositional optimism is assessed by asking people whether they expect future outcomes to be beneficial or not (Scheier & Carver, 1987).  Youth are able to expect future beneficial outcomes more easily following achievements.

3       One of the ways dispositional optimism (and pessimism) is measured is by the Life Orientation Test (LOT).  Another aspect of optimism distinct from dispositional optimism is the explanatory style, or the attributional style.  The attributional style theory suggests that optimism and pessimism are reflections of the ways we explain events.  The idea is that attributions cause these dispositions.  And these attributions, or explanations, are viewed as happening in response to internal versus external causes, stable versus unstable causes, and global versus specific causes.  As an example, optimism would be viewing a parenting reinforcement error as circumstantial (external), temporary (unstable), and specific (Gillham, Shatte, Reivich, & Seligman, 2001).  Parenting errors are opportunities to learn and grow and our attributions about those can increase our optimism, or pessimism (if we see our errors as internal, permanent, and pervasive).  Optimistic parents help children cope better, see problems as temporary, and look for ways to problem-solve more effectively.  For more information on how to grow optimism, read books by Seligman (1996, 2002, 2011) such as *The Optimistic Child: Proven Program to Safeguard Children from Depression & Build Lifelong Resilience, Authentic Happiness: Using the New Positive Psychology to Realize Your Potential for Lasting Fulfillment*, and *Flourish: A Visionary New Understanding of Happiness and Well-being*.

4       Dr. Carol Dweck of Standford has been studying other's beliefs and mindsets about learning for many years (2005, 2006, 2012).  She has concluded that most people have one of two mindsets toward learning – fixed or growth.  Some believe success is based on innate ability.  "My son was just born into being great at math."  This works in reverse as well.  "Manny was born with innate difficulties when it comes to math."  Of course, this example fits if we aren't talking about definitive learning or intellectual disabilities (i.e. brain damage).  Those who believe success is based on innate ability are said to have a "fixed" theory of intelligence.  Dweck called this a fixed mindset.  Those who believe their success is based on hard work, learning, training, and determination are viewed as having an "incremental" theory of intelligence, a growth mindset.  One's attributional style can

influence how this mindset is evident in their response to failures. Specifically, a fixed-mindset individual fears failure because it is a negative explanation about their abilities. In contrast, an individual with a growth mindset views failures as opportunities to see how their performance can improve and what kinds of things they can learn. This is another reason why parents can train their children on the value of failure in life. When kids fail, parents responding enthusiastically sets up kids for long-term success.

5       Some abilities like fluid reasoning or verbal abilities are more stable, but other abilities like working memory and cognitive processing speed change more over time. Generally speaking, IQ scores can improve by one standard deviation. Many studies have shown significant fluctuations in IQ with consistent changes with structural and functional brain imaging. In one study, researchers led by Professor Cathy Price at University College London showed that IQ is not constant (changes in 20+ points in four years); these changes occur particularly among youth and adolescents. Ramsden et al (2011) found that if verbal scores changed, corresponding regions of the teenage brain changed. Thus, an increase in verbal IQ score correlated with increases in density of grey matter in an area of the left motor cortex of the brain that is activated when articulating speech. Similarly, increases in non-verbal scores correlated with increases in the density of grey matter in the anterior cerebellum, which is related to movements of the hand.

6       In a study of 370 adult Americans who responded to these types of items (regret versus no regret), regret was strongly associated with increased anxiety and arousal (Roese et al, 2009). This partly explains why people avoid owning their regret as it can be anxiety producing. This is why Step 4 in 12 step groups (AA, NA, GA, etc.), taking an inventory of our lives, is so difficult. Facing our own demons can be a daunting dilemma. Do I dig in or do I distract myself in the technology of today? In our current digitalized society, it is becoming more difficult to develop a reflective life. Taking time to reflect, attend to the introspective life, and listen to one's interior life requires quiet and intentionality.

7       People who have lived a lot of life and reflected on the ups and downs of life know that there are psychological benefits of regret including learning from experience (Epstude & Roese, 2008). If you have 16 minutes, check out one of my favorite TED talks by Kathryn Schulz who gave a talk in November, 2011 titled

Don't regret regret.

8       Children and teenagers who are defiant, disrespectful, and bratty are more likely to become overweight or obese, compared with kids who have better behaviors such as showing respect and cooperativeness. Lumeng and colleagues (2003) found that slender kids who were persistently defiant and disrespectful were more than five times as likely to become obese, compared with equally slender kids who exhibited better behavior.

9       Dweck found that those with a fixed mindset tended to focus their effort on tasks where they had a high likelihood of success and avoided tasks where they

may have had to struggle, which limited their learning. For more information on the long-term effects of fixed mindsets and growth mindsets, see Dweck (2006, 2012).

10       Mueller and Dweck (1998) studied kids who received three treatments: praise for their intelligence, praise for their effort, and no additional feedback (control group). Kids were given very difficult problems and asked to explain their poor performance. Kids who were praised for their intelligence attributed their failure to a lack of intelligence. Kids praised for their effort attributed failure to a lack of effort. As a result, telling children that they are smart makes kids less likely to view themselves as smart, particularly after failure.

# (Chapter 5 Endnotes)

1       For more information, check out the website www.thefamilydinnerproject.org for great ideas on how to improve the regularity and quality of family dinners.

2       The locus of control was criticized because of its two-alternative forced choice technique. Regardless, this notion of internal versus external locus of control continues to provide insight into perceived control (Rotter, 1954). Healthy parents look for ways to reinforce an internal locus of control. Key conversations: In this situation, what is in your control and what is out of your control? In response to those things out of your control, in what ways can you respond to this situation?

3       One study showed that individuals who were successful in self-initiated attempts to stop smoking showed a more internal locus of control than individuals who were either unsuccessful in their attempts to quit or who never attempted to quit smoking on their own (Rosenbaum & Argon, 1979). Interestingly, a sample of 123 male and female responders showed that quitters scored more internal than either smokers or nonsmokers (Molloy, et al 1997).

4       One in three children are considered overweight or obese. More than one-third (35.7%) of adults are considered to be obese. Several factors influence this problem including processed foods, soda, excessive video games and TV. Additionally, there is a correlational relationship between locus of control and obesity (Neymotin & Nemzer, 2014). Obesity causes diabetes. Furthermore, research suggests that those with Type 1 diabetes are more external in their locus of control, held greater fatalistic attitudes and less trust in others (Trento et al., 2008).

5       Diet, smoking, exercise and medication compliance are factors affecting hypertension.
An example of an internal locus of control can be found in this quote from a hypertension study "Compliance with the treatment regimen is defined as an active

process with a sense of responsibility to improve health" (Taher et al., 2015). In a classic study by Stanton (1987), 50 adult hypertensive patients at a HMO completed questionnaires and participated in home interviews over 10 weeks. Results showed that greater expectancy for internal control over hypertension, greater knowledge of the treatment regimen, and stronger social support determined greater adherence which in turn influenced blood-pressure reduction.

6        One of the results of an external locus of control is helplessness when faced with medical problems. Nicasio and colleagues (1985) developed the Arthritis Helplessness Index (AHI), a self-report instrument designed to measure patients' perceptions of loss of control with arthritis. Greater helplessness correlated with several factors including lower self-esteem, higher anxiety, depression, and a lower internal health locus of control.

7        Research has shown that locus of control plays a role in adjustment and coping with cancer. A high internal locus of control over the course of cancer illness was associated with an attitude of a 'fighting spirit.' (Watson, Pruyn, Greer, & van den Borne, 1990).

8        The Internal Health Locus of Control (IHLC) measures the degree to which one believes one's health is influenced by one's own behavior. Research suggests that the relationship between locus of control and health-promoting behaviors is positive and important (See Lefcourt and Davidson-Katz, 1991). Each of these aforementioned studies point to the positive impact of both internal locus of control and taking one's health into their own hands. This is critical for parents because heathy eating and exercise (and other self-care behaviors) has a significant influence on health and being around for key milestones in the family's life discussed in this book.

9        In experiments with dogs, one of the study groups of dogs learned that nothing they did had any effects on shocks. The dogs simply laid down passively despite the pain of the shocks (Seligman, 1972). Dogs don't attempt to escape because they expect nothing they do will influence the shock. Experimenters taught the dogs to escape the shock by jumping over the barrier by physically picking up the dogs, moving their legs, and showing the actions the dogs would need to do in order to escape the electric shock.

10        Twenge and Campbell wrote a book titled *The Narcissism Epidemic: Living in the Age of Entitlement* (2009). "On a reality TV show, a girl planning her Sweet Sixteen wants a major road blocked off so a marching band can precede her grand entrance on a red carpet. High school students physically attack classmates and post YouTube videos of the beatings to get attention."        Research on entitlement suggests that self-centeredness and self-love is excessive. According to Twenge, narcissists lack empathy, overreact to criticism, and favor themselves over others. Because they need constant praise, immediate gratification and not taking responsibility accompanies entitlement. The most narcissistic generation of Americans is the most recent generation born between 1982 and 1999 (now

aged 13-30) and have been called Millennials, GenY, NetFen, and Generation Me. Parents raising the new generation will have to work particularly hard to reinforce selflessness, teach empathy, raise kids to receive constructive feedback, and learn to put others before themselves. Twenge has identified the latest generation, referred to as iGen, those born between 1995 and 2012, as shifting the culture in another dramatic direction. Data points to 2012 when this trend started; right after the recession of 2007-2009 and around the time when the majority of Americans began to own cell phones. A recent survey (2017) shows 75% of teens own a cell phone with the following preferred apps based on a nationally representative survey: (1) Instagram, 76% of teens, (2) Snapchat, 75% of teens, (3) Facebook, 66% of teens, (4) Twitter, 47% of teens, (5) and fewer than 30% of American teens use Tumblr, Twitch, or LinkedIn. Teens are delaying getting jobs, driver's licenses, and are going out with friends less because they are more isolated in their bedrooms using their smartphones. And teens are more unhappy the longer they are on their phones. Boys' depressive symptoms increased by 21% from 2012 to 2015. Girls increased by 50% from 2012-2015. Suicide has also doubled for both sexes in 2015 compared to 2007 with phones being a key variable – with isolation, cyberbullying, and other psychological distress like comparisons and appearance (i.e. # of likes) as all contributing factors.

11      Twenge (2006, 2011), Twenge and Foster (2010), and Twenge, Konrath, Foster, Campbell, and Bushman (2008a, 2008b) have provided careful analysis of data from the last 30 years indicating that narcissism has gradually increased among young men and women. See Campbell (2005) and Twenge and Campbell (2008) for thorough descriptions of narcissistic behavior patterns. As an alternative, Arnett (2013) argues against Twenge that emerging adults are excessively "narcisstic." In his article, *The Evidence for Generation We and Against Generation Me*, he suggests that emerging adults have high expectations and are confident in their abilities but suggests that narcissism has not risen based on scores on the Narcissistic Personality Inventory (NPI). See Twenge (2013), as she responds in her article, *The Evidence for Generation Me and Against Generation We*. In nationally represented samples of high school and college students, values have shifted toward extrinsic (money, fame, and image) values that are tied to an inflated sense of self and away from concerns identified as intrinsic (community, affiliation). The debate continues but the main goal of parents is to facilitate an environment that encourages selflessness to counter these developments in society. Closely tied to narcissism is selfishness which indications suggest is on a rise in western cultures (Campbell & Miller, 2011).

12      Like narcissism, research also reveals that selfishness is on the rise in Western cultures (Campbell & Miller, 2011; Twenge, 2006). Several authors have provided evidence of the negative impact of selfishness on relationships (Impett & Gordon, 2008; Stanley, Whitton, Sadberry, Clements, & Markman, 2006). There is a lot for healthy parents of the new generation to counter.

13      Rotter has been cited as one of the 100 most eminent psychologists of the 20th century. Rotter was 18th in frequency in citations in journal articles ac-

cording to a study by Haggbloom et al (2002).

14      Has Locus of Control changed? A cross-temporal meta-analysis of increasing externality in locus of control was reviewed by Twenge, Zhang, & Im (2004). Bottom line is that "The average college student in 2002 had a more external locus of control than 80% of college students in the early 1960s." Nowadays, teens view accomplishing goals as more based on luck, chance, and probability than effort and determination. This seems counterintuitive based on what you might expect from narcissistic teens with high self-esteem. This research breakthrough shows us the anxiety epidemic (just review the small sampling of stressors in Chapter 6) and why this epidemic is rampant in society. If teenagers believe that the "role of the dice," "the flip of the coin," or "being at the right place at the right time is all about luck" is more valuable than effort and determination, it is no wonder that anxiety is high.

15      Research shows that the average millennial had higher self-esteem than 86% of college men in 1968 (Twenge & Campbell, 2001; Twenge et al., 2008b). The average female college student during the 1990s had higher self-esteem than 71% of Boomer college women. There have also been significant changes in narcissism in recent years with the measurement of the Narcissistic Personality Inventory (NPI) with the average college student in 2006 scoring significantly higher than 65% of students in the early 1980s. Current college students are more likely going to agree with items such as, "If I ruled the world it would be a better place," I can live my life any way I want to," "I think I am a special person."

16      Campbell et al., (2005) provided a review of the problematic characteristics of Narcissism. The following is a list of characteristics that make it difficult in relationships: inflated self-views (i.e. smarter, more creative, more attractive), brag and draw attention to themselves (Buss & Chiodo, 1991), adopt "colorful personae (Hogan & Hogan, 2002), strive to associate with high-status others (Campbell, 1999), are more interested in their own status and success than their emotional closeness to others, and lack empathy for others (Watson, Grisham, Trotter, & Biderman, 1984). With Millennials now as parents, differences in how they parent compared to previous generations was reviewed by Steinmetz (2015) in a poll of 2,000 U.S. parents. Some of the results yielded: 36% of Millennials think their friends' children participate in too many activities compared to 50% of Gen X parents and 53% of Baby boomers; 60% of Millennials think it is somewhat, very or extremely important that their child's name is unique compared to 44% of Gen X parents and 35% of Baby boomers; 30% of Millennials are somewhat, very or extremely concerned about other parents judging the food their parents eat compared to 17% of Gen X parents and 11% of Baby boomers; 42% of Millennials say it is very or extremely important for a couple to be married before they have children compared to 49% of Gen X parents and 51% of Baby boomers. Interestingly, 58% of Millennial parents find the amount of parenting information available to be somewhat, very or extremely overwhelming. For more information on this study, visit http://time.com/4070021/millennial-parents-raising-kids-poll/

17      Oppositional defiant disorder and behavior conduct disorder are defined in the *Diagnostic and Statistical Manual of Mental Disorders*, fifth edition (DSM-V, American Psychiatric Association, 2013).   For a great resource when working with oppositional defiant disorder, see James Keim's work and his website at www.op-positional.com

18      Keim (1997) describes the ability to visualize the type of sequential steps necessary to achieve a desired end result as 'enhanced social perception.'  Consider Craig who knows exactly how to get his Mom to scream and leave the office so he can use the TV on his own. "It's easy. I tell her she is wrong. I mimic her voice and facial expressions. I nit-pick one detail and argue it.   When she raises her voice, I laugh." This five-step sequence for achieving his own TV time was easily developed by Craig.   Parents have to think two steps ahead and have to be prepared to not predictably follow the sequence.

# (Chapter 6 Endnotes)

1.  Diagnoses of children have risen in conjunction with the increased frequency of diagnoses in the DSMs.   For a review on changes in the United Sates over the last 50+ years, see Whitaker's Anatomy of an Epidemic.   Here are some of the key findings in his award-winning investigative journalism: (1) In 1955, there were 355,000 adults in state and county mental hospitals with a psychiatric diagnosis and over the next three decades, the number of disabled mentally ill rose to 1.25 million; (2) The number of disabled mentally ill adults more than doubled between 1988 and 2007 (more than four million adults); (3) The number of youth in America receiving government disability benefits because of an identified mental health problem drastically increased from 16,200 in 1987 to 561,569 in 2007.  Some of the key controversial issues that this book explores is whether the widespread use of psychiatric medications has actually been detrimental and influenced the increase in the disability numbers.  Just in terms of diagnoses, the number of identified diagnoses has increased by more than 300%, from 106 in the DSM-I (1952) to 365 in the DSM-IV-TR (2000).

2.   The American Association of Pediatrics reports that the typical adolescent averages 49 hours of media exposure per week.  More recently, common sense media (see nsensemedia.org)" www.commonsensemedia.org) reports that American teens (13-18) use an average of nine hours of media daily, not including for school or homework.  Tweens (8-12) use an average of about six hours of entertainment media daily.

3.   See the National Institute of Mental Health at www.nimh.nih.gov for fur-

ther statistics.

4.　Difficulty with sleep caused by electronic screens has been well-document-
ed. For an excellent resource, read *Reset your child's brain: a four-week
plan to end meltdowns, raise grades, and boost social skills by reversing the
effects of electronic screen-time* by Victoria Dunckley, MD. Dunckley details
how unnatural bright light from the screen of a digital device is transmitted
by the optic nerve which communicates a signal to the pineal gland that it is
daylight. The pineal gland does not produce melatonin for sleep because it
does not realize that it is nighttime. The sleep wakefulness cycle is affected
by this hormone delay and the over-stimulation of neurotransmitters and
hormones. Dr. Dunckley writes that unplugging from digital screens for 30
days can reduce or resolve behavior problems, poor grades, ADHD symptoms and other problems.

5.　In the past, it was thought that taking the perspective of others didn't develop until the ages of eight (Santrock, 2004). Nowadays, parents can build
empathy skills, social deftness, and perspective taking with regular practice
at a much earlier age.

6.　Kids go from speaking freely in elementary school to significant inhibition in
middle and high school with a 75% prevalence rate of public speaking (Hamilton, 2008). Something happens around the age range of 10-13 when children become overly concerned about being humiliated and embarrassed.
One of the things that happens is social anxiety. In fact, the mean onset of
social anxiety is 10 to 13 years (Nelson et al., 2000; Nelson et al., 2010).

7.　Numerous authors (e.g., Beck, 1995, Burns, 1999, Persons, 2008) have
written about the problems of cognitive distortions and the consequences
of treating one's emotions as an accurate compass in life and an accurate
reflection of reality. Accepting our emotions as a guide in life and a true
reflection of who we are can have deleterious consequences for how we approach life. One of the primary cognitive distortions that has been identified
as problematic for emotional disorders is emotional reasoning. This type of
thinking entails interpreting experiences through our emotions. In my case,
while vomiting at my ex-girlfriend's toilet following a break-up, I felt like a
loser. Using this rationale, the thinking is...If you feel like a loser, then you
must be a loser. If you feel ugly, therefore, you must be ugly... Any negative
thing you feel about yourself or others must be true because that is the
emotion. The problem with emotional reasoning is that emotions in and of
themselves have no validity. Emotions can come and go, shift like the wind,
and can be sometimes unpredictable. This is further complicated by individuals who believe that they cannot control their emotions, in reality, we have
some control over how we feel and can influence emotions. This is one of
the essential beliefs of cognitive behavioral therapy (CBT). Burns described
it this way, "Many people believe that their bad moods result from factors
beyond their control... Some people attribute their blue moods to their
hormones or body chemistry. Others believe that their sour outlook results

from some childhood event that has long been forgotten and buried deep in their unconscious. Some people argue that it's realistic to feel bad because they're ill or have recently experienced a personal disappointment… These theories are based on the notion that our feelings are beyond our control. If you say, 'I just can't help the way I feel,' you will only make yourself a victim of your misery---and you'll be fooling yourself, because you can change the way you feel" (p. 3).

8.　Mission Australia's 2015 National Survey of Young Australians aged 15-19 identifies the top teenage issues. For a great resource on understanding top teenage issues, visit the Raising Children Network at www.raisingchildren. net.au A different angle on the worry data shows the dangers that teens and kids face based on American parents' concerns for their children: 60% of parents say they worry that their child will be bullied, 54% worry that their child will struggle with anxiety or depression; 50% worry that their child will be kidnapped; 45% worry that their child will get beat up or attacked; 43% worry that their child will get pregnant or get a girl pregnant. For further information, visit the Pew Research Center at www.pewresearch.org

9.　Wegner (1989) randomly assigned individuals with generalized anxiety disorder, those who worry excessively, into two groups. Everybody in both groups were shown a white bear. One group was told to try not to think about it and the other group was told nothing. The group that was told to not think about the white bear was significantly more likely to think about the white bear. The difference was even more significant when they were told not to worry about their stressors. The group that was told not to worry about their issues had significantly more worry and stress. So, the old cliché "don't worry about it" is not supported by evidence.

10.　Researchers have explored the benefits and consequences of counterfactual thinking. Downward counterfactual thinking involves thinking about how the situation could have been worse, which often helps people feel a sense of relief (i.e. minor sprain as opposed to a broken ankle or fender bender as opposed to a total). Upward counterfactual thinking involves focusing on ways that the situation could have been better (i.e. If I dribbled up faster or passed the ball, then I wouldn't have been called for a backcourt violation) (Markman, Gavanski, Sherman, & McMullen, 1993). See Epstude & Roese (2008) for a thorough assessment of the counterfactual thinking idea; one of their key findings is that excessive counterfactual thinking is associated with excessive problem-focused thinking which is actually worry.

# (Chapter 7 Endnotes)

1.  Hofer (2008) found that 10.4 forms of communication were a part of the parent-child relationship.  With helicopter parents, this is initiated by parents.

2.  For more reading on the hedonic dip experienced in parenting, read Lyubomirsky (2008).

3.  John Gottman is a foremost expert on marriage research (Gottman & Silver, 1994; Gottman & Silver, 1999).  For more information on marriage tools and his parenting work on emotional intelligence, visit www.gottman.com

4.  Another classic book is *How to Win Friends and Influence People* by Dale Carnegie.  Carnegie listed a series of principles and one of those to help you interact effectively with other people is to "Try honestly to see things from the other person's point of view."  A recent study shows that perspective-taking relies on differing cognitive capacities in different situations (Ryskin et al., 2015). Perspective taking requires time and practice as a skill to develop.

5.  Ed Diener is known as "Dr. Happiness" as a leading researcher on positive psychology and coined the expression "subjective well-being."  Over the past 50 years, income has climbed steadily with the gross domestic product (GDP) per capita tripling, yet Diener (Diener & Biswas-Diener, 2008) has found that life satisfaction has remained flat.  In a cross-national study on teenagers, Diener found that "the most salient characteristics shared by the 10% of students with the highest levels of happiness and the fewest signs of depression were their strong ties to friends and family and commitment to spending time with them" (Diener & Seligman, 2002).

6.  See this article on 19 lottery winners who blew it all http://www.businessinsider.com/17-lottery-winners-who-blew-it-all-2013-5?op=1

7.  The main point here is that while rags to riches and back to rags is less common, the majority of lottery winnings don't maintain the increase in happiness following the win.  We adapt and tend to return to the pre-lottery happiness level.  Lottery winners' experiences fall under the umbrella of hedonic adaptation.  I fondly remember the 1980s opening of ABC Wide World of Sports as it shows highlights and stated "the thrill of victory and the agony of defeat."  In life, the thrill and agony subside over time.  Hedonic adaptation explains how the pleasure of a soccer championship, the sadness after a failed romance, the delight over a job offer, and the distress over bad news all pass with time.  Hedonic adaptation occurs in both positive and negative life experiences (Lyubomirsky, Sheldon, & Schkade, 2005).  And people tend to "recover" from both positive and negative life events (Suh, Diener, & Fujita, 1996).

8.     For an excellent resource on treating "tough adolescents," see Sells' *Treating the Tough Adolescent: A Family-Based, Step-by Step Guide*. The author provides a number of behavioral interventions and consequences that attempt to address the most ardent and difficult behaviors. Creative Interventions like the atomic bomb intervention are implemented when no other solutions are working for the toughest behaviors.

9.     Peterson & Seligman (2004) provided an alternative to the DSM, a book of psychiatric diagnoses that we use for diagnostic evaluations. While the DSM lists everything that could go wrong with people, Character Strengths and Virtues is written as a resource for what can go right. As a result, this empirical resource focuses on character strengths. An underlying rationale of positive psychology is that we have spent a large part of the last 100 years trying to reduce and lesson mental disorder. In contrast, positive psychology aims to build and strengthen what is good, rather than decrease what is bad or disordered. For a great resource for your children to measure their character strengths, go to www.authentichappiness.org. One of the engagement questionnaires is the VIA Strength Survey for Children which measures 24 character strengths for children. This can help your child think about their top strengths.

10.   This theory was put forth by Sonja Lyubomirsky's work (2008), a leading happiness researcher.

11.   Several studies deriving from Festinger's Cognitive Dissonance Theory and Bem's Self-Perception Theory have revealed that an effective way to change how you are feeling is to change the way you are acting. Instead of waiting to feel better, doing things like getting up out of bed, opening the shades and going for a walk can help people gain perspective. More specifically, if you want to be happier, then smile more and be pleasant with those around you. If you want to be more outgoing, then be more talkative and act more sociably. If you want to feel more loving, then express more affection. For reviews on the literature on cognitive dissonance and self-perception theory, see Cooper & Scher (1994) and Fazio (1987).

12.   For more information on shifting our attention to change happiness levels, see Dolan (2014). He suggests that deciding, designing, and doing reduces biases that maintain unhappiness levels.

13.   A good resource on succinct nuggets of wisdom taken from scientific studies was completed by Niven (2009), *Simple Secrets for Becoming Healthy, Wealthy, & Wise*.

14.   Several studies have shown how savoring increases awareness of the present and slows life down. Slowing life down is one of the challenges of parenting. An example of savoring is when we are mindful of our eating as chefs know the advantages of mindful eating. Savoring is the use of thoughts, reflections and actions to increase the intensity, duration, and appreciation of positive moments and experiences. Bryant introduced the concept of savoring as being mindfully engaged and aware of one's emo-

tions during positive events (Bryant & Yarnold, 2007).  As another reminder that money doesn't increase happiness, wealthier people report less savoring ability.  As an example, Quoidbach and colleagues found that when individuals were exposed to a reminder of wealth, people were less able to savor and enjoy a piece of chocolate (Qoidbach et. al, 2010).  Personalities and self-esteem also relate to savoring.  Bryant & Yarnold (2014) found that Type A people tend to not savor experiences as much as Type B people.  Type B also enjoy vacations more because of the savoring effect.  Wood et al (2003) found that individuals with low self-esteem tend to dampen their moods rather than savor positive experiences.

15.  Diener & Seligman (2002) also found that extraversion, low neuroticism, and relatively low levels of psychopathology form necessary conditions for high happiness.  Social relationships are necessary, but do not guarantee high happiness.  However, unhappy people have social relationships that are significantly worse than average.  This study was key in the happiness research because so many other variables did not determine happiness differences.  The key difference was how attention was placed, with very happy individuals centering their attention on positive events.  How does this relate to parents?  Happy parents have a network of relationships and center their attention on positive events.

16.  Achnor (2010) completed extensive research at Harvard University and explains how we can reprogram our brains to become more positive.  See *The Happiness Advantage: The Seven Principles of Positive Psychology That Fuel Success and Performance at Work.*

17.  The original study was completed by psychologists, Killingsworth and Gilbert of Harvard University and published in Science (2010).  2,250 subjects in this study ranged in age from 18-88, representing a wide range of socioeconomic backgrounds and occupations.  They found that people were happiest making love, exercising, or engaging in conversation.  They were least happy when resting, working, or using a home computer.  However, they estimated that only 4.6% of a person's happiness in a given moment was attributable to the specific activity he or she was doing, whereas a person's mind wandering accounted for about 10.8% of his or her happiness.  When volunteers were contacted at random intervals, they were asked how happy they were, what they were currently doing, and whether they were thinking about their current activity or some other activity that they classify as pleasant, neutral, or unpleasant. In other research (see Franklin, et. al 2013), mind wandering was categorized as interesting, useful, or novel.   When individuals wander about tasks that are either highly interesting and/or highly useful, they will experience more positive moods than when an individual's mind wanders about tasks that are of low interest and low usefulness.  This research suggests that mind wandering about some tasks while engaged in uninteresting tasks can bring on more positive moods.  However, mind wandering and negative moods are more likely to go together.  Furthermore, there

are clear benefits to reducing chronic patterns of mind wandering such as negative ruminations (Hofman and Smits, 2008; Driessen and Hollon, 2010). Additionally, there are clear benefits of mindfulness which is an absence of mind-wandering that is discussed throughout this book.

18.　The progression of P.E.R.M.A. Theory is best explained by Martin Seligman, one of the founders of positive psychology. His recent books from Authentic Happiness to Flourish reveal the progression of this key psychological theory on happiness.

19.　According to the Pew Research Center, 72% of teens play video games on their computer, game console, or cellphone. 59% of girls game, while 84% of teen boys game. The following are some additional statistics of interest regarding video games: (a) Talking with friends while playing a video game is a major way boys talk with friends; (b) More play is on-line than in-person—16% of boys play games with others in person on a daily or near-daily basis versus 34% play games with others online almost every day; (c) 57% of boys and 40% of girls play networked games with individuals they would not call a friend; (d) 71% of boys and 28% of girls voice chat during networked games. Source: Pew Research Center's Teens Relationships Survey, Sept. 25-Oct. 9, 2014, and Feb. 10-March 16, 2015.

20.　Evidence from a meta-analytic review strongly suggests that exposure to violent video games is a causal risk factor for increased aggressive behavior, aggressive cognition, and decreased empathy (Anderson et. al, 2010). For a great resource on the negative effects of video games, read Hooked on Games: The Lure and Cost of Video Game and Internet Addiction by Andrew Doan & Brooke Strickland. Doan is considered a leading expert in the area of neuroscience and its effects on gaming addiction. For a great resource on video games, internet addicts, and cell phone use, visit his website at www.hooked-on-games.com. There are advantages and disadvantages to video games. Some advantages include the stimulation of curiosity and imagination, opportunities to overcome challenges, and exchanging tricks and strategies with friends. See www.kidcrono.com for a good website on the advantages and disadvantages in this area.

21.　Doan and Walsh (2017) use an analogy to explain adults who are all thumbs in their thinking (adapted from Voss et. al, 2015). One can observe one's left hand. The thumb represents the brain areas associated with the benefits of digital media: quick analytical skills, improved hand-eye coordination, and improved reflexes. The index finger represents communication skills. The middle finger represents social bonding with family and friends. The ring finger represents the capacity to recognize emotions in oneself and in others (empathy). Finally, the pinky finger represents self-control. Folding the fingers, the adult is all thumbs in their thinking because there is not enough time to work on these other skills when we spend an average of 7 hours and 38 minutes in front of a digital screen for entertainment. Video game addicts end up with quick analytical skills and reflexes with poor communication skills, limited relationships, low EQ (empathy), and poor self-control.

22.   John Tauer (2015) discusses this successfully in his book *Why Less is More for WOSPS: Well-Intentioned Overinvolved Sports Parents*.  This book is a great resource that shows that decades of research indicates that young athletes do better with less involvement from parents.

23.   This column was eventually turned into a popular book.  This is a great resource on life's Lessons.  See Brett's (2010) book *God Never Blinks: 50 Lessons for Life's Little Detours*.

24.   Froh & Bono (2015) wrote *Making Grateful Kids: The Science of Building Character*.  They identified linguistic accuracy and vocabulary as influential in understanding how to build gratitude.  One of their ideas was drawing attention to the Whorfian hypothesis, which suggests that what you say influences how you think and what you do.  They suggest that a vocabulary of gratitude makes you feel more grateful.

25.   For more information on a review of new year's resolutions and behavior change, see Norcross (2012) on *Changeology: 5 Steps to Realizing Your Goals and Resolutions*.

26.   "The trend is toward greater emotional positivity with increasing age." This is a quote by gratitude expert Robert Emmons (2013) who authored *Gratitude Works! A 21-Day Program for Creating Emotional Prosperity*. As individuals get older, they maintain or increase emotional reactivity to positive information but their limbic system has less emotional activation to negative information.

# **References**

Achor, S. (2010). *The happiness advantage: the seven principles of positive psychology that fuel success and performance at work.* New York: Crown Business.

Ainsworth, M. D. S. (1973). The development of infant-mother attachment. In B. Cardwell & H. Ricciuti (Eds.), *Review of child development research* (Vol. 3, pp. 1-94) Chicago: University of Chicago Press.

American Psychiatric Association. (2013). Diagnostic and statistical manual of mental disorders (5th ed.). Arlington, VA: American Psychiatric Publishing.

Anderson, C. A., Shibuya, A., Ihori, N., Swing, E. L., Bushman, B. J., Sakamoto, A., Rothstein, H. R., & Saleem, M. (2010). Violent video game effects on aggression, empathy, and prosocial behavior in Eastern and Western countries: A meta-analytic review. *Psychological Bulletin, 136,* 151-173.

Arnett, J. J. (2013). Generation Me or Generation We? A debate. Emerging Adulthood.

Baumrind, D. (1971). Current patterns of parental authority. *Developmental Psychology,* 4, 1–103.

Baumrind D, Larzelere RE, Cowan PA (July 2002). "Ordinary physical punishment: is it harmful? Comment on Gershoff (2002)" (PDF). *Psychol Bull.* 128 (4): 580–9. doi:10.1037/0033-2909.128.4.580. PMID 12081082.

Beck, J. S. (2005). *Cognitive therapy for challenging problems: What to do when the basics don't work.* New York: Guilford Press.

Blankenhorn, D. (1996). *Fatherless America: confronting our most urgent social problem.* New York: Harper Perennial.

Bowlby J. (1969). *Attachment. Attachment and loss: Vol. 1. Loss.* New York: Basic Books.

Breslau, N., Chilcoat, H.D., Kessler, R.C., & Davis, G.C. (1999a). Previous exposure to trauma and PTSD effects of subsequent trauma: Results from the Detroit Area Survey of Trauma.

Brett, Regina (2010). *God Never Blinks: 50 Lessons for Life's Little Detours.* Grand Central Publishing; Reprint edition.

Bryant, F. B., & Veroff, J. (2007). *Savoring: A new model of positive experience.* Mahwah, NJ: Lawrence Erlbaum Associates.

Bryant, F. B.; Yarnold, P. R. (2014). "Type A behavior and savoring among college undergraduates: Enjoy achievements now—not later". *Memory.* 3 (113): 54–0.

Buri, J. R. (1991). Parental Authority Questionnaire. *Journal of Personality Assessment,* 57, 110–119.

Buri, J. R. (2006). *How to Love Your Wife.* Tate Publishing, Mustang, OK.

Buri, J. R. (2014). *Intentional Dating: When You're Ready to Leave Behind the Liars, Losers, and Lemons – 15 Keys to Finding Love for a Lifetime.* Tate Publishing, Mustang, OK.

Burns, D. (1999). Feeling Good: The New Mood Therapy. New York: Harper Collins.

Buss, D. M., & Chiodo, L. M. (1991). Narcissistic acts in everyday life. *Journal of Personality, 59,* 179-215.

Cameron, J., & Pierce, W. D. (1994). Reinforcement, reward, and intrinsic motivation: A meta-analysis. *Review of Educational Research, 64,* 363–423.

Campbell, W.K. (1999). Narcissism and romantic attraction. *Journal of Personality and Social Psychology,* 77(6), 1254-1270.

Campbell, W. K., & Miller, J. D. (Ed.). (2011). *The handbook of narcissism and narcissistic personality disorder.* New York, NY: Wiley.

Campbell, W. K., Bush, C. P., Brunell, A. B., & Shelton, J. (2005). Understanding the social costs of narcissism: The case of tragedy of the commons. *Personality and Social Psychology Bulletin,* 31, 1358–1368.

Carnegie, D., 1888-1955. (2009). *How to win friends and influence people.* New York: Simon & Schuster.

Christakis D. (2010) Internet addiction: a 21st century epidemic? *BMC medicine* 8: 61.

Christakis, N. A., & Fowler, J. H. (2013). Social contagion theory: Examining dynamic social networks and human behavior. Statistics in Medicine, 32, 556–577.

Cooper, J. & Scher, S. J. (1994). When do our actions affect our attitudes? In S. Shavitt & T. C. Brock (Eds.), "Persuasions" (pp. 95-112). Boston, MA: Allyn and Bacon.

Condry, J., & Simon, M. L. (1974). Characteristics of peer-and parent-oriented children. Journal of Marriage and the Family, 36, 543-5

Corneau, G. (1991). Absent fathers, lost sons: the search for masculine identity. Boston. Random House.

Davidson, J.R.T., Hughes, D., Blazer, D.G., & George, L.K. (1991). Post-traumatic stress disorder in the community: An epidemiological study. Psychological Medicine, 21, 713-721.

Diener, E. and M. Seligman (2002). Very happy people. APA, January.

Diener, E., & Seligman, M.E.P. (2002). Very happy people. Psychological Science, 13, 80–83.

Diener, E. and Rober-Biswas Diener (2008) Happiness: Unlocking the Mysteries of Psychological Wealth. Blackwell: Oxford.

Doan, J., & Walsh, C. (2017). Behaviors, Digital Media, & the Brain: Digital Vortex Survival Guide. F.E.P. International.

Dolan, P. (2014). Happiness by design: Change what you do, not what you think. Hudson Street Press, London.

Driessen, E., & Hollon, S.D. (2010). Cognitive behavioral therapy for mood disorders: Efficacy, moderators and mediators. Psychiatric Clinics of North America (33) 537-555.

Dweck, C. S. (2006). Mindset: The new psychology of success. New York: Random House.

Dweck, C. S. (2012). Mindset: How you can fulfill your potential. Constable & Robinson Limited.

Elliot, A. J., & Dweck, C. S. (Eds.). (2005). Handbook of competence and motivation. New York: Guilford.

Emmons, R. A. (2013). Gratitude works!: a 21-day program for creating emotional prosperity. Jossey-Bass.

Epstude, K., & Roese, N. J. (2008). The functional theory of counterfactual thinking. Personality & Social Psychology Review, 12, 168-192.

Fazio, R. (1987). Self-perception theory: A current perspective. In M. P. Zanna, J. M., Olson, & C. P. Herman (Eds.), "Ontario Symposium on Personality and Social Psychology" (pp. 129-150). Hillsdale, NJ: Lawrence Erlbaum Publishers.

Feinstein, B. A., Hershenberg, R., Bhatia, V., Latack, J. A., Meuwly, N., & Davila, J. (2013). Negative social comparison on Facebook and depressive symptoms: Rumination as a mechanism. Psychology of Popular Media Culture, Vol 2(3), Jul 2013, 161-170.

Franklin M. S., Smallwood J., Schooler J. W. (2011). Catching the mind in flight: using behavioral indices to detect mindless reading in real time. Psychonomic Bulletin & Review, (18) 992–997.

Froh, J., & Bono, G. (2015). Making grateful kids: the science of building character. Templeton Press; reprint edition.

George, C., Kaplan, N., & Main, M. (1985). The Adult Attachment Interview. Unpublished manuscript, University of California at Berkeley.

Gershoff, Elizabeth (2002). "Corporal Punishment, Physical Abuse, and the Burden of Proof: Reply to Baumrind, Larzelere, and Cowan (2002), Holden (2002), and Parke (2002)" (PDF). *Psychological Bulletin*. 128 (4): 602–611. doi:10.1037/0033-2909.128.4.602.

Gillham, Jane E.; Shatté, Andrew J.; Reivich, Karen J.; Seligman, Martin E. P. (2001). "Optimism, Pessimism, and Explanatory Style". In Chang, Edward C. *Optimism and Pessimism: Implications for Theory, Research, and Practice*. Washington, DC: American Psychological Association. pp. 53–75. ISBN 978-1-55798-691-7.

Goleman, D. (1995a). *Emotional intelligence*. New York: Bantam Books.

Gottman, J. M., & Silver, N. (1994). *Why marriages succeed or fail*. New York, NY: Simon & Schuster.

Gottman, J. M., & Silver, N. (1999). The seven principles of making marriage work. New York, NY: Crown Publishers.

Haggbloom S. J., Warnick R., Warnick J. E., Jones V. K., Yarbrough G. L., Russell T. M., Borecky C. M., McGahhey R., Powell J. L., Beavers J., Monte E. (2002) The 100 most eminent psychologists of the 20th century. Review of General Psychology, 6, 139–152. doi: 10.1037/1089-2680.6.2.139

Hamilton, C. (2008). Making Friends with your Public Speaking Anxiety Monster. A paper presented at the 2009 National Association of Communication Centers Mini-Conference.

Harms, P. D., & Credé, M. (2010). "Remaining Issues in Emotional Intelligence Research: Construct Overlap, Method Artifacts, and Lack of Incremental Validity". Industrial and Organizational Psychology: Perspectives on Science and Practice. 3 (2): 154–158. doi:10.1111/j.1754-9434.2010.01217.x.

Harms, P. D., & Crede, M. (2010). Emotional intelligence and transformational and transactional leadership: A meta-analysis. Journal of Leadership and Organizational Studies, 17(1), 5(13).

Henderlong, J., & Lepper, M. R. (2002). The effects of praise on children's intrinsic motivation: A review and synthesis. Psychological Bulletin, 128, 774–795.

Hofer, B. K. (2008). The electronic tether: Parental regulation, self-regulation, and the role of technology in college transitions. Journal of e First-Year Experience & Students in Transition, 20(2), 9-24.

Hofmann, S.G. & Smits, J.A. (2008). Cognitive-behavioral therapy for adult anxiety disorders: a meta-analysis of randomized placebo-controlled trials. Journal of Clinical Psychiatry, 69(4), 621-32.

Hogan, R., & Hogan, J. (2002). Leadership and sociopolical intelligence. In R. E. Riggio, S.E. Murphy, and F.J. Pirozzolo (Eds.), Multiple intelligences and leadership (pp. 75-88). San Francisco: Jossey-Bass.

Holt, J. (1982). How children fail (Rev. ed.). New York: Dell.

Hyde, J. S. (2005). The Gender Similarities Hypothesis. American Psychologist, Vol. 60, No. 6.

Hunt, J. & Fitzgerald, M. (2013). The relationship between emotional intelligence and transformational leadership: An investigation and review of competing claims in the literature, American International Journal of Social Science, 2 (8): 30-38.

Impett, E. A., & Gordon, A. (2010). Why do people sacrifice to approach rewards versus to avoid costs? Insights from attachment theory. Personal Relationships, 17, 299–315.

Keim, James P. (1997) Strategic Family Therapy of Oppositional Behavior. In Frank M. Dattilio (Ed.), Integrative Cases in Marriage and Family Therapy: A Cognitive-Behavioral Approach. New York: Guilford.

Killingsworth, M.A. & Gilbert, D.T. (2010) A wandering mind is an unhappy mind. Science, Vol. 330, Page 932.

Kohn, A. (1993). Punished by rewards: The trouble with gold stars, incentive plans, A's, praise, and other bribes. New York: Houghton Mifflin.

Lefcourt, H.M., and Davidson-Katz, K. (1991). Locus of control and health. In C.R. Snyder and D.R. Forsyth(Eds.), Handbook of Social and Clinical Psychology: the health perspective (pp. 246-266). New York: Pergamon Press.

Lepper, M. R., Greene, D., & Nisbett, R. E. (1973). Undermining children's intrinsic interest with extrinsic reward: A test of the "overjustification" hypothesis. *Journal of Personality and Social Psychology, 28,* 129 –137.

Lumeng JC, Gannon K, Cabral HJ, et al. (2003) Association between clinically meaningful behavior problems and overweight in children. *Pediatrics* 112(5): 1138–1145.

Lyubomirsky, S. (2008). *The How of Happiness: A Scientific Approach to Getting the Life You Want.* New York: Penguin Press.

Lyubomirsky, S., Sheldon, K. M., & Schkade, D. (2005). Pursuing happiness: e architecture of sustainable change. *Review of General Psychology, 9,* 111–31.

Main, M. (1996). Introduction to the special section on attachment and psychopathology: 2. Overview of the eld of attachment. *Journal of Consulting and Clinical Psychology, 64,* 237–243.

Main, M. & Solomon, J. (1990). Procedures for identifying disorganized/disoriented infants during the Ainsworth Strange Situation. In M. Greenberg, D. Cicchetti & M. Cummings (Eds), Attachment in the preschool years, pp. 121-160. Chicago: University of Chicago Press.

Markman KD, Gavanski I, Sherman SJ, McMullen MN (1993). The mental simulation of better and worse possible worlds. *Journal of Experimental Social Psychology.* 29:87–109.

Mehrabian, A. (1981). *Silent messages: Implicit communication of emotions and attitudes.* Belmont, CA: Wadsworth.

Molloy, G.N., Wolstencroft, K., King, N.J., Lowe, A.R., Gardner, P.L. & Rowley, G.L. (1997). Locus of control of smokers, nonsmokers, and non-practicing smokers. Psychological Reports, 81, 781-782.

Mueller, C. M., & Dweck, C. S. (1998). Praise for intelligence can undermine children's motivation and performance. *Journal of Personality and Social Psychology, 75,* 33–52.

Nelson E. C.; Grant J. D.; Bucholz K. K.; Glowinski A.; Madden P. A. F.; Reich W.; et al. (2000). "Social phobia in a population-based female adolescent twin sample: Co-morbidity and associated suicide-related symptoms". *Psychological Medicine.* 30 (4): 797–804. doi:10.1017/S0033291799002275. PMID 11037087.

Nelson, E. A., Deacon, B. J., Lickel, J. J., & Sy, J. T. (2010). Targeting the probability versus cost of feared out- comes in public speaking anxiety. *Behaviour Research and Therapy, 48,* 282-289.

Neymotin F., Nemzer L.R. Locus of control and obesity. Front. Endocrinol. (Lausanne) 2014;5 doi: 10.3389/fendo.2014.00159.

Nicassio PM, Wallston KA, Callahan LF, Herbert M, Pincus T. The measurement of helplessness in rheumatoid arthritis. The development of the arthritis helplessness index. J Rheumatol. 1985;12:462–7.

Niven, D. (2006). *The simple secrets for becoming healthy, wealthy, and wise: what scientists have learned and how you can use it.* Harper One.

Norcross, J. C., Loberg, K., & Norcross, J. (2013). *Changeology: 5 steps to realizing your goals and resolutions.* Simon & Schuster; reprint edition.

Ogawa, J. R., Sroufe, L. A., Wein eld, N. S., Carlson, E. A., & Egeland, B. (1997). Development and the fragmented self: Longitudinal study of dissociative symptomatology in a nonclinical sample. *Development and Psychopathology, 9,* 855–879.

Peale, N. V. (1996). *The Power of Positive Thinking.* Ballantine Books; Reissue edition.

Pearson, C. (1986/1998). *The hero within: Six archetypes we live by.* New York: Harper Collins.

Persons, J. B. (2008). *The case formulation approach to cognitive-behavior therapy.* New York: Guilford Press.

Peterson, C., Maier, S. F., & Seligman, M. E. P. (1993). *Learned helplessness: A theory for the age of personal control.* New York: Oxford University Press.

Peterson, C., & Seligman, M. E. P. (2004). *Character strengths and virtues: A classification and handbook.* New York: Oxford University Press/Washington, DC: American Psychological Association.

Peterson, Christopher; Seligman, Martin E.P. (2004). *Character Strengths and Virtues.* Oxford: Oxford University Press. ISBN 0195167015.

Pittman, F. (1994) *Man Enough: Fathers, Sons and the Search for Masculinity.* Perigee Trade; Reprint edition October 1, 1994.

Quoidbach, J., Dunn, E. W., Petrides, K. V., & Mikolajczak, M. (2010). Money Giveth, Money Taketh Away The Dual Effect of Wealth on Happiness. Psychological Science.

Ramsden, S., Richardson, F.M., Josse, G., Thomas, M.S.C., Ellis, C., Shakeshaft, C., Seghier, M.L. &

Price, C.J. (2011). Verbal and non-verbal intelligence changes in the teenage brain. Nature, *479*, 113-116. doi:10.1038/nature10514

Roese, N. J., Epstude, K., Fessel, F., Morrison, M., Small- man, R., Summerville, A. Galinsky, A. D., Segerstrom, S. (2009). Repetitive regret, depression, and anxiety: Find- ings from a nationally representative survey. *Journal of Social and Clinical Psychology, 28*, 671–688.

Rosenbaum, M., & Argon, S. (1979). Locus of control and success in self-initiated attempts to stop smoking. *Journal of Clinical Psychology, 35*, 870-872.

Rotter, J. (1954). *Social learning and clinical psychology*. Englewood Cliffs, NJ: Prentice-Hall.

Rotter, J. (1966). Generalized expectancies for internal versus external control of reinforcement. Psychological Monographs, 80, (Whole No. 609).

Ryskin, Rachel A.; Benjamin, Aaron S.; Tullis, Jonathan; Brown-Schmidt, Sarah (2015). Perspective-taking in comprehension, production, and memory: An individual differences approach. *Journal of Experimental Psychology: General, Vol 144(5),* Oct 2015, 898-915. http://dx.doi.org/10.1037/xge0

Santrock, J. W. (2004). *Educational Psychology*. Second edition. Boston, MA: McGraw-Hill.

Scheier, M. F.; Carver, C. S. (1987). "Dispositional optimism and physical well-being: the influence of generalized outcome expectancies on health". *Journal of Personality*. 55: 169–210. doi:10.1111/j.1467-6494.1987.tb00434.x.

Schulz, K. (2011). Don't regret regret [Video file]. Retrieved from https://www.ted.com/talks/kathryn_schulz_don_t_regret_regret

Seligman, M. E. P. (1972). Learned helplessness. *Annual Review of Medicine*, *23*, 407-412.

Seligman, M.E.P. (1996). *The Optimistic Child: Proven Program to Safeguard Children from Depression & Build Lifelong Resilience*. New York: Houghton Mifflin. ISBN 0091831199. (Paperback edition, Harper Paperbacks, 1996, ISBN 0-06-097709-4)

Seligman, M.E.P., Reivich, K., Jaycox, L., & Gillham, J. (1995). The optimistic child. New York: Houghton Mifflin.

Seligman, M.E.P. (2002). *Authentic Happiness: Using the New Positive Psychology to Realize Your Potential for Lasting Fulfillment*. New York: Free Press. ISBN 0-7432-2297-0.

Seligman, M.E.P. (2004). "Can Happiness be Taught?". *Daedalus*. 133 (2): 80–87. doi:10.1162/001152604323049424.

Seligman, M.E.P. (2011). *Flourish: A Visionary New Understanding of Happiness and Well-being*. New York: Free Press. ISBN 978-1-4391-9075-3.

Sells, S. P. (1998). *Treating the tough adolescent: a family-based, step-by-step guide*. New York, NY, Guilford Press.

Shakya, H. B., & Christakis, N. A. (2017). Association of Facebook Use With Compromised Well-Being: A Longitudinal Study. *American Journal of Epidemiology*, 185 (3): 203-211. doi: 10.1093/aje/kww189

Shanab, M. E., Peterson, D., Dargahi, S., & Deroian, P. (1981). The effects of positive and negative verbal feedback on the intrinsic motivation of male and female subjects. *Journal of Social Psychology, 115,* 195–205.

Shoda, Y, Mischel, W, & Peake, P. K. (1990). Predicting adolescent cognitive and self-regulatory competencies from preschool delay of gratification: Identifying diagnostic conditions. *Developmental Psychology, 26,* 978-986.

Siegel, D.J., & Bryson, T.P. (2011). *The whole-brain child: 12 Revolutionary strategies to nurture your child's developing mind, survive everyday parenting struggles, and help your family thrive*. New York: Delacorte Press.

Siegel, D.J., & Bryson, T.P. (2014). *No-drama discipline: The whole-brain way to calm the chaos and nurture your child's developing mind*. New York: Bantam.

Siegel, D.J., & Hartzell, M. (2003). Parenting from the inside out: How a deeper self-understanding can help you raise children who thrive. New York: Penguin Putnam.

Stanley, S. M., Whitton, S. W., Sadberry, S. L.Clements, M. L., & Markman, H. J. (2006). Sacrifice as a predictor of marital outcomes. Family Process, 45, 289– 303.

Stanton AL. Determinants of adherence to medical regimens by hypertensive patients. Journal of Behavioral Medicine. 1987;10:377–394.

Steinberg, L. (1987). The impact of puberty on family relations. Effects of pubertal status and pubertal timing. *Developmental Psychology, 23,* 451–460.

Steinmetz, K. (2015). How millennial parents think differently about raising kids. Time, October 15, 2015, http://time.com/4070021/millennial-parents-raising-kids-poll/

Strage, A., & Brandt, T. S. (1999). Authoritative parenting and college students' academic adjustment and success. *Journal of Educational Psychology, 91*(1), 146456.

Suh, E., Diener, E., & Fujita, F. (1996). Events and subjective well-being: Only recent events matter. *Journal of Personality and Social Psychology, 70,* 1091–102.

Taher, M., Safavi Bayat, Z., Niromand zandi, K., Ghasemi, E., Abredari, H., Karimy, M., & Abedi, A. R. (2015). Correlation between compliance regimens with health locus of control in patients with hypertension. *Medical Journal of the Islamic Republic of Iran, 29,* 194.

Tannen, D. (1990). You Just Don't Understand: Women and Men in Conversation. Ballantine Books, New York.

Tauer, J. (2015). *Why less is more for WOSPS: well-intentioned overinvolved sports parents.* Beaver's Pond Press.

Trento, M., Tomelini, M., Basile, M., Borgo, E., Passera, P., Miselli, V., Tomalino, M., Cavallo, F. and Porta, M. (2008), The locus of control in patients with Type 1 and Type 2 diabetes managed by individual and group care. Diabetic Medicine, 25: 86–90. doi:10.1111/j.1464-5491.2007.02319.x

Trumball, D. A., & Ravenel, S. D. (1996). Spare the rod?: New research challenges spanking critics. *Family Policy, 9,* 1-7.

Twenge, J.M., & Campbell, W.K. (2001). Age and birth cohort differences in self-esteem: A cross-temporal meta-analysis. Personality and Social Psychology Review, 5, 321–344.

Twenge, J. M., Zhang, L., & Im, C. (2004). It's beyond my control: A cross-temporal meta- analysis of increasing externality in locus of control, 1960–2002. Personality and Social Psychology Review, 8, 308–319.

Twenge, J. M. (2006). *Generation Me: Why today's young Americans are more confident, assertive, entitled—and more miserable than ever be- fore.* New York, NY: Free Press.

Twenge, J. M., Konrath, S., Foster, J. D., Campbell, W. K., & Bushman, B. J. (2008a). Egos inflating over time: A cross-temporal meta-analysis of the Narcissistic Personality Inventory. Journal of Personality, 76, 875–901.

Twenge, J. M., Konrath, S., Foster, J. D., Campbell, W. K., & Bushman, B. J. (2008b). Further evidence of an increase in narcissism among college students. Journal of Personality, 76, 919–927.

Twenge, J. M. (2013). *The evidence for Generation Me and against Generation We.* Emerging Adulthood.

Twenge, J. M., & Campbell, S. M. (2008). Generational differences in psychological traits and their impact on the workplace. *Journal of Managerial Psychology*, 23, 862-877.

Twenge, J. M., & Campbell, W. K. (2009). *The narcissism epidemic: Living in the age of entitlement* (1st Free Press hardcover ed.). New York: Free Press.

Twenge, J. M., & Foster, J. D. (2010). Birth cohort increases in narcissistic personality traits among American college students, 1982-2009. *Social Psychological and Personality Science*, 1, 99-106.

van Ingen, D. J., Freiheit, S. R., Steinfeldt, J. A., Moore, L. L., Wimer, D. J., Knutt, A. D., Scapinello, S. and Roberts, A. (2015), Helicopter Parenting: The Effect of an Overbearing Caregiving Style on Peer Attachment and Self-Efficacy. Journal of College Counseling, 18: 7–20. doi:10.1002/j.2161-1882.2015.00065.x

211

van Ingen, D.J., Moore, L.L. & Fuemmeler, (2008). Parental Overinvolvement: A Qualitative Study. *Journal of Developmental and Physical Disabilities*. 20: 449. doi:10.1007/s10882-008-9113-9

van Ingen, D.J. & Moore, L.L. (2010). How Parents Maintain Healthy Involvement With Their Adult Children: A Qualitative Study. Journal of Developmental and Physical Disabilities. 22: 533. doi:10.1007/s10882-010-9192-2

Voss, A., Cash H., Hurdiss S., Bishop, F, Klam, W.P., Doan, A. P. (2015). Case report: internet gaming disorder associated with pornography use. *The Yale Journal of Biology and Medicine.* Sep 3; 88(3): 319-324.

Warneken, F. and Tomasello, M. (2008) Extrinsic rewards undermine altruistic tendencies in 20-month-olds. Dev. Psychol. 44, 1785–1788.

Watson M, Pruyn J, Greer S, van den Borne B. (1990). Locus of control and adjustment to cancer. Psychological Reports. 66(1):39–48. doi: 10.2466/pr0.1990.66.1.39.

Watson, P.J., Grisham, S.O., Trotter, M. V., & Biderman, M. D. (1984). Narcissism and empathy: Validity evidence for the Narcissistic Personality Inventory. Journal of Personality Assessment, 48, 301-305.

Wegner, D. M. (1989). *White bears and other unwanted thoughts: Suppression, obsession, and the psychology of mental control*. New York: Viking/Penquin.

Wood, J. T. (2004). *Communication Theories in Action: An Introduction*. Belmont, CA: Wadsworth.

Wood, J. V.; Heimpel, S. A.; Michela, J. L. (2003). "Savoring versus dampening: self-esteem differences in regulating positive affect". *Journal of Personality and Social Psychology*. 85 (3): 566–580. doi:10.1037/0022-3514.85.3.566.

Yearly, Lee H. (1990). *Mencius and Aquinas: Theories of virtue and conceptions of courage*. Albany: SUNY Press.

Yuan, K., Qin, W., Liu, Y., & Tian, J. (2011) Internet addiction: Neuroimaging findings, *Communicative & Integrative Biology*, 4:6, 637-639, DOI: 10.4161/ cib.17871

# Resources

## Video Games

www.hooked-on-games.com
> Provides key information on video game addiction, 12-step recovery, blog & videos, and essential information on the multi-billion-dollar video game industry that is in the business of creating fun games that lead to addiction. Digital indulgences lead to life crumbling.

## Family Entertainment & Digital Safety

www.commonsensemedia.org
> Common Sense Media helps families make smart media choices. We offer the largest, most trusted library of independent age-based and educational ratings and reviews for movies, games, apps, TV shows, websites, books, and music.

www.dove.org
> A website designed to encourage and promote the creation, production, distribution and consumption of wholesome family entertainment. The website provides Dove reviews based on traditional Judeo-Christian values. There is a content chart and descriptions that gauge six criteria: sexuality, language, violence, drug and alcohol use, nudity, and other.

www.clearplay.com
> A resource for making movies family friendly. If you are concerned that certain scenes or language may be inappropriate for your family audience, ClearPlay helps filter movies.

www.stopbullying.gov
> A resource on bullying and cyber bullying.

www.cyberbullying.org
> The U.S.'s leading research center on causes, solutions, and statistics on cyberbullying.

www.enough.org
> Enough is enough is dedicated to raising awareness about the dangers of internet pornography and sexual predators, cyberbullying and other dangers.

www.fosi.org
> Family Online Safety Institute for Good Digital Parenting. Tips, tools and rules to confidently navigate the online world with your kids.

## Parenting & Behavioral Intervention

www.123magic.com
> 1-2-3 Magic is a popular parenting discipline program that teaches parents effective discipline.

www.oppositional.com
> Sometimes oppositional tendencies need to be handled with care. In those situations, additional education and reflectiveness may be needed due to the complexities. This website provides some good information on oppositional and defiant behavior.

www.authentichappiness.org
> Positive psychology is the scientific study of the strengths and virtues that enable individuals and communities to thrive. This field is founded on the belief that people want to lead meaningful and fulfilling lives, to cultivate what is best within themselves, and to enhance their experiences of work, love and play.

## Fitness & Nutrition

www.thefamilydinnerproject.org
> This website provides great ideas on how to improve the regularity and quality of family dinners.

www.choosemyplate.gov
> Education on food groups and making wise choices.

www.superfoodsrx.com
> Education on the SuperFoods. Key information on the 24 foods that will change your life.

## Relationships and Sex Education

www.stayteen.org
> The goal of Stay Teen is to encourage youth to enjoy their teen years and avoid the responsibilities that come with too-early pregnancy and parenting. Created by The National Campaign to prevent teen and unplanned pregnancy, the site features facts and resources to help teens make in-

formed decisions.

www.gottman.com
> This is a solid evidence based resource for incorporating emotional intelligence in our parenting as well tools on improving marriage relationships.

www.johnburi.com
> This resource is dedicated to the strengthening of marriage, family life, and the lifelong experience of love.

www.smartmarriages.com
> This website provides excellent information on marriage, family, and couples education.

## Driving Safety

www.teendriving.aaa.com
> A guide by AAA for teen safety behind the wheel.

www.teendriving.com
> Safety tips and advice for teen drivers, as well as their parents.

## Tobacco & Drug Prevention

www.thetruth.com
> Dedicated to putting an end to teen smoking with important facts everyone needs to know.

www.teens.drugabuse.gov
> Get the latest on how drugs affect the brain and the body. Featuring videos, games, blog posts and more, developed by the National Institute on Drug Abuse for Teens. Advancing addiction science for teens, teachers, and parents.

## Grief

www.toodamnyoung.com
> An online resource for grieving teens and young adults. The site features personal accounts, poems, and other creative pieces to process through trauma and grief.

www.dougy.org
> A collection of resources from the National Center for Grieving Children & Families for grieving children, teens, young adults, and families.

## Disabilities

www.autismnow.org
> A great online resource for information on autism.

www.hearinglikeme
> A wonderful resource for parents who have deaf children or hearing loss.

www.kidsandhearingloss.org
> A great resource for any parent with a hearing-impaired child.

www.smarkkidswithld.org
> Smart kids with learning disabilities is a resourceful website for parents with children who have dyslexia, ADHD, or specific learning disabilities in math, reading, or writing.

www.orthopedicimpairments.weebly.com
> Helpful information on orthopedic impairments such as neuromotor impairments like cerebral palsy and spina bifida, degenerative diseases such as muscular dystrophy, and musculoskeletal disorders such as juvenile rheumatoid arthritis.

www.brainline.org
> A useful parent's guide for helping kids with traumatic brain injury.

www.autism-society.org
> An autism website with resources on living with autism, the latest research, and includes opportunities for involvement.

www.autismspeaks.org
> Site with research, family services, and advocacy.

# About the Author

Daniel J van Ingen, Psy.D. graduated with a B.A. in psychology from the University of St. Thomas (St. Paul, MN) in 1998. He received his master's degree from Saint Mary's University of Minnesota in 2002. He received his doctorate in counseling psychology at the University of St. Thomas Graduate School of Professional Psychology in 2007. Dr. van Ingen is a licensed clinical psychologist in private practice in southwest Florida. He has worked with a variety of problems including depression, anxiety, addiction, trauma, substance abuse, and relationship problems for all age spans. He has worked with youth in sports psychology, performance anxiety, and blocking. He has served for many years as a youth sports coach in basketball, baseball, and soccer helping youth with goal setting, intrinsic motivation, and having fun for the love and joy of the game. His enthusiasm for life is contagious!

He has been dubbed the Sarasota Parenting Doctor for his work with families. Professionally, he has presented over 25 research papers at national and international conferences. He has published empirical research in the areas of anxiety, disabilities, and parenting. He is author of *Anxiety Disorders Made Simple: Treatment Approaches to Overcome Fear and Build Resiliency*. As a national speaker, he has trained thousands of clinicians in over 100 cities in 30 states on ways to prevent and solve the anxiety epidemic in youth. He is co-founder of Parenting Doctors (with his wife), an organization dedicated to helping parents find the heartbeat of their family. For more information on his practice, visit www.danvaningen.com and for more information on the Parenting Doctors, visit www.parentingdoctors.com.

He is married to Dr. Sarah van Ingen, the love of his life, and together they have three children. They love God, coaching youth, and building community while living life to its fullest in Sarasota, Florida.

Made in the USA
Middletown, DE
20 December 2019